T0367842

GOD Is Turning Your Miseries into Missiles

Your Tears into Joy

Rev. Mary Mercy

GOD IS TURNING YOUR MISERIES INTO MISSILES
YOUR TEARS INTO JOY

iUniverse books may be ordered through booksellers or by contacting:

iUniverse
1663 Liberty Drive
Bloomington, IN 47403
www.iuniverse.com
1-800-Authors (1-800-288-4677)

ISBN: 978-1-4917-5779-6 (sc)
ISBN: 978-1-4917-5781-9 (hc)
ISBN: 978-1-4917-5780-2 (e)

Printed in the United States of America.

iUniverse rev. date: 01/28/2015

CONTENTS

PREFACE

PEACE

THIS PROPHETICALLY COUNSELING BOOK IS FOUNDED ON THE BIBLICAL FAITH, TRUTH AND FACTS:

IT IS A BOOK GIVING GOD ALL THE GLORY, HONOR, AND ADORATION:

AND WILL KEEP YOUR VISION FOCUSED IN THE RIGHT DIRECTION

THE HOLY SPIRIT INSPIRED THE WRITING OF THIS BOOK TITLED:

GOD IS TURNING YOUR MISERIES INTO MISSILES

Read it and experience no more tears as GOD is turning your miseries into Missiles **and your Tears into Joy**! 1 Corinthians 10:3-5, Ephesians 6:10-18

You are going to learn how God will turn your mess into messages
Fear into courage;
Lack of faith into great Faith
Dishonesty to honesty in HIS Truth

Disobedience into obedience to GOD and to yourself
Dishonor to honor and to favor with GOD and men
Discouragement into encouragement
Discomfort into comfort
Disappointment to appointment with CHRIST JESUS and the right person or people that you need for achieving your goals.
HE is turning your victimization into great victory in JESUS HOLY Name; Amen!
This book leads the reader to the stage of thanks giving to the Most High GOD for all things: Psalms 100:4

And know that: "All things work together for good to them that love the LORD, who are called according to HIS purpose;" Romans 8:28.

Also, know this—that The Bible, as simple as it is, is above the intelligence of the offspring of Adam. Man, born in the imperfections of sin to death needs supernatural wisdom from above to grasp it and understand the benefits that lie in the WORD. The Bible is a complete tool for every human need.

And Rev. Mary Mercy says, IT DOES NOT MATTER WHERE YOU ARE, BUT WHERE GOD IS WITH YOU FOR IN MISERIES TO MISSILES THERE IS INSPIRATIONAL GOD GUIDING COUNSEL TO SEE YOU THROUGH YOUR TRIALS: GOD IS TURNING YOUR MISERIES INTO MISSILES AND YOUR TEARS TO JOY!

INTRODUCTION FROM THE AUTHOR

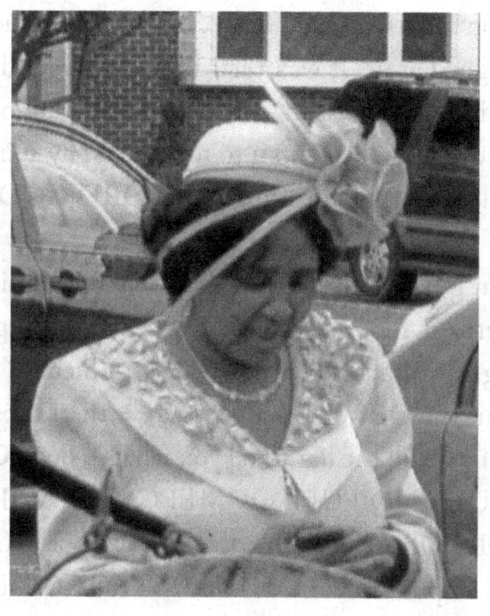

I am reading The Word of GOD, The Bible, as my family and I wait to be served early Christmas dinner at an Indian Restaurant in Columbia, Maryland USA. Here, I have received another new revelation on "Waiting upon the LORD;" Isaiah 40:31. It's all about the waiter. "They that wait upon the LORD, shall renew their strength," In order to serve HIM better. "They that wait upon," meaning "they that *wait* on GOD as HIS servants, serving

HIM diligently," HE makes them physically and spiritually rejuvenated to do exploits; Daniel 11:32. Read this book; Misery to Missiles, and you find a great treasure and wealth of knowledge from above. Rev. Mary Marcy, Pastor A Servant and Founder.

Let me tell you a little of my life story: in 1997 November I got to where JOB in the bible was in Job 1:13-22. I lost my all! I lost my two medical clinics and a hospital within three months. I lost my homes and we were left with nothing. The children and I almost went to live on the streets but GOD came to our rescue just before the devil laughed at us. It was a hard time but a harder time was yet to come. But GOD was in control of every situation. The only thing GOD did not allow Satan to touch was my spirit and soul. I was in a dilemma but worshiping my LORD GOD still.

The one great gift our GOD gives us at that tormenting moment is the strength to stay focused on HIM; worshiping HIM and not focusing too much on tortures and torments. The pain is there, yes, but the Deliverer is always closer than those problems brought by the devil; the liar. I tell you what— our LORD GOD IS FAITHFUL AND FULL OF MERCY. HE WILL NEVER LEAVE NOR FORSAKE YOU; IF YOU FAINT NOT! HE will never let you be put to shame. HE IS A STRONG DELIVERER AND HE WILL DELIVER AND ENRICH YOU AS YOU READ THIS BOOK! Yes HE will! And indeed, you will be as inspired and as encouraged as you read this book as I was inspired by the HOLY SPIRIT when writing it.

My miseries have been a whole train of how GOD turns miseries into missiles and how GOD has turned my tears to joy. Jeremiah 1:5-10 and 29:11-13, Isaiah 40:31, 41:9-20, 45:2-5, 54:1-17 with

2Timothy 3:16-17 is in full force and mine is to keep focused on Jeremiah 33:3, knowing that my Good GOD shall continually keep me in HIS Perfect Peace; Isaiah 26:3, with that Unending love, and Amazing Grace, I say, Amen and Amen!

The rest of the miracles before the incident which led me to this writing and thereafter you'll read as you go on with this book and in the other book which GOD is directing me to write. GOD Bless, prosper and increase you all for reading. AMEN!

My Great and special Gratitude and Dedication Goes To My LORD GOD ALMIGHTY, THE FATHER, THE SON AND THE HOLY SPIRIT, WHO Saved me and Gave me strength to write this; HIS Book. And also, I give my Special Thanks and Loyalty to my Dear Children for giving me Love and Support. You have supported me a lot while writing this GOD given Book and all the time you really support me, I am grateful to you. And I really give GOD all the Glory and Honor for giving you to me to be my children to Love and Cherish. GOD bless you and I thank HIM so much for giving us HIS life here on earth in Abundance and Life to come. AMEN!

MY SPECIAL THANKS AND ACKNOWLEDGMENT GOES TO

My Dear Mum who preached to me day and night and never got tired of praying for me to be strongly saved so that I can fulfill my destiny. She has never been tired of praying for me and my family. My Mother is such lovely believer of the Gospel of our LORD JESUS CHRIST and I have learned a lot from her. She inspires me on how to obtain true Love, Faith, Peace and Joy. Some people I felt hating because of how they treated us as a family, I saw my Mother loving them and treating them nicely and I wondered, doesn't she feel pain of what they did to us? After studying the WORD lead by the HOLY SPIRIT, I learned Mum knows how to obey GOD'S rules, Luke 6: 23-31. I prayed to GOD to give me the same spirit of obeying HIM. Mum has been blessed to see 4 generations of her Children and I believe GOD is giving her years to see the 5th. This year 2005, as I write this book she is 104 according to the years' events. The year 1900, British Colonial Government entered to build Embu City in Kenya. The year 1902 it rained after a long drought and as the great famine called Gatathoni was ending in that year, my Mother was born. She started preaching 1922. Dad paid dowry for her 1923 as per his records. I Thank GOD and give HIM all the glory for keeping her alive because she got some of us when she was still old to conceive and deliver according to human science but GOD did it.

We never noticed both our parents, Mum and Dad were old when they got the last eight of us. Thank you Mum for being there for us and teach us how to serve GOD in righteousness. GOD bless you and keep you despite all.

I wish to sincerely acknowledge and thank The World Wide Respected Ministry of Dr. Bill Graham for sponsoring me to the Ministry.

Greatly also, I thank Bishop Dr. Rogers Shaka and his Wife Minister Edina D. Rogers for Licensing me to Preach the Gospel of Our LORD JESUS CHRIST with the right Credentials after they recognizing my ministry unto our LORD GOD Almighty and HIS people. Dr. R. Shaka is also the President of TCB Association Ministry and an Author.

MY Bishop, Rev. Bishop Paul Mutua. The founder, Redeemed Church of Kenya, Machakos which has produced over 50 Churches in Kenya. He is my Spiritual Father, Pastor, Mentor, and a practical Teacher of Righteousness. He was my first teacher and coach on Gospel Outreach in righteousness. He re-ordained me with Oil and blessed my ministry licenses. I love and respect my Bishop and our Mum his wife. They are precious to me and the body of CHRIST. A role model of today's Church.

My Senior Pastor Rev. Dr. Crouch Lambert of New Horizon Baptist Church, St. Luke line Baltimore County Maryland USA. I served with Pastor Lambert as one of his Associate Pastors. He is one of the Pastors who reverenced and gave me license of the ministry after I ministered under his authority for years before I set my ministry and Church. I thank him and our Mum his wife Naomi so greatly for allowing me to preach and practice the Church work in their Church and under their authority here in USA.

I cannot forget those who played a great role in modeling My Faith Walk in Our LORD JESUS CHRIST: My Mum and My English and CRE Teacher Mrs. Naomi Wamai who taught me how to write excellent compositions and thesis and to walk in righteousness observing my Christian walk in this world. I really love her and her family. I still remember all that she taught us as a class and as an individual as she mentored me to grow in the Nature and Character of our Savior JESUS CHRIST. All the Ministers that followed took over from her firm foundation that JESUS had put in me through her excellent work. GOD bless her and her Family.

After that in my 20s as I was growing, Our LORD GOD sent to me Br. Dr. Reuben M. Kithuka and Brother Frances Karua who Baptized me in River Ena whereby the HOLY SPIRT Filled Baptizing and Overtaking my life with Fire. After that they then sent me to be mentored by these to great Men and women of GOD and Brethren Mr. &Mrs. Stanley Njagi and Mr. &Mrs. Dr. Daniel Mbiti who played the role of impacting my life into the Works of the Anointing of the HOLY SPIRIT. They played and do play a great role in my live as a believer and a co-work in the Ministry of CHRIST. GOD bless you and your families brethren, I love you.

ENDORSEMENT OF THE AUTHOR

by Pastor, Rev. Rose Faith a Dear Sister
and Co-worker in the ministry.

After reading and meditating all the Ocean of knowledge that is in this book, I have felt I must forward it to be printed so that many people will be blessed as I have been. In this book, there is wealth of knowledge with special Anointing as you learn what GOD does to those who believe HIM. Actually, as I read, I got healed of a problem that has been bothering me over years. Also, I felt assured by reading this book. I have known that all the knowledge that GOD has given to me is tool to turn all my miseries to missiles. Through this book, I have gained more confidence to wait on my Lord God.

I know Rev. Mary Mercy in the ministry as we minister. Her compassion for other people and love for GOD is great. She is ordained licensed Minister of the Gospel and Pastor of NCCIF Ministry registered in Maryland with a branch in Georgia, USA. She is a loving mother, Grandmother, Sister, Mentor, counselor and she was a loving wife to her late husband to whom JESUS CHRIST took over that love. GOD has given her anointing with wealth of knowledge and experience in many fields of life including, Biblical Counseling, the Gospel Ministry which she has been doing for over 38 years. Also, in medical areas, she is a licensed private medical practitioner in Kenya where she owned Mercy Medical Clinic; plot number 5 Manyatta, Embu. Also, owned a Hospital 88 bed capacity, Sunrise at Blue Valley Embu, Kenya. GOD moved her out of all that to serve HIM. HE created her in HIS Image and HIS Likeness; Genesis 1:26-27. JESUS CHRIST is the center and Lead of her life and she has nothing else to boast of but the fellowshipping of HIS suffering and the Love of HIS Saving Grace and the power of HIS Resurrection. She enjoys a lot of Power of HOLY SPIRIT who is her thorough chastener, guider, teacher, instructor, reproof, overcomer and the empowering force behind all her victory and success. GOD Almighty has given Pastor, Rev. Mary Mercy gift of love for others which drives her to the ministry of Gospel Outreach that our LORD JESUS CHRIST carried on while HE walked here on earth like us. She does the Streets, Shelters and Open Air Preaching Ministry which is our LORD JESUS CHRIST'S heart treasure. She did it in Kenya and she does it in here in USA as our LORD helps her to fulfill HIS Word in Matthew 9: 37-38;

By Pastor, Rev. Faith Rose.

SOME TESTIMONIES

Sister Shelly Bryan,

A Prominent Well Loved Sister in CHRIST and Coworker in the NCCIF/JCSS Ministry Testifies:

"My family and I praise and thank Our LORD GOD and Savior JESUS CHRIST Greatly for Pastor Mary. She is a true servant of GOD who has been used by GOD to be there for us day and night as a true Shepherd to us as a family and in the ministry. She has been a mother, a father, a counselor, a mentor and a teacher of our family and other families. Above all, she is such a giver that our ministry NCCIF/JCSS is a giving ministry even to other big known ministries. As the HOLY SPIRIT guides her to lead us to preach JESUS CHRIST and giving to GOD'S people living on Streets and Shelters in the City of Baltimore and other places, she lets GOD lead her in everything. We love you Pastor Mary and thank you too for accepting GOD'S Calling and Command to reach out for Souls with the WORD OF GOD and showing HIS Love by JESUS CHRIST and HIS Blood; and also, being there for us."

Sister Sharon a Beloved co-worker in the Ministry Testifies:

Pastor Mary has been there for me and my family day or night, it doesn't matter the time we call her for a problem she will answer and if need be come. I call her to pray or come when I'm under our enemy Satan's attacks, and I need a person to support me spiritually and physically, and truly, Pastor Mary is always available. Pastor Mary is always available for you whether you will be available for her or not. She really challenges me by her love for others. I am grateful to GOD and our Savior JESUS CHRIST for putting Pastor Mary in my life.

CHAPTER 1

Asking for Wisdom

One day, I was quietly worshipping the LORD and feeling all good about HIM. As I meditated on HIS Goodness, I heard a soft questioning voice: "supposing the LORD GOD asked you now, what you would like HIM to give you, what would you ask for?"

At that point in time, I needed money for a lot of things; all very necessary. I needed money for college fee, urgently, lest my classes be canceled. I needed money to pay the rent, money for my car payment, money for my basic necessities, money for my children and above all, money for Tithe and Offering. I was in a financial predicament. There were so many things lined up that I needed money for. As I was in meditation upon that question, I remembered instantly that when asked by God what he wanted, King Solomon asked for wisdom.

As I contemplated doing that, I thought, LORD, if I ask for man's wisdom, there is a lot that can be encompassed in man's wisdom that can bring disaster as was the case in Solomon's last twenty years of his life. I had studied the Word and come to know that despite all the wisdom GOD had given King Solomon, Solomon had misused it all. His great wealth and power became a snare to him and his reign, so that GOD got truly angry with him. As a result, the LORD GOD told Solomon that HE would have destroyed his kingdom, but that for King David, Solomon's father's sake, GOD would spare it for that moment, and have it divided during the reign of Solomon's son. (1 Kings 11:1-8, &9-13). Just read for yourself and you will see it. Start from verse 1 to 13.

At that moment, I said, My LORD and My GOD, all that I need now is JESUS CHRIST in me and me in HIM until HE comes to take me to heaven; my eternal Home. I said, if I have JESUS CHRIST in me, I will have GODLY Wisdom which cannot sin, and because I hate sinning against my LORD GOD, I will no longer struggle trying to lead a righteous life; JESUS CHRIST is my Wisdom, Knowledge, Understanding, Righteousness and Holiness, AMEN! Mine will be to rest in the One Who is in me and I in HIM and let HIM lead me to the path of HIS righteousness for HIS Name's sake.

In Psalms 23:1-6, the Psalmist knew this secret, and so he sang; "The LORD is my Shepherd I shall not want." As long as we have The LORD in us, we shall not lack for anything. I thought of the very wise men of the world today who are without JESUS CHRIST, they may do a lot and own a lot, but they are lacking Peace, Joy, and Love. They look for Peace where it cannot be found, for Joy where it has never been known, and for love from them that do not know how to love. And I said, **JESUS MY LORD, LET ME HAVE YOU AND I KNOW YOU WILL BE ENOUGH**

FOR ME; FOR I SHALL NOT LACK ANYTHING WHEN YOU ARE IN ME AND I IN YOU. FOR YOU ARE ALL THE LOVE I NEED, AND ALL THE JOY I NEED, AND ALL THE PEACE I NEED, AND ALL THE WISDOM I NEED, AND ALL THE MONEY THAT I NEED AND ALL THAT I WILL EVER NEED, AND EVERYTHING THAT I EVER NEEDED, AND EVERYTHING THAT I NEED NOW, TOMORROW, AND FOR EVER; AMEN! YOU ARE JESUS MY MASTER, MY SAVIOR MY RESCUING REDEEMER WHO LIVES FOREVER. And my LORD JESUS accepted my request that I may no longer live but that CHRIST Lives in me. I enjoy HIS presence, peace, love and joy in the HOLY SPIRIT. It is wonderful to know that **JESUS CHRIST IS ENOUGH FOR US, FOR HE IS OUR ETERNAL GIFT.** Hallelujah! Amen!

DO NOT SIT ON GOD'S PROMISES; STAND ON THEM INSTEAD

If you stand on GOD'S promises, ·by faith, you will tell that mountain, "mountain, be thou removed and be planted in the sea," and the mountain will be removed by your faith in GOD; Mark 11:22-24, Hebrews 10:8, 2Corinthians 5:7, Luke17:5-6.

The mountains of sorrows and troubles are physical manifestations of what Satan, our enemy, does in the spiritual realm. The powers of evil spirits are the real reason behind the troubles in your way; troubles of disease, poverty, marital instability, drugs and substance abuse; call it anything the devil brings your way to make you unhappy, and to give you heartache. Those sorrows bringing troubles are some of the mountains our LORD JESUS CHRIST told us that we shall tell them to be removed, by faith, and they shall be removed and be planted in the sea of forgetfulness. Yes, there are some real things that stand like mountains that need real removal for us to be provided, sheltered and feel comforted, but they all need mustard seed faith and they shall go in the Mighty Name of JESUS CHRIST; Amen!

Therefore, knowing this, we must not let troubles overwhelm us, lest we be sitting on GOD'S promises; promises which HE gave us as HIS beloved children. HE has given us promises from Genesis to Revelation and it is for us to stand still and claim them by faith.

Remember, Satan and his demons are spirits, just as GOD'S Clean Holy Angels are Spirits. We can only use the Word of GOD as a Missile to fight Satan and his demons. We cannot use the physical weapons of bombs and guns. Your Missiles are in your tongue, when you call out to the Mighty Name of JESUS CHRIST, you are throwing bombs to devil and his kingdom. You have to use them as the Word of GOD teaches in Mark 16:17-18, Luke 10:17, John 14:12-14, 15:7. Do not use your own words and curses; words of your own mouth will fail you. Use the WORD OF GOD as it is in the BIBLE.

This is why we must learn the Bible through the Power of the HOLY SPIRIT who inspired the Writing of the WORD in THE BIBLE. Do not allow Satan to lie to you with the teachings which people who do not believe in GOD have received from Satan. I have often heard some people teach others that "you should not mention God or his word at your workplace because you are imposing religion upon other people." Others say that when you exclaim, "Oh my God," you are using the name of the LORD in vain. Those are lies from hell, manufactured and released to confuse those children of GOD who do not read or do not concentrate and meditate in the Word. Read the Word and know our GOD'S will and HIS intent towards you; Deuteronomy 6:13 says, "Swear by no other name but your LORD GOD…." So long as you know who your GOD is and HE knows you, then you are not cheating or blaspheming HIM. HE is your Father, HE feels proud of you and HE wants you to feel proud of HIM and talk of HIM every moment of your life by mentioning HIM all the time.

When you see or hear something that surprises you, don't exclaim or proclaim "gosh or jeez, or my goodness" for who is gosh, or jeez and where is your goodness? Who are those? They are not your GOD! They did not create you in their image and in their likeness they are only stealing your Creator from you. Why are you proclaiming or exclaiming their name in whatever circumstance it is that you are calling or mentioning them. Devil will soften it for you and tell you, "It's just an exclamation everyone is using." Who is everyone? And how are you related to that 'everyone' who is saying it that you must follow? Where did that exclamation come from, and what was the reason behind it? That much I can tell you. In the same way and in the same method that was used to remove the Bible and prayers from the schools and public places is the same way the Word that can Praise the LORD GOD from your mouth has or is being removed from you and from the communities. It is up to us to stand and proclaim the Name of our LORD GOD in public by exclaiming HIS name in every surprised or sudden exclamation we make. Let us exclaim, "Oh my LORD GOD ALMIGHTY" Or "Oh JESUS CHRIST," Or "Oh LORD JESUS!" And that way, we are going to remember the devil and his devices. If you know your GOD well that HE is your "Father Who Art in Heaven, Hallowed be Thy Name" you have HIS Divine permission to use HIS name under whatever circumstance; Deuteronomy 6:1-25. Remember, in the Ten Commandment, from the first command, GOD emphasized on us not to have or worship any other god but HIM alone; Exodus 20:-7.

The Word was there even before HE was written on the scrolls. HE was already with the world, helping the world to live, but "the world knew HIM not!" Nothing was created without the Word; JESUS CHRIST, yet, HE IS THE WORD; we read in John 1:1-5. Therefore, HE knows everything even what we are going through right now. If it is good, HE knows, if it is bad, HE knows it too. There is nothing new to JESUS CHRIST. Before HE came to the physical world as a Man GOD, HE still existed and lived in the Spiritual realm, and HE was still at the top of everything. All things are subject to HIM and nothing takes HIM by surprise. When HE is in you and you in HIM, you have more than all you need. Amen!

CHAPTER 2

Temptations to Victory

AS A CHILD OF GOD, WHY DO YOU HAVE TO FACE BATTLE AFTER BATTLE? This is a question asked by very many people. Some believers in JESUS CHRIST and even some who are not believers in JESUS CHRIST ask the same question.

In Luke 10:19, our LORD JESUS told us, "I have given you power to tread over scorpions, serpents, and over every power of the enemy." And in John 10:10 JESUS told us that "the thief comes to steal to kill and to destroy." A thief is an enemy. And JESUS wants us to fight with our enemy using HIS Power in order to exercise that power HE gave to us and defeat the kingdom of our enemy Satan using that power; the missiles. Again, remember that our enemy is Satan and his demons; and not other people. Those demons are the ones JESUS called scorpions and snakes. What we need to bear in our minds is that there is no battle without pain, but pain while we are in GOD'S Grace is full of Peace that passes our understanding, John 14: 27-31, 20:15-31, Philippians 4:7. Our brother Paul, inspired of the HOLY SPIRIT, learned this and recorded it in Philippians 3:10, in Romans 5:17-19 and 8:17-18 but every suffering and pain that has a great reward is worthy it. Therefore, if we suffer now but gaining in double measure everything we lose, as did Job in Job 42:10-17, and a hundred fold; here on earth and in the life to come: life in abundance of what we lose, and with joy, peace, love without an end; Mark 10:30.

Through the prayers and tears you are shedding every day for your heart-felt pain, GOD is going to turn all into joy and use all that prayer and tears as Missiles to destroy your enemies' plans, and assignments, and frustrate all Satan's work and efforts towards you. Therefore, fear not, Isaiah 41:10, 54: 15-17.

Remember that all the battles you have been going through have their origin in the Garden of Eden. You and I are just victims of that circumstance, but victors because our ***LORD JESUS CHRIST fought for us to make us more than conquerors, Romans 8:37.*** But if we don't watch, we can become victims of ourselves for lack of knowledge; Hosea 4: 6. How victims of ourselves? If we engage ourselves in disobedience, that leads us to unholy anger, bitterness, doubts, discouragement, malice, envy, rage, and all that comes from Satan. Then we become victims and slaves of those sins and sin becomes our master. GOD Forbid! Genesis 4: 7-12 records the result of sin that had followed as a result of giving the wrong offering without repentance. Cain's sin of murder was as a result of doing the wrong thing, and not accepting GOD'S correction to repentance; hence, envy was conceived in him. Envy then produced malice, anger and bitterness, which brought up end products of murder and eternal condemnation. 1 John 3:15 says, "whosoever hates his brother is a murderer: and you know that no murderer hath eternal life abiding in him."

Actually, every repented sin has no power over the person who has committed it. But every sin that is not repented is carried forward even to the 4th generation of the sinner. See Exodus 20:5 in the Ten Commandments.

Simple Mathematics from Heaven:

When Adam sinned, his sin affected his first born son, and was carried on to each generation handing over to the fourth generation from Adam, and Cain to their fourth generation of each father until the flood. And after the flood, the sin continued with Ham and from Ham sin kept on spreading from each father that sinned, and each father that sinned handing over his un-repented sin to his children's generation to the fourth generation of each man in his generation up to his fourth generation. That is now clearly to say the un-repented sin can go from one generation to another forever. I pray that The HOLY SPIRIT will help you to see it the way HE has made me see how the sin can remain in a family forever if it is not repented. And our LORD JESUS CHRIST in Matthew 5:17 asked us, "think you that I have come to destroy the law, and the prophet? No, I have come to fulfill it." Meaning, what is written in the Old Testament, **JESUS came to reinforce.**

Many Christians proclaim that there is no carrying of sins from generation to Generation. So, they go on living with un-repented sins of their great grandfathers to their grandfathers and fathers without taking notice of it to repent even if they may not know what evil deed was done by their forefathers. Mostly, they can see something is going wrong within their families. Their children may not be doing very well in the community and in school, and they have a lot of behavioral problems. It is appropriate for the parents of such children to go down on their knees and repent their forefathers' sins. That is repenting of the known to unknown sins. We know of Adam's sin because it is recorded and we repent it. But does it harm me if I repent what I do not know about my great grandpa, my grandpa to my father so that it does not get to me and to my children?

Indeed, I repent all in the Mighty Name of JESUS CHRIST MY LORD and my Savior. The reasons to repent are as even nature teaches us: why do we see a man who was an alcoholic helplessly watch his children and his children's children become alcoholics? Why do Medical Doctors take down your family history? Why is it that in almost 99% of families with a history of murderers, the evil is repeated from generation to generation? Even in most cases of mental illness, why do you find it repeated from parent to child? Some families have a line of drug addicts from grandfathers down to the grandchildren. Why? How is it that some families where the grandfathers divorced, sons have grandsons who then follow the same path. The answer is simple; it is because of unrepented sin. Whoever committed the sin first did not care to repent it, turn away from it, and follow JESUS CHRIST to break that curse. Learn and notice that evil thing which was done in your family and repent it as Daniel and Nehemiah in the Old Testament.

When we received CHRIST JESUS in our lives our old nature died. It died to sin starting from Adam's, which caused us to commit all manner of sin before our Heavenly Father GOD. The moment we receive the Blood of JESUS CHRIST we get Born Again and become new creations in CHRIST JESUS. "Behold, the old has passed away and the new has come." 2 Corinthians 5:17.

If after being born again we do not find change in our lives then there is something we need to repent sincerely, and not hold it lightly. But if we do not repent, or if we repent and then go back to the same or some other sin, then sin and Satan gets dominion over us and our families. Therefore, that sin becomes the devil's anchor. It becomes as a hanger for the devil to hang his sins in our families for generations. May GOD forbid that this should happen to us!

A famous story is told of a man who was selling his house without a realtor's assistance. This man put a condition on any buyer who wanted to pay $50,000.00 less than the asking price. The condition was put in writing. "A buyer who pays $50,000.00 less than my asking price must allow me to put a nail in the living room near the door, and allow me to hang my coat there when I need to." None made an offer until one young man thought that he could make a big saving on a beautiful house that was also spacious enough for his family. Looking at the terms of purchase, he thought he had a good deal. He had a free financier ready to pay the whole amount but the young man took the money from the financier and he bought the house less $50.000.00. And the story goes, after one week, the seller passed by and hang a dirty coat on the nail which he had driven through wall at the time of the transaction. The young man and his wife looked at that coat; felt bad, but they could not say or do a thing because of the agreement.

After few days he came back with some rotten sheep skins dripping with some stinking blood and hanged them on the same nail. When the young man, the owner of the house came home he found his wife and children outside in the cold because the house was stinking unbearably. He looked at the skins and the stuff dripping down his floor, and right away went to his seller. He offered to give him that figure he had earlier discounted of $50,000.00, if only he would leave him and his family alone. But the man said, my friend, for me to sign another agreement, you would have to give me $100.000.00, then I will move my skin out of the house. The seller still had the legal rights to the house. So long as the first agreement of the nail remained he had the right to hang whatever he wanted to hang! The deal was no longer a sweet money-saving deal but a loss. Because of the condition that the young man had accepted; to leave some space in his new house for the seller, life in the house became so difficult that he and his family could not bear it. He compromised his family's comfort for $50,000.00. For him to get that comfort back he had to lose $50,000.00 more! He thought of the Financier who had offered him to the full selling price of the house, and the way he had declined the offer so that he could save $50,000.00, and he felt nothing but regret at the lost opportunity.

JESUS CHRIST our Chief Financier is ready to buy us wholly, at the asking price, (and indeed has already set the full payment for our souls) but if we want a cheap life where the devil can hang his dirty stinking coat on a nail in our spiritual house, we compromise our faith and belief with him. There can be no comfort in such a house, only regret. A family with unrepented sin is like a family that bought a house but allowed the seller to have legal rights over a nail on which he could hang whatever he wanted. The seller is the devil, and the unrepented sin is the nail on which he places miseries of all kinds to torment your life and the lives of your children unto the fourth generation.

Some members of that family will continue to get saved and to backslide, never knowing that the devil has set up an anchor and a nail to hold onto in their lives while he is destroying them due to the generational un-repented sins of their forefathers, which they are now the victims of. If we are sinners by Adam's sins, and we are required to get saved from Adam's sin, how much more should we repent the sins of those with whom we have direct blood-link? The Ten Commandments are the Word of GOD and cannot be changed by anything else. Only repentance harmonizes our lives with the life of our GOD, and nullifies the curses of generational sin. Now, we have the Blood of JESUS CHRIST for the remission of our sins. But if one does not repent according to the Word of GOD in the Bible, one will revert to that sin.

Repentance means to say sorry and to never do it again. There are some kinds of sins that remain alive and strong for the devil to hold legal rights to and use when attacking a family. This goes on until one member of that family hears the Word of GOD and obeys and repents of that sin and breaks that curse.

In fact, if one of the key members of a family such as the father or the mother practiced sorcery and died in those spirits there is a likely hood of that family following sorcery. Unless another key member of that family who is Born Again breaks that curse of sorcery by repentance, and by pleading for the blood of JESUS CHRIST to wash, cleanse, purify, sanctify and cover the family, Satan has an anchor and a hanger in that family. The devil will hold firm, claiming his legal rights over that family until he destroys that family with the sin of disobedience.

I have done this research thoroughly, and found this to be true. If you observe carefully, you will see that my revelation is certain. The families which started out in true Christianity, these have a long line of Christians in the family and it is carried on and on. Likewise, those families who prosper in the LORD, one only need look at their background, check into their roots. One will find that they originate from a GOD- fearing man who was worshiping the real true GOD; very obedient and disciplined, and who prospered, like our Patriarch Father Abraham.

Abraham's prosperity is carried forward by the Children of Israel, and the devotedly obedient Christians from the first disciples to us. We may go through tribulations, but we are still prosperous in all ways if we quit not. Those who quit miss the mark of perfection, hence, they lose out like Adam and Eve did when they quit and ran to hide. Prosperity is not only signified by material acquisitions and money. It is indicated also in our spiritual and physical well-being.

When Adam and Eve sinned, they gave up to Satan all the dominion, power and authority which they had been given by GOD; Genesis 3:1-14. They in turn received from Satan the spirit of fear and bondage. They let their blessings be stolen by Satan, through his lies. From that time on, a curse fell upon earth. It is that curse that we need to repent from.

We need to break it by the Blood of JESUS CHRIST the only HOLY Man; who lived here on earth without a sin. JESUS CHRIST came on earth as man born of the woman, Mary, yet completely GOD. Matthew 1&2, Luke 1&2 1 John 4: 15-21, 51-15, 2 John 1: 7, 1 John 1, 2&3. When you study the Word you get enough missiles to use when crushing the devil and his spirits of curses.

When we accept JESUS CHRIST as our LORD and Savior, we receive the blessing of victory that the LORD GOD pronounced in Genesis 3: 15.

Here, the LORD GOD promised Redemption from the sin of disobedience through the Messiah JESUS CHRIST. The LORD GOD said, the Messiah will come and crush Satan's head and Satan will bruise the Messiah, JESUS' heel. The battle at the cross, which started as early as the last supper at the upper room with JESUS and Judas Iscariot used of the devil, continued to the Garden of Gethsemane to fulfill that promise. And indeed, JESUS CHRIST, sinless as HE was, He was bruised on HIS heel as they crucified HIM on the Cross. Then when HIS Body was separated from HIS Soul, HE descended to hell to crush Satan's head. HE fought for us, crushed the devil's head, took the keys of hell and death and won the battle for us. And by the way, JESUS CHRIST had won this battle before the foundation of the earth. However, to save us, HE had to come and live with us as Man; Son of GOD, the LAMB OF GOD, shed HIS sinless Blood to wash our sinful blood and nature and to demonstrate the righteousness of GOD HOOD to mankind; and to turn our miseries into missiles to fight and completely destroy that enemy whose head HE crushed.

Ask then, why do we have to fight and yet JESUS CHRIST won the battle for us? The revelation of the answer to that question is found in Philippians 3:10. My brother Paul wrote, "That I may know HIM and the power of HIS resurrection, and the fellowship of HIS suffering, being conformable unto HIS death;" That is the battle we fight, but we are on the winning side. We must suffer the same despise, rejection, and ridicule our LORD JESUS went and goes through on earth while HE is doing good things to those who hate and despise HIM. Look at the whole world that HE gives free oxygen and water how they have equipped themselves with religions that are far from HIS LOVE, PEACE AND JOY: Far from the Will and Love of GOD, busy battling HIS very elect.

We cannot lose, do not fear! We never lose, for JESUS CHRIST did not lose. It is a battle already overcome.

JESUS broke the curses for us. But we have to take on that gift of life which HE gave us by so doing. By the help of the HOLY SPIRIT, in order for this action JESUS CHRIST performed on the Cross by HIS Death to be perfected in our lives, we have to repent by approaching the Throne of Mercy and Grace; each one of us carrying one's cross. Repentance is the highest degree of Humility that pleases GOD.

Our LORD JESUS said, "Deny yourself, take up your cross and follow me. And whosoever will love his life will lose it, and whosever shall confess me before men I will confess him before My Father who is in heaven and whosever shall deny ME before men I shall deny him before My Father which is in heaven" Mark 8:34, Luke 9: 22-26, Matthew 10:32-33. Once you commit to follow Jesus and confess HIM as your LORD and Savior, you are on the winning side and you can never be defeated. All that you need to do is to wholly surrender to HIS Divine will for you and HE will become good companions, Psalm 46: 1-11.

What Satan brought your way so as to heap misery upon you, GOD is going to turn around and make your weapon. You will use the very same weapon to fight Satan and defeat him. It is by Faith only that this can be done. Work in cooperation with The HOLY SPIRIT IN CHRIST JESUS and you will be surprised at how fast GOD is going to defeat Satan for your sake. Joyfully, you will carry a testimony of triumph; of overcoming.

Remember, our LORD GOD said, HE will never leave you nor forsake you, Joshua 1:5, 2:7. Whether the body wants it or not; surely you have to cooperate and keep focused on the author and the finisher of your faith; JESUS CHRIST, Hebrews 12:2: And this can only be made possible by keeping on worshiping GOD even when things are very sore. Worship and Praise unto the everlasting Father is the key. But this must be done by full faith, and love. Give GOD the Glory and honor for all things and stay in HIM and HIM in you.

Let JESUS CHRIST have a dwelling place in you at this moment of your sorrows and thereafter. John 17:9-26 CHRIST JESUS Prayed that GOD The Father may keep us from falling or failing; and give us protection with HIS Glory. JESUS asked our father to keep us in HIM as HE is in the Father. What a great honor to have our Master JESUS praying and interceding day and night for us.

Let me encourage you, sorrows may be the only thing you have known in your life, but joy comes in the morning, Psalm 30:5. And remember, the darkest hour is before dawn. The road gets tougher just before arrival.

The morning of the LORD GOD ALMIGHTY may not have arrived for you but it is on the way. It may tarry but it will surely come. Feel encouraged, even though things may not look so good as to encourage you. Take JESUS at HIS Word for HE is the Word of life. Be encouraged; John 6: 68-69; and remember HIM at the Garden of Gethsemane and Calvary, how he sorrowed for you so that you may not sorrow forever. HE travailed for you to bear and present you safely before the Father's Throne of Mercy at the Ark of the Covenant. Only for a moment will you be in sorrow, and joy will come in the morning. For all your miseries are being turned into missiles to destroy all that is causing you to be miserable.

Very soon some people around you will be wishing that they too had gone through what they have taken you through. Others who were watching or hearing what you are going through will wish to have entered into the trials and temptations that you went through. Soon Satan will regret that he caused all that happened to you. He will wish he did not kindle the fire he kindled on you. Very soon devil will say, "I did not know I was opening avenues for his/her blessing, and promotion with fame." Those who joined your adversary Satan to punish you will regret and desire to be your best friends. Your present employer will wish he/she did not treat you so badly when you are in a better position. But you have to be faithful before your LORD GOD like those who were before you; they remained faithful and grateful even when they sorrowed.

The Saints before you went through and more of what you are going through right now; 1 Corinthians 10: 13, and in it all, they never complained. Therefore, they were chosen to be good examples of the sons of A Mighty GOD. They remained faithful to their GOD without knowing the outcome. They did not sin as they waited upon the LORD, as some today will tell you when you caution them against sinful deeds, they will say, "I know, and I am waiting on him." Then you wonder what sort of waiting this is, if one is living on alcohol, smoking, drugs, fornication, or adultery so as to "calm their minds." Living in sin, yet say, "I am waiting upon the LORD." A waiter is committed to serve the person, the master he/she is waiting upon. "You cannot serve two masters effectively," said our LORD JESUS.

There is a price to pay in salvation by being faithfully despite all, if you are a truly committed Christian. Tests will come to test your faith, and in the tests, there are numerous problems, but sin not. Stay clean and holy until the LORD'S rescue comes. Sin not! Stay waiting upon the LORD sinless. Some say in these perilous days, they are waiting upon the LORD; yet, they are living in sin.

It is sad to hear one asking, why is GOD not doing for me what HE has promised? Or why is HE not fulfilling HIS promises to me? How do you expect GOD to be positive to your requests if you do not honor HIS Word? For a while HE may have been kind to you and did you good even though you may have not been faithful to HIM. But now, HE wants you to learn and stop lying to yourself, and to others that you are waiting upon the LORD.

Be faithful, and do not worry what people are saying about you. Just be faithful to your GOD. You will soon see HIS reward for you. Sometimes, we are caught up by some issues which might make us get into some deals which we think are clean business, only to find yourself in a big mess; repent seriously and quit it. Do not stay in sin once you identify it as sin. You may stand to lose a lot of money, and property for quitting the sinful way, but you are better off that way! I tell you, you had better lose those things than lose your life forever.

Remember Joseph, the 11th son of Jacob in Genesis 42 to 45, who was thrown in a pit by his brothers and sold to some Ishmaelites who happened to be passing by. Well, after 13 years of being into captivity, his brothers, upon finding him, now risen to the rank of Deputy King/Pharaoh, wished they had been thrown into that pit instead!

Your lordship is on the way if you quit not. I may not tell you when because I am just a human being like you, but our LORD GOD, the omniscient, the all-knowing GOD, knows when HE is going to get you out of the pit, out of slavery and into the rank of king. The HOLY SPIRIT will reveal HIS time to you as you read The Word.

GOD is faithful, and can never forget you in that pit or in that slavery, nor in that prison. Amen! Remember, CHRIST came to set the captives free; Luke 4:18-19. GOD can never forget you, Isaiah 49:15-16, 61:1-3. But you must know that, "the trying of your faith works patience but let patience have perfect work, that you may be perfect and whole wanting nothing," James 1:3-4. Romans 5:3b-5, "knowing that tribulation works patience, and patience works experience and experience works hope and hope makes not ashamed." Most of the time when we go through tries and temptations we tend to think either GOD hates us or HE has forgotten us, or HE has allowed Satan to torture us because we have sinned much. No! That is not the case. The apostles went through a lot of tribulations, and they had not sinned. It is because they were righteous and doing what the LORD GOD wanted them to do. JESUS being CHRIST, the anointed One of GOD and the Son of the Most High GOD, was tortured by the devil and tried as we are, but HE never sinned. All that we need is to ask HIM to give us the Power that kept HIM on earth without sinning. The devil was punishing the Apostles so that they could stop preaching and winning souls for GOD'S Kingdom, so that God's children may not inherit.

However, there are times we are chastened and that is alright, it is because GOD is a Loving Father who disciplines HIS children. When we are not being chastened, we are being tried as gold is forged through fire, and we must pass through the furnace so as to be refined. At other times, it's our testimony that has been given the devil Satan by our LORD GOD. When Satan accuses us before our Heavenly Father, and our Father says to him, no; they are wholly righteous, keeping to what I the LORD GOD desires from them. The devil, Satan, is not happy about such a testimony.

He must work hard to fail us and disapprove our Father GOD'S testimony. At that moment Satan starts to bring disasters to us that will make us ask, where is our GOD! Does HE really care? Look at this storm! It is so big that it's going to carry us away! Where is our GOD? The disasters are too many, and I cannot make it any more! GOD has left me! Then Satan will send your loved ones to tell you that you have been left by GOD and you better quit HIM and start helping yourself. Never listen to them! Your adversary Satan has brought all those disasters your way so that he can disapprove your love for GOD.

Satan has said "you are not righteous; you do not love GOD for no reason, it must be because GOD has been protecting you and kept you comfortable." Read Job 1:1-22 and 2:1-10. Thank GOD for Job. He never cursed GOD, much as he did not know why he was going through hell. All tribulations will cause much pain, but stand still and pray so that our LORD GOD may help you to stand on HIS Promises. If you get tired and sit on GOD'S Promises, you may not be able to make a step forward when HE wants you to make a move towards your miracles, Exodus 14:13.

At the Red Sea, Children of Israel were told to stand still; although it was not easy to stand still and helpless watching their enemy advance towards them to throw them into the sea. At the same time the LORD GOD told them, keep on moving. How were they to keep on moving while standing still? And where were they to go: to the sea or to the enemy Egyptians behind them? Remember, these were men with their wives, their young ones and everything else that belonged to them. It was a hard, trying moment for Moses and the Children of Israel. Nevertheless, GOD came in good time.

Our GOD is never late, HE Comes in very good time, never too early lest you miss the blessing and fall, nor too late lest you perish. In Exodus 14: 15 the LORD told Moses "speak unto the children of Israel that they go forward." If they had sat or slept with fear and anxiety, it would have taken time for them to wake up and move forward. "Stand still and keep on moving forward towards your LORD GOD Almighty and see GOD'S Salvation" which HE is going to bring to you and your Beloved ones, Amen.

My prayer for anyone who will read this Miracle Book: My Dear Loving Father, I pray by faith knowing that you do hear me when I pray, whoever will read this book; please let him/her receive an instant miracle of Salvation and everything that they have been waiting for. I am also waiting to receive miracles which carry numerous testimonies immediately I finish this miracle book, in JESUS HOLY NAME I PRAY. AMEN! AMEN!

This book is written for you and for me, where it is written you, read, I to apply it to your needs. I read Psalms 91 like this, I Mary, "who dwells in the secret place of the MOST HIGH, shall abide in the shadow of the Almighty." And I continue embracing the whole chapter emphasizing it on me. If I may say this, King David and all those writers of the Word of GOD were inspired to write for those who were to come after them. For where they are the Word in Psalms 91 and in the whole Bible is not necessary. The Word worked for them at that period in time as they lived. Now, it is for us who need the Word until we get to heaven. So, apply the Word in your life as you read HIM now. It's now you need the Word. When you get to heaven, you will not need the Word to apply in your life, you will be completely living with HIM. But now, you need the Word to live in you to defeat the enemy, and to apply in your life for better life's encouragement and comfort. You cannot enjoy peace, joy, and love in the Holy Ghost if you have no Word inside of you. Otherwise, you will live a defeated Christian life full of discouragement and struggles John 1:1-5.

At that time that you are going through very hard unbearable pains and miseries of different problems; remember, GOD is in you and on your side and you need to stay focused on HIM and be on HIS side too. "For when GOD is on our side who can be against us," Romans 8:31, or "whom shall we fear," Psalms 118:6, 27: 1-6. "Seeing that GOD did not spare HIS only begotten son for us, but give HIM for a sacrifice of our sins," how can HE let you go through what you are going through if HE is not going to get you out safely blessed with victory? Isaiah 54:17, "No weapon formed against you shall prosper, and every tongue that shall rise against you in judgment thou shalt condemn." In other words, you have the permission of the LORD to condemn that tongue, for that is your inheritance as a child and as a servant of GOD: for your righteousness is of HIM. And 1Corinthians 10:13 continues to say, "there hath no temptation taken you but such as is common to man: but GOD is faithful, who will not suffer you to be tempted above what you are able. But will with the temptation make away to escape, that you may be able to bear it."

Only, not by trying to help yourself out of your problem, for as a child of GOD, you cannot help yourself in any way without GOD doing it for you.

So many times I have gone through some trials until I ask my GOD, Dear LORD, is even this common to man? And HIS answer is, yes! You may be asking yourself the same thing as I have done, but I have learned big to wait upon GOD; I have seen HIS faithfulness whenever I go through temptations. When I wait and faint not, HE comes quickly to deliver me. Yes, HE really does!

The time of waiting feels like forever, but still, GOD'S coming is timely. Indeed, HE will carry us through even the most painful times of our lives. When we are climbing mountain of problems, HE carries us through and over those mountains. When we're going downhill in the deep pit of lacking, HE is holding us tight lest we die of fear. When we are sleeping in the pool of tears, HE is there with us to comfort us lest our tears fall for nothing. When we are not able to swallow food because the pain in our hearts blocks our throats, JESUS is there with us to encourage lest we give up.

When such a time comes for you, remember the Woman in Luke 7:36-48 who washed and anointed LORD JESUS' feet with her tears, and know that our LORD feels for us as we wash and anoint him with our tears. That woman may have gone through a lot of humiliation and struggle but when she washed and anointed JESUS with her tears, I believe that that was the end of her struggle. She received the Love she had desired and deserved, and the approval from the Most High Priest.

The high priests and the Pharisees at the Jerusalem Temple would have ordered for her to be stoned if she had gone to them. But the Everlasting and Ever Loving Highest Priest, JESUS CHRIST, gave her life and love instead of death. Here, we need to say a big...Hallelujah! JESUS advocated for her from men who were condemning her at that moment and at any other moment. HE cleansed, purified and sanctified her there and then. To sanctify means to make a clean separation for a great purpose. There and then, she was separated from the rest of the worldly women and made a child of the Most High King, the KING of Kings, and the LORD of Lords. No more struggle; no more tears. Her misery was turned to missiles there and then by her LORD GOD.

Most probably, if you had met that Lady before she washed JESUS with her tears you would not have looked at her twice. But after the encounter with CHRIST JESUS THE LORD, she became a celebrity. Her problems were over and her miseries were exchanged with missiles to destroy and put the devil to great shame. Likewise, JESUS will turn your misery into missiles to destroy all the works of the enemy, Satan, who has caused you to have such a painful life. Just continue to worship and wait upon HIM. See Luke 7:36-50, Hebrews 4:14-16.

Boldly, stay unto our LORD GOD the Father, and the Son and the HOLY SPIRIT. You are very important and you are very soon overcoming the tribulation you are going through. Do not forget at HIS calling, JESUS said, if you follow HIM, you will get everything in 100 folds but with tribulation and persecution; Mark 10:29-30, Matthew 19:28-29.

And in everything "count it joy when you follow in to divers temptations," James 1:2. "And we knowing that, all things work together for good to them that love GOD, them that are called according to HIS purpose," Romans 8:28.

CHAPTER 3

Look At Gilgal

Gilgal is a place of restoration, and plenty. At Gilgal the reproach of Egypt is take away and the new life of great victory in JESUS CHRIST Begins. Gilgal is a place of New Beginning in the LORD. All new beginnings are sweet only in JESUS CHRIST. Outside there, only miseries that will never turn to missiles but remains miseries to miseries leading to bitterness and to bitterness until you learn to surrender all to JESUS CHRIST The owner of life and you start your Gilgal of waiting for your restoration and victory.

At Gilgal, there are many threats and uncertainty but you have to have gained enough faith to be able to stand against all the threats of the enemy. Gilgal is a place appointed for you to meet with JESUS CHRIST The Captain of The LORD of Host, and where you have to, I mean, you must learn very well to hear, know, and understand your GOD properly so that you do not mistake your, vision, mission and ministry. Here, at Gilgal is where JESUS CHRIST is going to appear to you as a mighty warrior in any form and you might start casting and rebuking HIM thinking HE is the enemy. But it is HIM who has come to reveal the whole of Godliness to you so that you may learn to recognize the ways and things of GOD patiently like Joshua, and never draw a sword to GOD when HE is about to save, deliver, and restore you. You see, Joshua did not allow the fear to lead him shout and draw his sword to the military/ soldier like man that stood before him with HIS Sword drawn at Gilgal, Joshua 5: 13-15. For Joshua had known, no fear any more GOD is on their side and to him the man looked like GOD'S Messenger.

You may be at your Gilgal Now! Joshua 5:9-15. What are you supposed to do at your Gilgal? Crying in misery for the fear of Jericho wall and the inside the walls Canaanites? Or praising GOD with joy of your Missiles that HE has given you from HIS Word and the past miracles? Take your Prayer of Worship and worship the LORD by the Power of the HOLY SPIRIT to defeat Satan your enemy. Reminding the enemy Satan the many Red Seas that GOD has dried and crossed you and the defeat of his army. The past Manna, the provisions of food, water, shelter, clothing and finances to do the things that need money. And thank GOD instead of lamenting with fear, self-pity and long standing anger.

Do not allow Satan to take control of you through bills and debts which Satan has brought to you. The devil wants to take full control of your life. It is for you to refuse and stand boldly as a soldier who knows the power and ability of his Captain JESUS CHRIST. Our Major General can never be defeated. We fight a battle which is already won. The Jericho wall and its army of bills or sickness or whatever problem standing against you was sunk for you by our LORD GOD before it was built; you are seeing the image of a dead wall.

All your debts were paid at Calvary. There at Calvary, there was a great settlement done. All the negotiation was completed between Gethsemane and Calvary. And finally, while all the bills and the debts were being paid, every one heard the voice of the Master JESUS saying, it is finished! It is over!

No more unpaid bills, no more unpaid debts for you to pay miserably! "I have paid all for you, only believe!" Said JESUS CHRIST OUR LORD AND SAVIOR! You do not know how since you cannot see the money right now, but very soon, you will see the settler settling every bill for you and leave you debt free. The Children of Israel were not able to foresee the Red Sea hoisted to the level of that painfully threatening ground they stood on as the army of Pharaoh tried to come closer to overthrow them.

Do you see how the children of Israel stood on a painfully threatening ground? They did not know where to run to, or where to go next. With the Red Sea before them and the enemy, the Egyptians' army behind them spread all over surrounding them side by side, where could have they gone to? They saw nothing but death encompassing them. But GOD saw great praise after HE accomplishes what HE was doing. Exodus 7:3-5. Wait faithfully, and patiently, GOD is going to be glorified as you enjoy HIS Victory on what HE is doing in the problem encompassing you.

The children of Israel stood helpless and fearful, but Moses stood faithfully hopeful, knowing that his GOD did not need their help to deliver them. Just remember, they did not see when GOD cemented and elevated the depth of the sea to make a smooth road for them to cross safely. Just imagine, the children of Israel were not asked to help clear the stones, coral, logs, man eater sea fish and sea animals after the water was moved on both sides to make the way passable.

Had the LORD asked them to help out; that work would not have got finished. And they would not have been able to cross that Sea before they are either eaten by sea man eater creatures or the enemy overtake and capture them. Our GOD does not need our help at all. And so HE will never ask or require us to help HIM to do HIS Miracles. HE is a wonderfully very good director and a very successful powerful worker. Don't limit HIM at all.

Can you see the magnitude of the Red Sea Miracle? People think of the parting of the water only, but it was a whole huge of job which would probably have taken over 40 years if men and their machines were to do it. Moving of the water on both sides and making that water stand solid was one big mighty wonderful and inexplicable miracle. Then, lifting up that ground under the water to be at the same level with the sea shore, and putting those animals, fish, coral stones, and logs and the drying the thick deep mud and plaster it was another mighty huge Work to be done within very few hours of the night.

Above all, that miracle was followed by many other mighty processions of miracles. Making that dry road from such a deep sea full of sea animals, whales, sharks, crocodiles, mighty stones, huge corals, deep mud and sea plants, name what else is in the sea that has never dried from the creation of the earth, was the next step.

By the time the plastering of that sea was done and the safe crossing of the children of Israel, to the swallowing up of the enemy the Egyptians by the same water was complete, the children of Israel had seen a Mighty Hand at work. And our LORD GOD had made HIMSELF known by all the nations of the earth in mightier way.

Read Exodus 14 and 15, and you'll see a Mighty Hand at work for your Red Sea. Only believe like Moses, and you will see GOD'S Salvation. "The enemy you see today, you will never see him anymore." The problems which have caused you to cry day and night, you will never see or hear of it any more. I do believe like Moses that all that I need to do is to stand still, keep on moving towards my promised land and see my GOD'S Salvation. There may look like there's no way or hope but GOD has a way out of every problem and every situation.

Now you can sing this chorus with me "LORD I believe, LORD I believe, all things are possible, LORD I believe, all things are possible with you, yes I believe my Jehovah Jireh. Hallelujah! Is this applicable! Yes it is! Here, the key point is to know who your GOD is: And how you relate with HIM. And that your GOD changes not. Our GOD is not like a chameleon that today he will be a white chameleon and tomorrow dark green or brown. When you know your relationship with your LORD GOD who changes not, then you will have overcome it all.

No Human Mind Can

To go back to Joshua as he lead the children of Israel upon the death of Moses, all through, Joshua knew his GOD very well, and his relationship with his GOD. In Joshua 1:2-9, The LORD GOD promised and commissioned Joshua to be a leader to HIS people, so Joshua was following this great commission.

The enemy knew who Joshua was but did not imagine that Joshua knew who he was in his Father GOD. Satan thought Joshua was like Adam and Eve; that he might lure him with deceit. We had better be careful lest Satan see a loophole in us and try to entice us with his questioning lies.

Satan thought that if he put doubt into Joshua, then he was going to defeat him. But Joshua knew how to wait upon the LORD his GOD. Joshua focused unto HIM that had chosen, anointed, ordained and sent him. Joshua knew that his GOD had never failed them all the way from Egypt to that point, only Israel had failed GOD many times. Joshua also remembered the many times Israel had failed GOD. All the way from exiting Egypt to the trans-Jordan phase they kept on failing GOD. But in his heart, Joshua had promised not to fail his faithful loving GOD. Joshua remembered miracle after miracle from Egypt to Soji-Jordan (Across Jordan). You and I need to remember all the miracles that our GOD has performed for us. Breathing in and out with lungs and the whole respiratory system being clear is alone a great miracle for which we should be grateful to our GOD.

As a human being at Gilgal, Joshua must have been in deep prayer with great distress because of the task which was ahead of him. Just like any of us; of course, Joshua was not a supernatural man, he was a natural man waiting on the One who is supernatural, the LORD GOD ALMIGHTY.

If you want a supernatural life, you have to wait on the author of the supernatural life who formed HIMSELF into a Supernatural Son to be conceived of a virgin, Mary, and to be born supernaturally, and to die a supernatural death even though it looked natural on the Cross, and to produce a supernatural Blood to supernaturally cleanse and save those of us who will believe in HIS only begotten Son.

Salvation in JESUS CHRIST is a supernatural act in the lives of believers. And that is why a carnal mind cannot comprehend how we are saved, and boldly say; we are Born Again and live on, proclaiming the same all the years of this life on earth.

That is why we believers are supposed by all means to lead a supernatural life: a life full of Godly Worship in Righteousness, and Holiness without doubt that our GOD is going to do it for us supernaturally.

Remember, here, we are talking about the life of Joshua as the second leader of his brethren the children of Israel after crossing Jordan. At this juncture, Joshua and the whole family of Israel are waiting to go to attack the great wall of Jericho. When they look at that wall, and they see the sophisticated ammunitions hope is kind of going out of them. And that is why they have to supernaturally be circumcised afresh in order to be able to wait for the supernatural act of getting into Jericho.

From Egypt, to Jordan, Joshua had known A LORD GOD of miracles, and he had witnessed HIM work supernaturally.

I feel in the spirit that this is a stage every believer needs. That we observe our walk in the LORD and when we see that our LORD has helped us cross our Red Seas, and helped us live in our wilderness without failing HIM; we need to get to our LORD and let him circumcise us afresh. Why be circumcised afresh? The wall ahead of us is mighty and the battle can be vicious unless we are able to wait upon Our LORD GOD ALMIGHTY for a supernatural deliverance.

Joshua stayed focused on the promises of GOD, by standing still, looking and waiting to see the power of his GOD'S deliverance. With all the miracles that Joshua had witnessed GOD perform on their way to Canaan; Joshua knew that the same power would be manifest on the wall of Jericho and on the army atop the wall. He knew that those inside the walls would perish, as it was with the Red Sea and the Egyptians.

Therefore, you too, need to wait on GOD like Joshua. It is a terrible frightening moment, but real believers have nothing else to do, but to wait. The waiting Moment is not one of the sweetest moments on earth! But GOD knows all that.

Remember, you are not alone. Our LORD JESUS prayed for us to be given a comforter, the HOLY SPIRIT. It‘s hard, but wait in HIM! Don‘t you quit, you are not of them that quit. No, you are not! And even if you feel like quitting, don't. Wait! Even if you feel like GOD is gone away and HE is very far from you, it is not by feeling nor by seeing; it is by faith that you are going to wait. It may feel foolish, but wait!

There are moments when even prayers do not come easily. You just feel like GOD is too far from you, and you are about to let go. No! Do not let go! You are not sure if you are able to wait for what you cannot see today, but you had better wait. Our Father in heaven can see what you are going through. You do not need to see HIM to believe that HE is going to do it for you and leave you safe. Just believe that HE IS, and that HE is seeing you and HE is holding you tightly. And HIS Holy Angels are surrounding you so that you cannot fall, and be hit by the devil's stones. At this terrible moment of your life, that is all that you need to do. Wait on HIM that you cannot see or feel: just shall live by faith; Habakkuk 2: 4, Romans 1:17, 2 Corinthians 5: 7.

John 10:10b, JESUS CHRIST who promised you life in abundance is not asleep, and HE does not sleep nor slumber; Psalms 121:1-8. The best thing that was happening to Joshua, and that should happen to you now, is to have in memory all the miracles that you have seen in past.

Joshua had in him memories dating back to the deliverance of the Passover in Egypt, to the Red Sea, and in the wilderness, to where they had now reached in the land of Canaan. All was fresh in Joshua's mind. Joshua had not forgotten the conquer of Trans-Jordan and HE knew that the same GOD who had conquered all the enemies of Israel to that point where they were knew what to do with that great-looking wall of Jericho and the people inside it.

The wall stood there, at 50ft by 50ft and standing at its top were mighty men of war. Seeing those commanders, and their methodically trained soldiers, waiting, heavily armed, in readiness for battle against the inadequate Israelites, Joshua in his natural human mind would have withdrawn and run for his life. And mark this, never forget! At that moment of waiting, the most obvious thing was happening to Joshua's mind. The enemy of believers, Satan, was visiting Joshua's mind every minute of the waiting period with forceful questions to cast doubt in him. Looking at his unarmed army of Israel, it was not easy for any human mind to work out how they were going to seize that city.

Joshua knew that the battle was not his, nor was it the children of Israel's. We too must remember that the battle is not our own. For we are not able to fight our enemy Satan in any way, but Our Redeemer LORD JESUS CHRIST has assured us that the battle is not ours; it is HIS to fight and finish for us. Ours is to receive the victory if we faint not.

Our part on this earth, which Our LORD GOD asked us to play is to only believe HIM and trust HIM; and to believe in HIM that HE loves us so much that HE cannot leave us neither forsake us. And that HE is A Mighty GOD in every way; HE cannot let our enemy's weapons fall on us. Also, Our Heavenly Father wants us to know that we are only frightened by the noise of the bullets. All that we hear is the noise! GOD cannot allow us come to the battle field! It is too hot for us!

In reality, the actual battle is in the air, and what get to us is only the sound and the dust of ammunitions. When the devil comes to you with multiple financial problems which you don't know how to solve, or the loss of that very well paying job, tell him you know your redeemer lives. Or if he comes with a disease called cancer, leukemia, osteoporosis, lupus, active peptic ulcers, pneumonia, and any other name Satan gives his products, he is aiming at your faith, and the love you have for your GOD. Rebuke him hard and tell him to carry away his products and to never bring them back to you again!

You are clean through the Word of GOD and by the Blood of JESUS CHRIST. You are the child of GOD and are created in HIS Image and Likeness. Your body is the Temple and the Indwelling place of the HOLY SPIRIT, Praise LORD GOD ALMIGHTY! You are a child of MOST HIGH GOD and not devils' plaything.

Satan knows our GOD is an all-loving GOD and Omnipotent; there is nothing Satan can do to distract GOD'S love from you. He can do nothing to stop GOD from helping you out. Surely -- nothing! Satan knows very well that the only way he can distract GOD'S love from us is through causing disobedience to GOD. If he, the devil, can cause you to doubt GOD'S ability to perform miracles for you, he has won you over. And this is the way in which Satan is trying to work on your mind. At this moment of numerous troubles which he has brought to you: DO NOT let him win; refuse in the Mighty Name of JESUS CHRIST. Tell him No, devil, I am more than a conqueror through CHRIST JESUS Who loves me! "From the days of John the Baptist to this day, the Kingdom of GOD suffers violence and the violent take it by force" Matthew 12:12.

The Lie

First, the deceiver is lying to you that there is no miracle you are waiting for in such circumstances. This is how and what Satan says, "Is heaven going to open and GOD give money to you?" Or

"Have you seen it done the way you say GOD is going to do it for you? Do you think GOD is going to do it again the way HE did it for you last year? Are you sure this time you are not mistaken? Don't you remember last year you had at least some source of income but now you have nothing? Don't you know even if GOD heals, not all people are healed and not all the diseases are healed? "All these are his lies to steal your focus on your Father LORD GOD. Rebuke him hard and cast him away in JESUS Name.

For, when he has left you with no faith in GOD and no faith in what you believed, then he will start giving you his opinion and provisions which are nothing but lies. At that moment, he knows he has already gotten the whole of you and now he can easily kill you, and destroy everything that GOD gave to you. Satan will even go as far as rallying other people against you, and harm you for no apparent reason other than to ruin the very little faith that may be found in you so that you do not heed the word of GOD. For, if the devil manages to get you through his constant lies and sees that he has stolen your faith, he will laugh and clap his dirty hands and dump you to die miserably.

My advice to every one of us believers is: it does not matter what Satan is telling you, watch and look at the Victory of the Cross at Calvary. Look unto JESUS CHRIST standing on the Right Hand of The FATHER and know that HE is interceding for you daily before the Father; Romans 8: 31-39.

Remember, Satan does not aim at or waste his time fighting people of no faith. He is busy fighting those who are faithfully waiting for GOD'S promises. He dishes out the lie that, 'since what you are going through is very painful, there are some easy dirty satanic ways which you can go through to get out of your situation." My friend, devils' ways can never be safe, for they will lead you to destruction now and for all eternity. Watch out and follow JESUS CHRIST to the Cross of Salvation, and you will be safe. I beseech you, do *not* fret or quit. Your situation may feel very bitter, painful, discouraging, and tiring, but do not quit or fret.

Psalms 37:1 starts by saying, "Fret not thyself because of the evildoers, neither be thou envious against the workers of iniquity. For they shall soon be cut down like the grass, and wither as the green herbs." That is a very strong statement, one which aims at giving us some sound teaching and imparting in us a lot of wisdom. As I say to you my friend, quit not, my dear, from our GOD'S Kingdom of marvelous protection and provision. Our GOD does not slumber neither does HE sleep; Psalms 121: 1-8. HE watches over you day and night. HE is watching over you even when your heart is so pained, troubled, and discouraged, GOD has not forgotten you. If GOD had forgotten you, you would have been consumed in a fraction of a second.

Think about the times you have gone through sleepless nights, lying in your bed with your heart aching with despair, and yet, despite the discouragement, you have gradually sunk into sleep and woken up in the morning alive and well. Amazing, isn't it? Amazing how we can go to bed so discouraged and still find that we are alive and well and of sound mind; not gone insane over stress. It is because the One who watches over us would not allow it happen to us. Our LORD GOD wakes us in the morning fully protected from mental attacks.

I am sure you know that excessive stress is one of the most common causes of depression, which manifests itself as great sadness. It is a state of unhappiness and hopelessness which may cause a psychiatric disorder showing symptoms such as persistent feelings of hopelessness, dejection, rejection, poor concentration, lack of energy, inability to sleep, and, sometimes, suicidal tendencies. When you experience such feelings know that you are under severe attack from the enemy. Do not neglect it or let the sent demons deceive you, saying, "It is normal sickness so go and get diagnosed and then take some medicine for it." Yes, medicine, rather medical treatment will relieve the symptoms for a short while and then the symptoms will recur, again and again, such that you repeatedly take antidepressants until you became dependent on them.

I have been through a similarly severe attack from the devil and I know how easily those demons push their way into one's brain. This they do through problems that Satan and his demons device to fight us with. Remember, problems are the devils missiles; weapons forged from lies aiming at stealing your LORD GOD given peace, joy and love; hence, faith.

The devil knows that when you have no faith in your Father, GOD, he and his demons have a lot of power over you. Don't let those symptoms rest in you, they are not just symptoms. They are manifestations of the enemy Satan and his demons, attacking you from right inside your brain. Psychiatric medicine cannot locate what part of the brain they are lodged in. Medical science does not see demons unless they manifest themselves in the form of microorganisms such as bacteria, parasites, bacillus, protozoa or worse, viruses which happen to be invisible microscopically.

I know some medical people may try to disprove this finding but it is the truth. I have carried out research on the devil and his demons in connection with diseases, and what we call causative organisms, since 1977. I have found that without a doubt it is the devil who manufactures germs that sicken. He counterfeited the normal germs (normal florae) that our LORD GOD created to support our bodily functions, and made his sickness-causing germs, giving names to the diseases they cause; names such as pneumonia, flu, whooping cough, arthritis, Aids, tuberculosis, and so on. Satanic spirits can also get into a body and cause dysfunctions. But we have got power over them in the Name of JESUS CHRIST; Luke 10:19, Mark 16: 15-20, JESUS gave us power over all the powers and works of our enemy Satan and his demons.

Therefore, come up against those demons of depression and stress in the Name of JESUS CHRIST, bind them and cast them back to their bottomless pit in the Mighty Name of JESUS CHRIST. Defeat them and cast them out of your mind, your brain, and your entire body in JESUS HOLY NAME; Amen! Overcome by the Blood of JESUS CHRIST knowing that the LORD GOD ALMIGHTY watches over you, and HE cares for you. You are not alone; our Righteous LORD GOD who can never lie is inside of you, waiting for you to manifest HIS True Word upon your life.

Tell the devil you know who you are and that he has no power over you. GOD has already turned your miseries into missiles. Start shouting Satan and his kingdom down with the heavenly bullets of GOD'S Word in the Mighty Name of JESUS CHRIST! Get excited as you bind every demon of anxiety, stress and depression, telling them to go out speedily in the Mighty Name of JESUS CHRIST. Tell him you are child of the Most High GOD and heaven is your eternal home, Amen. And in the Mighty Name of JESUS CHRIST, remind Satan of his future.

Your body belongs to the HOLY SPIRIT and it is the indwelling of GOD the Father, the SON, and the HOLY SPIRIT; Satan has no share in any part of your body; Amen! When you know this secret; that our LORD GOD ALMIGHTY only lets such things happen so that you may learn to surrender yourself to HIM and learn to lean on HIM alone, then you will live a very successful life even when hardships come. You will be able to speak to the situation and circumstances around you. HE who lives forever and HE Who changes not, is watching over you, to help you come out of the situation you are in safely, and prosperous having turned your misery into missiles. Only trust HIM wholly; Psalm 118; 17. Yes, surely; it is only HIM Alone, the LORD GOD ALMIGHTY who is able to do that for you for HIS Holy Name's sake.

You are HIS child and he cannot put HIS name to shame. For Our GOD is a Father that cannot give HIS children scorpions for eggs, nor snakes for fish, nor stones for bread, Matthew 7:9-11. Neither is HE going to let you receive debts for credits or sickness for health, Jeremiah 33:3, 17: 7-8-14, 29:11-14,30:16-17,Isaiah 53:4-5, 54:1-17, 55:1-9;12-13,59:19, John 14:12-15.

Your account, stolen by the devil, now has GOD crediting it with money the amounts of which you have never held in your hands. Nothing is impossible with GOD, only believe. All your bills will be paid in full and you will have enough to serve the LORD your GOD with. And LORD let it be so now, in JESUS

HOLY Name Amen. I ask and I believe now it is done in JESUS Precious Name; Amen!

Tithe:

Our LORD JESUS told Peter, “go to the lake, cast in a hook, and take the fish that comes first, open its mouth, you will find enough money for ME and you,” Matthew 17:27. When you get what the LORD GOD will bring your way, remember the Tithe and Offering for the work of your GOD. Do not be consumed by your needs, give your Tithe and Offering to your Pastor or Church where you fellowship then pay the bills. And remember, you must apply GOD’S law while you wait. You must ask to be given, seek to find, and knock for the door to be opened, Matthew 7:7-8, John 14:12-14. HE is your shepherd and you shall not want, Psalms 23:1-6. Meditate upon HIS word so that you gain strength to wait on HIM. AMEN!

CHAPTER 4

Past Miracles Stir up Waiting Miracles: Hebrews 11: 1-6

The past miracles prepare a waiting stage for oncoming miracles. Do not allow Satan to take advantage of you by causing you to forget the previous precious miracles because they stir your today's miracles for your future miracles. Your yesterday's miracles will help you build up your faith-wrought missiles out of your misery. Remember faith is the substance of the things hoped for and evidence of the things not seen. Instead of you sleeping on that bed lamenting in deep misery, you will remember what GOD did for you yesterday, last month, last year and ten years ago. And you will be able to tell Satan, "devil you are a liar and you have no power over me! In the mighty Name of JESUS CHRIST I Command you out of here now!! Stop your nonsense and go away right now in JESUS HOLY NAME! Go away devil!" Tell him, "This is not your territory! You have no legal right to stay here bringing lies to me! I am child of GOD and I am waiting for my Father's provision! "If it is sickness he has brought to you, tell him to take away his baggage of all that sickness it carries and go with it to his place! And you are commanding him to do that in the name of JESUS CHRIST your LORD and Savior Amen! JESUS CHRIST paid it all for you and the devil has no share in your life any more. Satan and his dirty work of sickness, poverty, and all his problems are inadmissible in your life. Only the HOLY SPIRIT has the right to dwell in your body. Tell Satan who you are in the LORD JESUS CHRIST. Let the devil know that you know who you are in The LORD and he should know you as he knows JESUS CHRIST, Paul and other Apostles.

Acts 19:15, Here, Satan in a madman told the seven sons of Sceva, a Jew and chief of Priests, "JESUS we know, and Paul we know, who are you?" These sons of Sceva were not Born Again, and that was their biggest mistake; to think that they could cast out devils in the name of JESUS CHRIST as Paul and other Apostles were doing. By the way, the devil comes to every one of us in different ways. When you are righteous, and holy waiting upon the LORD, then Satan will send his demons to torture you with many types of problems to steal your trust in GOD. The whole purpose of the devil's deeds is to frustrate our LORD GOD and the complete precious work of our LORD JESUS CHRIST at the Cross of Calvary. You have not done anything wrong, you are alright but stand still and wait for your salvation

Also, while waiting, you must know the relationship between you and JESUS CHRIST; that is, you must stay cleansed, purified and sanctified in order to command and cast demons out of yourself, your area, your property, your body, and even out of other people. You can't just use the Name of JESUS CHRIST without HIS Divine quality and character in you. You must be CHRIST LIKE; Acts 11:26.

To be able to tell Satan off, you must have no link with him at all! If you are not Born Again and you do not have the right identity by the Blood of JESUS CHRIST, then you cannot get power to expel the devils out of your dwellings and they can really pester and even destroy you.

At this juncture, please consider this that if you are not sure that your name is written in the book of life; receive JESUS CHRIST in your heart right now, so as to be allowed to use HIS Mighty Name: JESUS CHRIST. (YESHUA MESSIAH)

Just pray this simple, but important prayer with me now and your life will change for good, if you pray and stick to your confession, JESUS will dwell in you and HE shall allow you to use HIS Name against the enemy, Matthew 16: 16-19, Mark 16: 17. Romans 10:8-11 says, "We believe righteousness in our hearts and confess salvation with our mouth."

<u>Pray A Prayer of Faith into Redemption:</u>

SAY: DEAR LORD JESUS, PLEASE SAVE ME, AND ACCEPT ME BY WASHING ME WITH YOUR PRECIOUS BLOOD THAT YOU SHED AT THE CROSS OF CALVARY FOR ALL REPENTING SINNERS, I ACCEPT THAT I AM A SINNER. AND BY NATURE I WAS BORN A SINNER, AND ONLY YOU CAN SAVE ME. I AM REPENTING ALL

MY SINS THAT I KN0W AND THAT I DO NOT KNOW I AM ASKING YOU KINDLY TO FORGIVE AND SAVE ME, DEAR LORD. WRITE MY NAME IN THE BOOK OF LIFE, MY LORD, GIVE ME THE POWER OF YOUR HOLY SPIRIT TO ENABLE ME STAND AGAINST Satan's power, LEAD ME DEAR LORD, AND KEEP ME SAVED IN YOUR BLOOD UNTIL YOU COME AGAIN, IN JESUS HOLY NAME I PRAY AND BELIEVE; AMEN!

If you are born again, just believe that you have enough missiles to fight. Take up and put on your whole armor of GOD and fight the victorious worthy battle in the Name of JESUS CHRIST without fear, Amen.

You are about to overcome because even before you noticed that there was battle, your LORD GOD was fighting it for you, HE had already sent enough Angels in the air to fight for you. All that is reaching you is the gun powder, the dust and the noise of the bullets.

Every time you are in battle, remember Job chapters 1 and 2. How Satan went to present himself before Our Creator and asked permission to tempt Job. Also, remember Job chapter 42, how GOD had restored to Job everything that the devil had destroyed and restituted all in double measure.

GOD did not give back to Job only what he had before, but Job was paid and repaid, properly all that the devil had destroyed. I mean fully compensated for everything in double measure, and with more beautiful children and with his body healed and restored to a younger person than he was before the disasters and given another 140 years to live with his children to the fourth generation, Job 42:10-17.

Now that you have been attacked on all sides, and you cannot fight strongly, remember Job, Paul and all the men of GOD who have been there before you. They were fought and fought, but they never gave up; they held to the Peace of GOD, in pain. This battle is not physical, and your friends may not understand what you are going through. They will even add you sorrow if you try to explain to them what is amiss. They wonder why you should have that problem which is so acute. But know that Job went through that before we did so that we could learn to wait.

The Apostles too went through a lot so that GOD may teach us patience. You can never know how to wait until you have been on long wait; then what you have been waiting for eventually, miraculously comes with all the Heavenly beauty. You can never know what patience is until you have been put on a waiting list that is extremely long and in the midst of waiting without hope, without knowing when it will happen, GOD performs a miracle and there you are. All that you have been waiting for comes with all the Heavenly joy and the beauty there in. From then, you just become a very good teacher of how to handle Mr. Patience and Mr. Waiting.

Actually, even now, there are others who are going through worse battles than yours. So wait, and having done all, wait on GOD'S promises which cannot fail. Therefore, stand still and you will soon see GOD'S deliverance on you. Pray without ceasing, 1Thessalonians 5: 17-25 even for others about whom you do not know what they are going through and where they are. Also remember, Ephesians 6:10-17&18-19 tells us, "we wrestle not against fresh and blood, but against principalities, powers, rulers of darkness in this world, and against spiritual wickedness in high places. Therefore, stand and having done all, stand, with the whole armor of GOD and fight "praying for the saints" and those who are preaching the Gospel of the kingdom of GOD here, far and wide that the LORD GOD "will give us utterances as we preach."

CHAPTER 5

Satan talking behind your back

Remember the devil with his demons were talking negative of JESUS CHRIST OUR LORD'S sacrificial death from the Garden of Gethsemane to the Cross, the tree of death at Calvary to restore us to Garden of the tree of Life.

JESUS refused to listen to Satan and all his dirty conversation full of lies. At that moment, Satan was trying to convince JESUS that HIS death on the Cross would be fruitless. Satan was saying, you and I can never be saved and no one is going to believe and accept that JESUS died for their sins, so HE should refuse to die.

Satan was ridiculing JESUS CHRIST telling HIM that he, Satan was the winner from the time that he had deceived Adam to the time he had deceived all those people who were against JESUS CHRIST as they shouted, crucify, crucify, crucify Him! And how he, the devil had hardened people's hearts not to heed JESUS'

Word as he preached even with numerous miracles and taught the Word of Life to them for 3year.

That day, that devil was busier in the Garden of Gethsemane than he had been in the Garden of Eden. Satan was trying to convince JESUS not to die because he knew that the moment JESUS accepted to die, then that would be the end of the devils' power over believers. He knew that miracles would have more meaning in believers' lives than ever before. He knew we were going to be "more than conquerors through CHRIST who loves us." Satan knew that the moment JESUS CHRIST sheds HIS Blood, a New Covenant was going to be established in us, the believers, as it is written in Jeremiah 31:31-35; that would be the end of power of devil's kingdom. His lies would be over! His kingdom would now be powerless! However, despite his defeat, he still continued with his old dirty game of deceiving and he will continue until CHRIST will come to take us home. It is us to keep to the standard of the Covenant of our LORD JESUS CHRIST by humility with prayers of thanksgiving and supplication.

Therefore, you and I must be aware of his lies and mark when he comes to whisper and lie to us. We must know that his is an old trick to put us away from our Father's relationship. We must keep on focused on our relationship with our LORD JESUS and HIS Divine Work of Calvary for our Divine Salvation. That is the miracle number one. And then we keep on remembering all the miracles that JESUS has done for us. That makes us keep our ears from listening to the lies of Satan, and his demons. Our ears will be closed to his devices; the WORD of GOD will be alive in us. When our LORD GOD Says, "Fear not;" we shall hear it clearly, daily.

When Satan talked at the back of Joshua's mind, Joshua would overcome Satan's discouragement by the renewal of his mind, Ephesians 423-24, Philippians 2:5-11, for that Great Miracle of crossing of Red Sea was still fresh in Joshua's spirit.

In Joshua 2:1-24,3:1-15,5:1-12, all this time, Joshua had to wait upon the LORD for one more mighty thing he had not seen done by his GOD, the demolishing of that mighty strong wall of Jericho and the conquer of the mighty men of war inside that Jericho city.

At least, crossing of Jordan was not so much Joshua's concern because he had seen the miracle of Red Sea. But entering Jericho must have been a concern to him because they had not fought a fortified-walled city with skilled great men of war before.

At that trying moment, what kept Joshua from fainting was refusing to listen to the voices of the enemy, Satan. Instead he meditated on the past miracles. In order to remain obedient, Joshua would remind himself all the mighty works that the LORD had done on their way from Egypt to the crossing of River Jordan. River Jordan was a very great wide and deep river and especially that area around Jericho where they were crossing, it overflows the high banks. I have been to Israel many times and I can tell you that you couldn't just cross that river in the days of Joshua. Now, technology has made it easier for a traveler.

If Joshua's brain were to be opened to us today, to see what Satan was trying to put in his mind, we would wonder at how he had managed to wait to carry on that task and obediently overcame ...Oh victory in the LORD! He must have sung a song of victory in the LORD.

Here; the secret is, the HOLY SPIRIT would see the determination of Joshua to obey the LORD his GOD. And HE would encourage him the more to remember miracles that GOD performed for them in Egypt and all the Miracles in the wilderness.

Joshua never let his present pains and miseries carry away memories of past miracles which he had seen and experienced since the deliverance had started with Moses' going back from exile to the land of Egypt. The Book of Exodus expresses Israel's deliverance from Egyptian's authority to GOD'S Authority starting with the birth of Moses to the crossing of Red Sea; Exodus 2 to 15. And many more other deliverances continued on the other side of Red Sea. This kind of journey is experienced by the True Born Again who waits upon the LORD day and night. Waiting upon the LORD or for the LORD does not mean sitting back and wait. No! It means, working for the LORD and looking upon HIM as a waiter serves looking upon the master for payment. Again let me say, Our LORD GOD employs, engages and entrusts only HIS children with HIS Ministries.

Joshua constantly remembered how some of his brethren who had thought themselves better leaders of Israel, and doubted GOD'S work through Moses, had been killed by the LORD in the wilderness. Examples in the Bible of folk who had forgotten past miracles were those of Korah and Dathan and their followers; Numbers 16: 23-33. Others in the New Testament were Judas Iscariot, and most of those who shouted that Jesus be crucified.

After they had received healing and other miracles, they shouted, crucify him.

Many times, we let past miseries bring fear to the present misery and carry away the memory of the past miracles that GOD intended to bring us to the Jericho conquer, our holy land of plenty. Jericho was a mighty fortified city of great wealth in the whole of Canaan Land. The kingdom of Jericho was well saturated with wealth and was well protected as far as man was concerned.

Security was greatly tight, and the wall was as mightily fortified and over 50ft high and over 50ft thick. Cars, trunks, and any kind of vehicle would have driven on top of the Jericho wall as though it were a dual carriage highway. That is how mighty that wall was. On top of the wall, there were guards' houses with the most sophisticated missiles that Israel had ever seen, and might not have known how to use.

But GOD knew that the battle was HIS and it was to be for HIS Glory and Honor. Remember, the children of Israel; just like you and I were not men of war, they had just come from slavery into wilderness where there were no army training barracks. But our Heavenly Father is a Man of War, and HE teaches us how to war when need arises, Psalms 18:34-39.

Politically, Jericho was under the cover of a good relationship with the king of Egypt; hence, Jericho was like a part of Egypt. The relationship was such that when Jericho was attacked, Egypt was attacked. They had a way of sending their 9-1-1 signals and alarm whenever necessary. And the need had arisen to fight, kill and destroy the children of Israel to stop GOD'S covenant from being fulfilled.

You and I follow in this same category of the Children of Israel. The kingdom of Satan is like the wall of Jericho to us. And the link of communication between the Canaanites and Egyptians was like the link the demons have. It does not matter how far the nation is from the other, Satan and his demons will still communicate on how to destroy.

In these later days, the kingdom of Satan seems to be greatly fortified and well informed round about our lives. Whatever we touch, whatever we try to do, the devil and his demons are there trying to destroy. They are there trying to stop anything GOOD coming our way.

All is looking miserable on your side. Nothing on your side seems to succeed. Your children are scattered all over with no success. But GOD! At the beginning, when you started this heavenly journey of salvation in our LORD JESUS, everything looked very good and promising, but all of a sudden, hell fell on you, and now! Oh LORD! You seem to be sinking and it looks like the devil has organized it such that you will sink deeper than ever before.

But Remember, the deeper you go the deeper your redeemer goes, therefore, you can never sink beyond where JESUS CHRIST can save you. But before you sink even one leg into the devil's sea, call our 9-1-1. It is quicker than any nation's 9-1-1 on earth. "Call upon the name of the LORD and you will be saved," Romans 10:13, and whatever you shall ask in the Name of JESUS CHRIST, HE will do it, John 14:13-14. Our 9-1-1 is JESUS CHRIST and HIS Precious Blood.

JESUS is not going to let you sink. When Peter was caught up with fear and lost his faith, he started sinking, but immediately, he called the most effective 9-1-1 JESUS CHRIST! LORD, save me! He was saved from sinking immediately.

The hidden enemy Satan is trying to lie to you, so that you can doubt the ability of your Heavenly Father to provide for you. On the mountain of Moriah, Abraham did not know that GOD had already set to save Isaac. Thank GOD for what Abraham had previously confessed without knowing; "GOD shall provide HIMSELF a lamb of sacrifice my son," Genesis 22:8.

The moment Abraham took the knife up to kill Isaac for a sacrifice, the LORD appeared with a Lamb for a sacrifice. Our GOD is an instant provider, and a care taker of every situation. HE is not going to let you sink into that bottomless pit the devil has dug for you. It is Satan and his kingdom which is going to fall in there and be forgotten like the army of Egypt was when it followed the Children of Israel into the middle of the Red Sea. They got swallowed up as the sea closed in on them.

The Egyptians had no idea that the road in the midst of the Red Sea had specifically been made to save Israel and to destroy Israel's enemy. Likewise, the pit Satan is directing you into is for saving you and for destroying him; Amen! Woe unto anyone who is taking part in what devil is doing to you.

Again remember, the devil is a liar and the father of all lies. Some of his lies at first seem like the truth, but they remain lies and can never turn into the truth!

Satan is a liar from the beginning and he himself is nothing but a spirit of lies. No other term can describe him better. He himself is a lie, for there is no truth in him. All that beauty that Satan had in heaven as Lucifer, when he had the position of archangel, became a lie, after his enticing and deceiving other angels that he was their god. He was thrown down with one-third of the angels who had chosen to follow him and his lies. Those fallen angels are the demons which device all the evil for humanity.

"Everything that the devil says is a lie", says our LORD JESUS (John 8:44).Much as he is there and he was the Lucifer created by our GOD as an archangel, his arch was taken away by his assuming that he could become the most high and replace GOD, Isaiah 14:12-15.

But our LORD JESUS CHRIST is the Truth, the Life, and the Way unto Our Father GOD ALMIGHTY, John 14:6. By distinction, JESUS is the Truth and the Light of the world! Period! Full stop! We do not need anyone else but JESUS CHRIST in us and we shall dwell well in our hearts, overcoming every suggestion of the devil and his demons. Whatever the devil tells you, it is a lie; do not believe him. Read the Bible constantly to keep yourself focused, and you will be a winner, and a blessed winner. FOR JESUS IN YOU IS A WINNER; WHY SHOULD YOU LOSE? Often I have gone through some tough times, but whenever such times come, I get mad at the devil and Worship my Father like I will never get any other chance to Worship HIM. At that moment, some people may think you crazy, but you will know what you are doing and what I are achieving.

I do not allow Satan to start settling his lies in my mind by telling me how I am finished and done, how I am going to fail and so on. I refuse all his lies as polished from hell and released to confuse, corrupt and destroy peoples' minds.

I refuse all those lies from the devil in The NAME OF JESUS CHRIST MY LORD AND MY SAVIOR, THE ONLY HOLY ONE! AMEN! Sometimes before I remember that it is the enemy trying to oppress me through his manufactured problems, I feel stressed and wonder if my GOD IS still there, but the moment I ask, "where is my GOD?" I hear the Spirit of my Father telling me, "in the midst of your Worship, you will find HIM." The HOLY SPIRIT is very

Sensitive and we need to keep focused on HIM. HIM in us and us in HIM, AMEN! Let me say this, we can worship GOD in the midst of all that we are doing. Ask The HOLY SPIRIT to infuse your mind and to have control of your thoughts and to give you a CHRIST-Like mind.

The devil brings things that will make you look like you are a liar like him. He wants you to look like you did not tell the truth when your LORD GOD gave you that which Satan had stolen from you. That is why he wants to you to talk about problem after problem after problem. When you focus on your problems, you forget that the devil is the hidden enemy who is fighting your success. You forget that he is fighting the salvation in you.

Bear this in mind, that the oppression in Egypt and the battles that the children of Israel fought in the land of Canaan, and any other battle that the children of Israel had, was more spiritual than physical. Often we make the mistake of thinking that the journey and the life of Israel, including all their battles, were physical. They were spiritual battles manifested as physical. Why is it important for us to understand what happened to the Israelites, whose struggles may seem far removed from our everyday lives?

We need to know that all we who are Born Again are the New Israel and that CHRIST came to unite us with the First Israel so that we can all be blessed children of Abraham. As it is written, Abraham will be a father of many nations and a blessing to all the families of the earth, Genesis 12:2-3.

The Brethren of the first Israel are our role model. All that they went through was for our benefit; that we may learn as the New Children of the Covenant. Israelites are the First Children of the Covenant. Today, Born Again Christians are the New Children of the Covenant of our LORD JESUS CHRIST, regardless of their country of origin. New Covenant was laid on the Cross through the shedding of Jesus' Precious Blood.

CHAPTER 6

Israel's Battle; is the True Christian's Battle: (The Born Again.)

Israel's battle, which is the same as the battle that everyone who believes in CHRIST JESUS goes through; was set at the Garden of Eden in Genesis 3:15. Here, the LORD GOD told Satan, who appeared in the form of a snake, "I will put enmity between you and the seed of the woman." The seed of the woman signified JESUS CHRIST who was to come and be our Savior, the Messiah. And make us seed of woman like the prophets who were before us that GOD had revealed the battle between GOD and the devil. Of course, GOD fighting for us weak deceived creatures, yet without gratitude that our heavenly Father, our Creator fights for us day and night. Not because HE cannot do without us. No! GOD can do without us but HE has a special love for us: for HE created us out of that special love and devil is jealousy of that love. That is why devil seeks to destroy us by many methods and most of it is by making us sin against our Father so that he can frustrate HIM.

The promised nation which was to bring us the Messiah was Israel. As a fulfillment of the promise, they offered or give JESUS CHRIST to the Gentiles as a HOLY Offering to be sacrificed by gentiles for our redemption and cleansing us from all manner of sins. He was the Israel's Holy Sacrifice for us to our LORD GOD so that we can join them to be the children of GOD through Abraham. He was offered up for a sin offering, being the Firstborn Son. You remember when on Mount or hill of Moriah, Abraham was about to slay his own only son of promise Isaac for a sacrificial offering to the LORD GOD. GOD gave Abraham a Lamb, in the place of his son. Symbolically, the Lamb that Abraham was given was JESUS THE SON OF GOD for Abraham's sins and that of his physical genealogy but for the whole world to have a redeemer, JESUS CHRIST was offered up by GOD, to die in our place, so that we may not perish from sin (read Genesis 22:10-12 & 17).

We gentiles had no righteous sacrifice to offer for our sins. It was the seed of a righteous Abraham through Isaac and Jacob which was to be a blessing to all the nations of the earth, and that is why GOD appointed JESUS CHRIST to be born of the children of Israel, the stock of David and of Abraham. The assurance of this was a Covenant between GOD and Abraham, in which GOD promised Abraham that he would make him a father of all nations Genesis 12: 2-3

As a fulfillment of that Covenant, JESUS CHRIST was born of Israel, the chosen nation, and Israel gave HIM up for a sacrifice, so that Gentiles too may profit from the same.

You see, as a true Christian, you are a victorious child of GOD and not a victim of the devil because you have blessed Abraham's seed by loving JESUS CHRIST. And automatically you love other people, for you cannot Love JESUS and be able to hate others. True love for JESUS CHRIST allows HIM and the Father, GOD, to have abode in you (John 14:23). When this happens, the devil and his kingdom will hate you with perfect hate, and try to torment you so that you can give up on your salvation. But stand still -- you will see your salvation coming as light as is the day.

Your Victory is on Its Way

The devil and his kingdom are succumbing to the missiles which have been forged from what were your miseries. You have frustrated Satan by accepting JESUS CHRIST and you have become Number One enemy of the devil. He must therefore make sure that you suffer. But our GOD will bring quick deliverance with great victory and blessings.

When the wall of Jericho was flattened by our GOD miraculously, Israel not only had a beautiful place to live in, but also abundant food and wealth. They had enough for themselves for Offerings and Tithes.

The worst you and I can do is to forget what our LORD GOD has done for us in the past, or even for others that believe in HIM. Look at Israel, numerous miracles were performed for them from the day that Moses the servant of the LORD stepped into Egypt. But most of them did not have remembrance of these. They neither recalled nor acknowledged GOD'S work upon their lives.

Having seen what GOD had done for them in Egypt and at the Red Sea; making a smooth, wide road in the midst of the Sea waters, for them to cross with their children, and chickens and turkeys and ducks, and all the animals that they carried, they forgot it all. Instead, they kept on murmuring and grumbling whenever a problem came up, big or small. In actual fact, they ought to have prayed for GOD to help them to be contented, and be thankful in every situation they found themselves in, knowing that a dark past of slavery in Egypt was past.

So, my brother, my sister, no matter what you are going through at this moment, and no matter what may come tomorrow, **pray that the HOLY SPIRIT will lead you to remember to thank GOD for what HE has done for you in the past.** Every one of us, saved and not saved, goes through a lot here on earth. The difference is in that the saved one is being tempted, while the non-saved one is being punished by the enemy of the human race and being deceived that it is GOD doing evil to her/him.

Sometimes, I go through some issues that cannot be mentioned unless GOD allows it. When such have come as it is today 11/17/2005, I thank my LORD GOD ALMIGHTY and Worship HIM with all my heart, my body and my spirit, and in HIS SPIRIT AND TRUTH. For GOD is A Father who is A SPIRIT and the "true worshippers must worship HIM in Spirit and in Truth," (John 4: 23). HE manifests HIMSELF through us who believe in HIM while we worship HIM.

Look at the prison, in Acts 16:25-26, when at midnight, Paul and Silas prayed and sang praises unto the LORD GOD: and the other prisoners heard them singing. See what happened in that prison because of the praises unto the LORD. "And suddenly, there was a great earthquake, so that the foundation of the prison was shaken: and immediately all the doors were opened and every one's bands were loosed." (Acts 16: 25-26).

My dear friend, do we see what happens when we become worshipers, praying and praising GOD? The LORD will open the doors that were closed and loose the people that were bound. I beseech you, let us worship and praise our GOD instead of talking about our problems. May the LORD GOD ALMIGHTY really help us to worship HIM no matter what comes our way, AMEN!

Wake Up Now!

Wake up now and worship The ALMIGHTY LIVING GOD, don't stay miserable in that bed or on that couch. You're a child of GOD the KING of kings, and the LORD of lords. JESUS CHRIST is telling you, "I am the Captain of the host of the LORD and I have come to fight for you." Joshua 5:14-15

The battle is too blistering and vicious for you! You cannot make another step without him! You feel like you want to lie down and die, but death is not coming fast enough. And then you consider all the things you need to do; and that it would be a great predicament for you to die now because you would leave your loved ones in a quandary.

You have come to the point of asking, "Dear LORD, what is this, where am I going to hide, I wish something could conceal me so that no one would see me ever again!" All those who have been watching as GOD was lifting you up yet again and were unhappy are going to laugh and to heap scorn on you, when they hear that you have sunk again.

DO NOT WORRY! FEAR NOT, (Isaiah 41:10). You will not sink! GOD is in control, and you are HIS child. HE is your closest friend at the time of trouble and HE knows the right time to rescue you from all your troubles, before you sink (Psalm 46). And it does not matter if they laugh, it will only be for a short while, and then they will start wishing they were like you.

My sister, my brother, remember Job in Job 1-42 and Hannah, wife of Elkanah in the book of l Samuel 1:2-3, they were both laughed at and scorned, but GOD was on their side at every moment, "GOD was their refuge and a present help." (Psalm 46: 1)

Let the HOLY SPIRIT Illuminate your life at this moment of your troubles. When you have no source of income and you can barely make it; when your children are sick and you do not have health insurance because your health insurance was cut off when you lost that good job; your mortgage or rented house is almost going and you do not know where to turn to; when there is not enough food because even the food that your Church gives you is not enough for your family; you open the refrigerator and close it because it is empty; it looks like all that you have, despite the fact that it is GOD who gave it to you, is going to go away and you will be left homeless; you can't bear it anymore. It has been a long-standing battle; it has been coming from one side to the other in many different versions.

You have prayed and fasted until you do not know how to do it anymore. Fasting to pray has become a fashion of your life. When you eat you feel like you are sinning. But remember, from the time Israel left Egypt there were many battles and the struggle started as soon as they left Egypt. They were caught between the Red Sea and the wilderness by their enemy the Egyptians, but GOD knew how to overcome for them and deliver them.

The biggest problem we have is that we want to see ahead, that we may know how it is going to happen and how we are going to be delivered from our troubles. But we are not the miracle-working GOD; so we cannot see the miracle that is soon coming our way.

We should learn to wait patiently by faith for the miracle worker to perform HIS miracles and take us across the Red Seas that are before us, and for HIM to destroy our enemies who are behind us(Exodus 14:21-31). Moses and the whole company of Israel saw their enemies destroyed as they watched. Many are the afflictions of the righteous, but GOD delivered him from all (Psalm 34:19).

Psalms 91:1-16 covers us my dear friend, "How?" and "When?" You ask. There are questions which pull us down should we meditate upon them. We must not brood over the body or the heart or the mind asking, when and how? (2 Kings 7:1-20 Elisha gave the Word but King's adviser doubted the Word of GOD in his crafty). Those questions will cause us to fail and make us forget to meditate upon what our GOD has said and done for us in the past. The Children of Israel had something that their

GOD who is our LORD GOD too, had done in Egypt which they would have meditated upon when they got to the Red Sea: to remember and meditate on all GOD'S Mighty Works in Egypt. Instead of complaining and murmuring, they would have thank GOD, praised and worshipped the One who delivered them from slavery and trust that HE is able to deliver them from the Sea and Egyptian army. They would have said in their praise to GOD, "our GOD who killed all your firstborns and left you crying as we carry all your possessions is very much able to deliver us from you defeated army of Egypt. We shall not fear or fret."

For their sake, GOD brought into Egypt many plagues, and finally killed all the firstborns of Egyptians to deliver HIS people Israel. Our GOD knows how to keep HIS promises; in Genesis 15:1-21, HE promised Abraham that after 400 years Abraham's seed, Israel, shall come out of Egypt with great substance, to the land that GOD had given Abraham and that is exactly what happened; when the Children of Israel were leaving Egypt, they left with Great substance.

If you look at your past life, unless you let the devil, Satan blind you with his lies, you will see what GOD has done for you in the past. Actually, that GOD has chosen to save us from eternal damnation is more than enough. For JESUS CHRIST, being GOD, to leave heaven for you and me, this we really need to kneel and thank GOD for. Let us thank GOD for what HE has done for us in the past, and the present shall be taken care of by the same GOD. Romans 12: 1-2, tells us that the only reasonable service we can give to our Father, GOD, is to present ourselves to HIM as a living sacrifice that is Holy and acceptable unto HIM.

If we learn to worship GOD at that time when we are not feeling very happy, then HE will turn our anguish into weapons such that once we have fought and are out of trouble we shall be able to worship him joyfully.

There is worship that GOD receives very swiftly; this is the worship full of praise. Just like you and I, when we have a friend who tells us all good things, we take time to appreciate and show him our affection.

So is our LORD GOD, HE appreciates it when we praise HIM and lift HIS Name higher than anyone else. Now we can go to Psalm 103: 1-5 and praise and worship our Dear and Loving Father GOD by blessing HIM. Let us not forget HIS benefits and all that HE has done for us. HE has healed us; HE has given us life and "renewed our youth and strength as he does eagles," HE has supplied "our needs according to HIS riches in Glory by CHRIST JESUS" (Philippians 4:19).

Our LORD GOD is the Highest Supreme Authority and Love. There is none like HIM and there will never be any other like HIM. HE is our all in all. The only one we need and ever needed. Let us now approach HIS Throne of mercy with humility, with thanks giving and praises to worship him alone with all our hearts and all our might. Let us give HIM all the respect because HE alone deserves the Glory and honor. After worshipping our LORD GOD then we can tell HIM all that we need from HIM and I tell you my dear friend, the LORD will respond very fast and hearken to your prayer and give to you whatever you have asked for.

Sometimes, the LORD may say: wait. When HE says, wait, please do so. Or HE may say no. In such a case, go back and ask HIM what HE wants you to ask for or how he wants you to ask, because sometimes what we ask for is not always fit for us. But in many cases, if we ask according to HIS Word, HE is very careful to answer us and give us what we have asked for.

The one thing needful is that we ask according to HIS word and HIS will. But it is good for us to know that it is HIS will to give us the **desires of our hearts and he can never give us scorpions for eggs, or stones for bread, or snakes for fish**. HE is not that kind of a father, HE is all-loving, righteous, full of mercy and careful. HE is not like the fathers of this world.

Look at what GOD says in Deuteronomy 28:1-14, and know that you are a child of the KING of all Kings; Amen. Verses 1-3 say, "And it shall come to pass, if you diligently obey the voice of the LORD your GOD to observe all HIS commandments which I command you today: that the LORD your GOD will set you high above all nations on earth: and these blessings shall come upon you, and overtake you because you obey the voice of the LORD your GOD. Blessed shall you be in the city, in the field, in your stores, in your banks, and everywhere you will be, the LORD your GOD shall cause blessings upon your life. Verse 7 says, The LORD will cause your enemies that come to you in one way to be scattered seven ways." Verse 12-13, "the LORD will open to you HIS good treasure, the heavens, to give rain and bless the work of your hands. You shall not borrow but you shall lend many nations. And the LORD will make you the head and not the tail. You shall be above only but not beneath, if you hearken to the commandments of the LORD your GOD, which

I command you today; and be careful to observe, and not to turn aside from them."

You can see how willing and ready our Heavenly Father GOD is to bless us. I wonder whether you are ready for GOD'S Blessings. Beloved Brethren, Plenty of valuable and beautiful promises are our GOD'S blessings towards us who are HIS children. But there is nothing that is valuable that is without a cost. It is true that at Calvary, on the Cross JESUS paid all our debts, but we have our ultimate part to play or to fulfill as the children of the Most High and Righteous Holy GOD who is above all. We have to be very careful to obey our GOD: for where there are blessings, there are curses, if obedience does not follow. Deuteronomy 28 from verse 15 prescribes what follows a believer in the event of disobeying GOD: it says, "if you disobey and do not keep my commandments that I command you this day, these curses shall follow you: cursed shalt thou be......:"

Surely, we do not want curses to follow us instead of blessings. Therefore, we must know and obey; this is why JESUS CHRIST came on earth to hang on the Cross so that he can become the curse for us, and take away all our disobedience in HIS Precious Blood. Galatians 3: says, "Cursed is every one that hangs on a tree." Our LORD JESUS being GOD took on a human body and was hang on that cross so that HE could take away our curses of sin. By the way, it's only sin that brings curse. The reason is; sin is the manifestation of disobedience.

JESUS became the atonement, making amends for us: the making of reparation for our sin and mistakes. When we simply obey and repent our sins, HIS Blood cleanses us from the filth of our sins and carries away grieves of our sins.

But we cannot receive that atonement or reconciliation between GOD and men unless we accept that we were born sinners and that this is the reason we find ourselves in a cycle of sin and repentance. The Christian belief that reconciliation between GOD and man was brought about by the death of JESUS CHRIST, is true and wonderful. But the faith that makes this belief effective comes by acceptance that we are sinners by the first fall of Adam and Eve. Denial of that truth would not make us better people but worse human beings.

It is through identifying this first sin as our eternal problem we get reconciled with GOD by our Remorseful repentant and then we become new creations in JESUS CHRIST. And thereafter we live a holy life in CHRIST JESUS which gives us back our cleaner and better identity.

CHAPTER 7

The Lost ID

Is your misery the result of YOUR LOST IDENTITY?

Do you feel as if you have lost your ID? Do you feel as if you are no longer the same person that you used to know? Has a person whom you trusted betrayed you so that you feel like you will never trust anyone again? Is your heart is aching with the pain of betrayal and you do not know how or where to start again?

Look unto JESUS and call upon HIM. Sing a new song unto the LORD, and say:
I must tell JESUS--X 3
That I am not happy
And HE is gonna make me happy-- X 3
For HE alone understands--my heart's pains X3
And then sing:
I must tell JESUS that I am HIS—
And I must tell JESUS that I am HIS---
And I must tell JESUS that I am HIS-----

Here below is your answer:

First, know you are not alone. JESUS is with you and you are not the first one to go through this kind of trouble. "For there is no temptation that has come to you which is not common to man:" 1 Corinthians 10:13, "But GOD is faithful, who will not suffer you to be tempted above that ye are not able bear, but will with the temptation also make a way of escape, that ye may be able to bear it" 1 Corinthians 10-13.

Secondly, you have to know this that when you started feeling betrayed and lost that is not when your Identity got lost. Every one born of a woman on this planet called earth is born with a lost Identity, Genesis 3:1- 8. Only one Single Person born of a virgin woman, Mary, was born with HIS Identity and never lost it, and that is our LORD JESUS CHRIST. We all lost our identity when Adam and Eve fell into the sin of disobedience.

And that is why HE was given the name that was above every other name, (Philippians 2: 8-11). JESUS CHRIST, HE HIMSELF is that ID because HE never sinned all through HIS life here on earth. HE lived a life like us with all the temptations that we face but never sinned. And by JESUS we become newly created in righteousness and true Holiness; by the renewal in the spirit of our mind, Ephesians 4:23-24.

Thirdly, JESUS CHRIST is a specialist in fixing, improving to perfection the lost identity. Meaning, JESUS will never fail and HE is going to fix that problem for you and you will soon give a testimony of victory. You must believe by faith HE is for you to receive.

Hebrew 9:11 records, "But CHRIST being come an High Priest of good things to come, by a greater and more perfect tabernacle, not made with hands, that is to say, not of this building," like us. Hebrews 4:14-15 tells us, "Seeing then that we have a great high priest that is passed into the heavens, JESUS the Son of GOD, let us hold fast our profession. For we have not an high priest which cannot be touched with the feelings of our infirmities, but was in all points tempted like as we are without sin. Let us therefore come boldly unto the throne of grace that we may obtain mercy and find grace to help us in the time of need." Just like now dear LORD!

By the way, do not blame anyone for what you are going through lest you fall into a greater problem of bitterness and unforgiving spirit. It is your adversary Satan who has organized all that and GOD has let it happen because HE knows HE will give you a spirit to bear it until you overcome, for you are HIS child and you love HIM.

GOD is happy with you, but HE is not happy with the pain you are going through, and that is why HE is going to pay you for all that you have lost twice over and more. In Job 2:3B, Job lost his Identity; you will get a better identity and a name more praiseworthy than you ever had before.

No one knew you before, but after this, you are going to be known by many far and wide. There is not one godly person I know through the Bible who has not gone through great tribulations. Not one that I know! They have all gone through hardship of some kind, majority having gone through what we call shame and loss of identity, but GOD has turned that shame to HIS Glory.

There is no one who had lost his Identity as much as Job did, read and see his conversation with his three friends. They all say, wrongfully, that Job must be a sinner and that he is being punished by GOD for his sin. Look at the end of Job's journey of tribulations, all his agony was turned to joy.

Job was made a high priest to those friends who had scolded and scorned him to the last. It was only after Job prayed for them that GOD forgave them. Those friends thought they were very righteous and could not see how Job would recover after losing his wealth and his health. They were counting days until they could miserably bury Job and forget about him. Little did they know that Job's was suffering was temporary, and that Our LORD GOD was going to turn Job's misery into Missiles!

However, should the spirit tell you that you are being chastened, when going through such tribulations, please do not slack to repent and seek the LORD for forgiveness. HE is faithful and just. He will cleanse us of all our sins and put us right again, as for the old sins, those are forgotten and you do not need to remember them again.

Do not let Satan kill your joy and worship by reminding you of your past. Remind him of his future! Tell him, "Satan, I am under the Blood of JESUS CHRIST and if the blood of goats and bulls could cleanse them of GOD in the old days, how about me who am cleansed in the Precious Blood of JESUS CHRIST MY LORD! How much more shall the Blood of JESUS keep me clean? Much in fullness of GOD"

<u>JESUS CHRIST is My Righteousness and My Holiness.</u>

Devil, I am clean and righteous! And therefore Satan, don't you try to condemn me! I am not condemnable; I am baptized in the Blood of JESUS and in the power of the Holy Spirit.

If you have not bẹen baptized in the Power of the HOLY SPIRIT, this is the time to kneel and say, My LORD GOD, IN THE MIGHTY NAME OF JESUS CHRIST MY LORD AND MY SAVIOR, BAPTIZE ME WITH POWER AND FIRE AS YOU PROMISED. I ASK YOU TO BAPTIZE ME WITH YOUR HOLY SPIRIT AND LET ME EXPERIENCE THE POWER OF YOUR HOLY SPIRIT AS ON THE DAY OF PENTECOST, AMEN!

JUST AS THE 120 DISCIPLES EXPERIENCED IN THE UPPER ROOM WHERE THEY WAITED, DEAR LORD, LET ME BE BAPTIZED BY YOUR HOLY SPIRIT AND RECEIVE POWER TO BE ABLE TO LIVE A RIGHTEOUS AND HOLY LIFE FULL OF YOUR PROMISES. DEAR LORD, HELP ME TO BE ABLE TO RECEIVE YOUR POWER FOR YOUR GLORY AND I WILL LIVE TO GLORIFY YOUR NAME FOR THIS MOST EXPENSIVE GIFT THAT MADE YOUR SON JESUS TO DIE FOR ME. LORD I WAIT TO RECEIVE YOUR POWER IN THE HOLY SPIRIT.

GOD is faithful, if you pray this prayer constantly without ceasing, and as the Spirit of GOD leads you, our dear LORD GOD is going to baptize you. Many believers do not receive this promise even though they may be clean and washed by the blood, and are fully determined to lead a holy life after the Blood and water Baptism. The reason is that they ask of the Father in a hurry. They want to pray in hurry and with just a few words, and then they want to be baptized right away. It has never happened and it will not happen that way.

The Baptism of the HOLY SPIRIT is a Precious Gift, you and I have to labor for it. For the overflow of the Power of the HOLY SPIRIT comes by the baptism and the infilling of the HOLY SPIRIT OF GOD ALMIGHTY!

You need to sacrifice your time so that you can spend quality time with the LORD your GOD. Those disciples who waited for the first time as they were promised by the LORD JESUS before HE was taken up to Heaven, they waited patiently for ten days after JESUS was taken up John16:7-8, 14:16-18, Acts 1 and 2.

You See, they were praying, and not doing other things. Their business was only to pray and wait as they were instructed. That instruction is still in full force. It was not for Peter, John and the other disciples only; it was for every disciplined Born Again Believer. You must properly know the one that gave that promise and HIS purpose for it. It is a divine promise of GOD to Baptize HIS believers with the HOLY SPIRIT and with FIRE; Matthew 3: 11B as it was in the wilderness.

Moses was baptized several times. Then followed Aaron and his sons, and later the 70 men whom Moses chose were baptized also. This promise was of old. All the true prophets were baptized in the SPIRIT of truth and boldness. Every believer of our LORD JESUS needs to crave, yearn and covet with the whole heart to be baptized in the HOLY SPIRIT. Baptism of the HOLY SPIRIT is not a religious movement called the Pentecostal Church, no! It is the Promise of GOD which goes together with salvation by repentance.

Can you see from the Bible in Matthew 3:11 that that promise was not spoken of at first by JESUS CHRIST! JESUS was not the first to speak about the Baptism of the HOLY SPIRIT and FIRE. Neither was it spoken of by a Pentecostal believer.

One Pastor preaching in a Baptist Church in Maryland caused laughter in congregation when he said, "baptism of Fire and the HOLY SPIRIT should not be preached or taught by the Pentecostal preacher, for it was a Baptist preacher, John the Baptist, who first spoke about the Baptism of the HOLY SPIRIT with FIRE." This preacher was speaking with humor and some sarcasm out of the realization that most of his congregation believed contrary to what the Word of GOD said. He wanted them to understand that it was not the Baptist believer, John the Baptist, and not JESUS, nor Apostles, nor even Pentecostal Pastors, but all true believers of the Bible who should be baptized.

I remember that one afternoon in September 2, 1973 when the LORD GOD baptized me in HIS HOLY SPIRIT and with HIS FIRE! Oh JESUS CHRIST MY LORD, I will never forget the power, peace and joy that I received that day.

I was praying and praying constantly, I had forgotten everything else outside that room. I was there not thinking but seeking. We were in a fellowship after the water Baptism, and I desired nothing but the power of the HOLY SPIRIT. I could not move from where I was kneeling for more than two hours. I cried in full desire to be Baptized, I had just come out of the Water Baptism with great Power and with an urge to be SPIRIT Baptized.

But I had heard several times the controversial, contradicting spirits of the devil preaching the gospel of rebellion that speaking in tongues ceased with the Apostles. But whenever I read the Bible in as many languages as I could read and understand, I did not come across a place in the Bible where it was written; the tongues ceased with Apostles. Whenever I read 1st Corinthians 13, the HOLY SPIRIT would be saying that all other gifts would cease, but only because when we get to heaven, only love, peace and joy shall abide forever.

All these other gifts of the HOLY SPIRIT: Faith, tongues, prophesies; teaching, longsuffering, self-control, gentleness, goodness, prosperity and healing, will cease because we shall not need them in heaven. It's only now that we need them when we are in this body and in this present time. Or do you think you will need healing? No you will not need it, you will never be sick in heaven. And you will always be good, and no poverty will be near you. What a home we are waiting for! Thank you LORD for what you are preparing for us; "the eye has not seen nor has the ear heard" says the LORD in I Corinthians 2:9.

After CHRIST comes for us, we will have no need for faith, hence, no need for healing. And therefore, as much as we need faith now, so much more do we need to speak with new Tongues. The reason being; it's the only language that the devil does not understand. It is a mystery to the devil and them that do not know it.

What is the advantage of speaking in tongues? When you speak in tongues, your prayer line is not hindered by the enemy as happens when you speak in the normal language. In tongues, you can intercede for a long time in the SPIRIT very clearly without repetitions and interruptions. In 1 Corinthians 14:1-40 Paul by the power of the HOLY SPIRIT continues to teach, Verse 1, "follow after charity and desire the spiritual gifts, but rather that you prophesy, for he that speaketh in an unknown tongue speaketh not to men but unto GOD:" in Verse 18 he says, "I thank my GOD, I speak with tongues more than ye all: Yet in the Church I would lather speak five words in understanding, that by my voice I might teach others also, than ten thousand words in an unknown tongue." Paul was teaching that kind of teaching because many brethren had started misusing the speaking of tongues by speaking as if it is just another foreign language to show off to people. They did not speak to pray or prophesy with an interpreter. They used the tongues to preach, and pray for needs, yet they did not care whether they were being understood by others or not.

In other words, they were just speaking as they got consumed by the Holy Spirit, and they failed to exercise control. So it came off as some kind of pride and not for the glory of GOD. From the time I got baptized in the HOLY SPIRIT and I started speaking in tongues, I have been to very many churches and with very many brethren that do not speak in tongues, but I do not despise them, nor do I speak in tongues to show off in a disturbing manner.

The HOLY SPIRIT IS A GENTLEMAN. HE has never troubled me and I feel very comfortable in fellowship with all believers. I am not afraid to teach them the way of the LORD AND to share what I know ABOUT THE BAPTISM OF THE HOLY SPIRIT. In Verse 39 Brother Paul continues to teach, "Wherefore brethren, covet to prophesy, and forbid not to speak in TONGUES." Verse 40, "let all things be done decently." If the speaking of new or heavenly tongues was to cease before CHRIST came TO RECEIVE US IN HIS GLORY, HE would not have taught about it as one of the important signs that would follow us after we believed and got Baptized, (Mark 16:15-18).

Cornelius, who was not an apostle, was baptized by the LORD in the HOLY SPIRIT even before the water Baptism. This shows us that baptism in the HOLY SPIRIT was not just a gift of the Apostles only. By the way, every believer has GOD'S Spirit-filling in his/her spirit, but the Baptism of the Holy Spirit that comes with power and fire to consume the other powers around is the immersion or burial into the Holy Spirit.

During the time of the Baptism of the HOLY SPIRIT, one is completely immersed and covered by the SPIRIT of our GOD to consume all the evil. This is not a onetime experience like water immersion. The HOLY SPIRIT will immerse you as many times as you need or as you humble yourself before HIM for refilling and rebaptism. The anointing that comes by the immersion is not supposed to be a onetime experience, but laziness makes many believers stay with only speaking with tongues without the anointing.

What I mean is; once you have been immersed inside the HOLY SPIRIT for the first time, you need to continue cleaving, craving and thirsting with great hunger for more and more Power and

Anointing with Fire. That way signs and wonders will follow because it is JESUS CHRIST manifesting HIMSELF in you. The anointing of the HOLY SPIRIT you received to lead you to salvation was to give you knowledge that JESUS CHRIST is the son of the Most High Living GOD, Matthew 16:15-17. But the works of the LORD with signs cannot follow without the Fire and the Power of the HOLY SPIRIT'S Baptism.

We all need the Power and that Fire to continue in and with us as believers. Acts 10:34-43, and 44 say, "while Peter was speaking these words, the HOLY GHOST(HOLY SPIRIT) fell on all which heard the Word:" After this happened, the human flesh started fighting with GOD'S Spirit (just as it does today) to refuse the holy things of the Kingdom of GOD. The Jewish brethren started questioning Peter. They thought that he had taken away their gift of the HOLY SPIRIT and shared it with gentiles. Man is strange! He always fights for what he calls his; even what he cannot understand. This Baptism of the HOLY SPIRIT is a promise that the LORD GOD had revealed to Prophet Joel over eight hundred years before JESUS CHRIST was born on earth. And the HOLY SPIRIT Baptism is as alive today as it was on the day of Pentecost. And it was not a onetime gift for those Jewish Brethren alone; it was for the gentile believers like us too. Further, it is a gift that precedes the coming of Jesus; and so when JESUS was promising HIS Disciples that he would them the comforter; the spirit of truth, HE was talking about what GOD had already promised through the mouth of Joel the Prophet.

The power of the HOLY SPIRIT will enable you to know your identity and to speak the Word boldly. The Holy Spirit will always help you to withstand and cast the devil out and make it known to Satan who you are in the family of the Most High GOD. It is not a bad kind of pride to be proud of your Heavenly father for HE says, "Let him that boasts, boast not that he is rich, fat, goodly looking, but boast that he knows ME." Jeremiah 9:23-24, "Thus says the Lord: Let not the wise man boast in his wisdom, let not the mighty man boast in his might, let not the rich man boast in his riches, but let him that boasts boast that he knows and understands that I am the LORD" David, while he was a youth of about 17 years, boasted about his GOD before Goliath, Philistines and his brethren in the army of Israel. He called Goliath an uncircumcised Philistine and told him that he is defiling the Army of his GOD. In some Christian Churches, they would not want to hear a believer speak like David did to Satan. Some believers beseech Satan as if they were friends.

In 1 Samuel 17: 34-47, David explains to King Saul all the mighty works of the LORD through his hands. He assures Saul that, all is going to be alright because the LORD GOD whom he believes in is the same GOD who delivered him from the paws of a bear and a lion, two mighty animals.

David said; "the same GOD is able to deliver me out of the hands of this Philistine and give him in my hands to deliver HIS army, Israel. David continued and told Goliath, "you come to me with a sword and a spear, but I come to you in the Name of the LORD of Hosts, the GOD of the armies of Israel, whom you have defied. And this day, will the LORD deliver you unto mine hands; and I will smite you and take thine head from you; and I will give carcasses of the host of the Philistines this day unto the fowls of the air, and to wild beasts of the earth; that all the earth may know that there is a GOD in Israel. And all this assembly shall know that the LORD saveth not with the Sword and Spear: for the battle is the LORD'S and he will give you into our hands."

That speech could not have been uttered by someone who was not proud of his master. Neither could it have been made by one who did not know the relationship he had with his Master. Or even one who did not know the power of his Master, and the love of his Master and Father. David knew that GOD was his supreme Master and above all HE was his Eternal Father. David, while he was a boy, knew that GOD loved him so much that HE could not let a devil worshiper such as Goliath kill him. If you know the power of your Eternal Father then speak of HIM boldly and let people know who you are to HIM that lives forever. And if people talk ill of you, the HOLY SPIRIT will always remind you who you are, and help you get rid of fear of a lost identity.

THE HOLY SPIRIT will remind you that there is "no weapon formed against you that shall prosper, and every tongue that rises against you in judgment thou shalt condemn for this is the heritage of the servant of the LORD, and their righteousness is of ME, says the LORD" Isaiah 54:17. You will be able to stand against Satan in the Name of the LORD, when he comes to defy your life.

The devil is not after anything else, he is after your Testimony and your Identity. That is what bothers him so much because he knows, so long as you know how to identify yourself with the LIVING GOD as your Father; you then know JESUS CHRIST and the Power of HIS Cross, and HIS Resurrection. Therefore, you have a testimony and the cover of Blood of JESUS CHRIST which defeats Satan; Revelation 12: 11.

CHAPTER 8

Self-esteem Experience

Again, let's examine: what causes you to be miserable? Is it a lost Identity? **JESUS CHRIST IS Your Forever Identity!** Now, remove that feeling of lost Identity so long as JESUS CHRIST is in you, you have an identity that will never be stolen, or be lost. To be identified with the LORD of lords and the King of kings is more honorable than that other identity you were crying for. ALL THESE OTHER IDENTITIES ARE TEMPORARY. GOD WANTS YOU TO DWELL ON A FOREVER IDENTITY; JESUS CHRIST, WHO IS GREATER THAN ANY OTHER IDENTITY YOU CAN EVER GET. The KING of Kings and LORD of Lords!

IS IT LOVE THAT YOU NEED? JESUS loves you so much that HE died for you! You can never have a better lover; one who will love you to death. Only JESUS CHRIST died for you!

He left HIS Father's Throne to come and die for you, so that you may have life and have it more abundantly. When you have life in abundance, what don't you have? Who can take away what you have? Is it People? Or is it Satan? None can take it away unless you give it away. And if you give it away without realizing it, then your Heavenly Father will give you power to take it back in the Name of JESUS CHRIST AMEN!

Is it that you feel like you have "No Good Name?"

Are people talking about you, and making up things that you don't even know about, and are they derisively talking about you? Have you been painted on you many colors that are not you? Has that man, or woman disappointed you and got your name tarnished? Are you, as a consequence, in distress? Have you lost everything you had and now you have nothing to hold on to?

The answer is; GOD is in control of all your miseries and all your heart and bodily pains. Direct your worry about all that is going on around you to JESUS CHRIST who loves you and who died for you. Also, look unto JESUS CHRIST "the author and the finisher of your faith." Encourage yourself by this, you are not the first, nor are you going to be the last to go through discouragement; I Corinthians 10:13

Look at King David in his early days of leadership; at the camp in Ziklag! Here he had felt very disappointed. He had lost everything and his camp was burnt down by his enemies, the Amalekites. His army of men were going to stone him because they had also lost everything while David was their leader. The men had turned against him as if he were the one who had made the Amalekites attack the camp. Everything had turned sore for David.

Remember, at this point in time, David has not yet become King over Israel. Yet here he was being blamed by his followers. At this point in his life, he was running away from King Saul of Israel; his native land. He was in exile, hosted by the enemies of Israel, the Philistines. While David was out of camp Ziklag with his followers, the enemy struck the camp of his refuge, and all that was his had been taken by the Amalekites. <u>But David looked at the LORD who sees beyond such moments, and he saw GOD'S Power. He was able to encourage "himself in the name of the LORD his GOD!"</u>

And he moved towards the LORD his GOD to enquire of HIM that knows all things. See 1 Samuel 30:1-8. You must look at CHRIST JESUS at this time of your unhappiness and learn to enquire of the LORD when the enemy surrounds you, or when he strikes and carries away everything as he did to David. David's followers knew only to look at David, but David knew what was best: to look unto the LORD the Author and the Finisher of his faith, even JESUS CHRIST. Remember, this is an old story, the story of Satan attacking GOD'S children from all the sides so that he could torment them and push them to hell if it were possible. But thank GOD! It is not possible for our LORD GOD to let the devil take control of HIS children

GOD has never left his children fatherless. HE is a very careful Father and the people of the world may be used by the devil to strike us, but our GOD will never leave us nor forsake us. While our GOD can never leave us neither forsake us, what do we do ourselves when problems become too much?

When problems multiply around GOD'S children, we tend to murmur, grumble with bitterness, leaving our Father, and forsaking HIM, forgetting that he is an able GOD. After receiving lies from the devil, we run away from the Kingdom of GOD and go away from HIM to be tormented by the enemy with his lies and be kept under captivity by Satan. GOD Forbid that we do that, and if we have ever done it let that be the last time we forsake our Eternal Loving and Mighty GOD, whatever problems and circumstances may come our way.

Let us learn to fully trust our GOD for HE is faithful. I have a testimony of our LORD GOD that HE is a faithful GOD. You may ask this commonly asked question: what makes GOD, who is such a Supreme Authority, allow Satan to strike and punish HIS children? Well, you are not alone; neither are you the first one to ask that question. I used to ask the same question and almost blamed GOD for being a weak GOD. If you may allow me to say this: That question is misguided. It need never be asked by one who reads the Bible! But meaningless as it is, most of us do ask it. However, our GOD is such a loving LORD, HE only looks at us and smiles with a very wide and Fatherly smile.

Do you want to know the answer to the question? The answer is simple: because when we get into problems, these problems often find us busy with other day to day things and not worshiping GOD. And devil the thief, he knows when we are too busy with our own things without listening by Worship or Singing Praise to our GOD, we are far from protection. So he comes and strike!

Then we fail to worship in the midst of our problems and start wondering where we should go! Mostly when problems strike, when we are busy with our daily routine jobs, we forget what we read in the Bible yesterday. We become like the wife of Job in the book of Job 2: 9, then we fail our test by asking that silly question. Actually, that is exactly what the devil wants us to do. To blame our GOD for all that evil the devil does, and that evil beast goes laughing at us on its way, reassured that we do not know his tricks. The devil is a liar. He is also very crafty. When the devil comes to strike, he wants you to blame GOD for it, so that he can go away with his mischief and continue laughing at you while he is punishing you. See how bad and terrible he is!

The worst thing about the devil is that even when you are blaming GOD, Satan will still punish you because he knows that you are not aware of his dirty games and you have forgotten who you are and who is your Father and the Power of your Father GOD.

Devil is crafty and very subtle; remember he is that same Lucifer who was once the archangel of GOD. It was he who exalted himself high and wanted to overthrow the Heavenly Kingdom so that he could be the ruler of what he never created. You can never be in league with Satan. It would be the worst thing you could do to yourself: for them that are already serving him, he has nothing good to offer to them except evil, shame and hell as their destination. Satan hates those of us who love JESUS CHRIST because being on GOD'S side, we have only good things offered to us and Heaven is our final destination.

We should also hate Satan completely with all that is within us.

There are those about whom Satan is not worried because they are serving him day and night. That is why he never bothers them. They look as if they are doing very well, and just getting richer and richer, happier and happier, Psalm 37:1-40 In their barns there is nothing lacking. But wait until he turns around on them and starts demanding everything from them, they are left with nothing and they die in their miserable bed of desperation and depression, Psalm 16:5. The devil, that evil Satan will never help those who serve him diligently. Rather, he pays them by bringing them calamities: for that is his duty. There is no one to help them unless they call upon the name of our LORD GOD and be saved. Don't blame GOD for their failures, GOD does not interfere with people's decision or possession. When the possess devil to work with him so that they can be rich, GOD just looks at them with sympathy and wait to see if one day before they die; they can hear HIS Still Voice that says, Come unto me, you who labor and a heavy laden! Come!

My friend, you and I are already the children of the Most High in the Mighty Kingdom of our GOD. It is one which the devil has tried to break for millennia, by causing us fail. Our most grievous failure comes when we forget to acknowledge the Goodness of our GOD.

Although, Satan knows very well he can never sabotage to overthrow our GOD'S Kingdom, he never tires trying to penetrate through by using us, trying to make us give up our GOD, and follow him to hell. We must always keep in mind that Satan, being God's enemy can never love us. He spends sleepless nights looking for whom to devour. He is jealous of us. He is furious at our keeping away from him and for not being under his captivity.

It causes him great pain to see GOD'S Kingdom prosper, with happy joyful people, and with his knowledge that his days are numbered to be cast in the everlasting lake of fire.

He puts in a lot of work, in a bid to change our destination from Heaven to hell. Let this knowledge stay deep in our mind as our treasure. The devil stands as a saboteur of the LORD GOD our eternal creator, and he tries to frustrate HIM by punishing us.

The devil is a nonentity. He has no power with which he can defeat GOD Almighty. His jealousy is insurmountable and his defeat causes him unspeakable anger. Satan knows he is forever a loser and he can never inherit the Kingdom of Our GOD.

In the knowledge that GOD spares no effort trying to get us out of the clutches of the devil, Satan works at his hardest to frustrate these efforts. In this, he has been very successful due to the ignorance of many. He has used those humans who are not aware of who he is. He uses them to punish you and me who are outside his kingdom of eternal darkness, trying to get us to blame our GOD and give up our eternal Joy that is in CHRIST JESUS.

Therefore do not be surprised when believers do you wrong. When they are busy about character defamation of you, me and others, they are just victims of the enemy. He is using them to dishearten you and me. They have no way of knowing that they have been put to use as vessels of character assassination. They are blind to the fact that they are serving Satan.

Actually, they need sympathy and our prayers more than anything else, so that they can be delivered from that evil and be saved. You and I are alright as they talk about us. So long as we face Calvary and claim our rights, we are alright. Their actions and talk cannot injure us, we are covered by the Precious Blood, and we are not victims, we are Victors. Therefore, worry not but be thankful to GOD that HE has not allowed you to be a victim, but a Victor in HIM who lives forever 2 Samuel 16:5-12.

In fact, this reminds me about my father and mother. Those two wonderful people never cared what nosey neighbors said about them: so long as they knew they were doing the right thing before GOD and that they had not done anything to hurt anyone, they went on about their business while the rest of the village passed time gossiping and idling away. They were role models in the village and much admired by many.

They were so averse to gossip that if a person came and told either one of them that so and so had talked about them behind their backs, they would ask that person. "So what?" They would then go on to show that person the folly of hearsay. In jest my father was in the habit of commenting that the piece of gossip had had its merit in as far as it had brought the gossiping person to him, so that my father could now talk to him about more serious useful issues of life.

"We talk about JESUS CHRIST being our LORD and a good GOD to us." They would tell the person, "If you had JESUS CHRIST in you, you would have told us about HIM, but let us tell you, we love you and we love that person you are telling on, who talked about us behind our backs, and JESUS CHRIST loves you and him too. When you get to that person, say hello and that love him and JESUS CHRIST loves him very much that is why HE died for him."

That way, these wonderful people kept peace with everybody and became the teachers of the community. GOD also honored them because they had more wealth in that community than anyone else. They gave large portions of their land to the community for the building of a Church and a school. My dad was the proprietor of the modern education in that community. My Mom is still alive but Dad went to be with the LORD at the ripe old age of above 100 years and my Mom is 109 this year. She is not able now to cope with the work they used to do on their farm, but they together had the best of their time. Why? I believe it is because they were saved by the Blood of JESUS CHRIST and believed in the LORD GOD the giver of all things and adored HIM more than anything else.

If we obey GOD and keep HIS commandments, HE will hear our prayers and heal our problems and keep us from the attacks of the enemy. Deuteronomy 28:1-14, promises us all that prosperity we may need when we obey GOD and keep HIS Word. I am not suggesting that I never saw my parents having temptations, trials and tribulations. No! That is not what I am saying, I am saying, through it all, they trusted the LORD their GOD and GOD to guide them through their mountains safely. As it is in verse 7 of Deuteronomy; "the enemy will come in one way but seven ways shall he flee and be scattered." And Isaiah 59:19 says, "The Spirit of our GOD will raise a standard against Satan when he comes in raging like a flood." Our GOD is very careful to save us from all troubles and shame.

My parents may probably have had more tribulations than the rest of the people in the community around them but they were managing so well that you would not have known it from outside. You would have had to be very close to them to know what they were going through. Their employees didn't think they had ever had any problems in their lives. But both my parents were orphaned at an early age, and after they got married, my mother did not conceive until after 7 years. So she was declared by people barren, a thing thought taboo in those days. With the kind of insensitivity that existed then, she was greatly mocked. But my mother trusted GOD for children. After she had had her first two, a boy and a girl, they both died mysteriously and she had to wait for another 15 years and over before she could have more children.

I thank GOD for HIS mercy which endures forever. Also I thank GOD for HIS care of us because the same calamity which had befallen my first born brother and my older sister, killing them, was never very far from us. It could have struck any of us and killed us too, but GOD is so caring and so protective that HE will continue to care for us. Dear LORD; even now, keep us in Your Right Hand of Your Divine protection and in Thy mercy and grace covering us at every moment of this life until you come again; Amen. We need your cover and protection daily, dear LORD.

I believe GOD has a purpose for every one of us, and it is my prayer that HE will use us to serve HIM for HIS Glory. It is good to be saved despite all. There are many things that happen under the sun. Nevertheless, GOD is kind and blessed are they that know their GOD, and trust HIM. They shall be strong and do exploits, Daniel 11:32b

My sister, my brother, if you are going through the affliction of lost Identity, don't worry, JESUS will fix it for you and your later Identity will be better than the first. If you have knowingly broken a commandment, repent sincerely and JESUS will cleanse you and make you as pure as gold and as clean white as snow.

JESUS is a specialist at fixing lost and damaged Identities. Mary Magdalene had an ill reputation, but when she came to JESUS her Identity was changed in an instant and her reputation got completely mended. She became the first person to see and preach the name of JESUS after HIS resurrection.

How about the Samaritan woman at the well of Jacob? Here was a woman who had gone through so much that she had had five husbands. Each had probably thrown her out because she could not bear children, or due to some other reason. But when she met JESUS at the well, her life got changed completely and for good. She became the second from Prophetess Anna the 88 year Widow in the Temple to evangelize and preach about the Messiah. She was the first person JESUS, as an adult revealed HIMSELF to. He told her in person that she was speaking to CHRIST the Messiah.

What a wonderful thing to have JESUS CHRIST the son of the Most High GOD speak to you face to face; John 4: 7-29. When JESUS Talks to you, and makes HIMSELF known to you, it makes all the difference in your life. All that was bad goes away and a new thing starts in your life.

Can you imagine speaking face to face with JESUS THE SON OF THE MOST HIGH GOD! Instantaneously, what negative ideas about getting to know HIM that the deceiver may have put in one's mind would be wiped out, and what would prevail would be that Glorious Image of GOD! Your self-esteem would soar and your identity would attain perfection; patterned after GOD'S image. All your sins would fade away; they would be buried in the sea of forgetfulness. Amen!

Do you know we are living at a time when we do not need to buy the restitution of sins with money or with our property as did the people in the Old Testament? Yes, we are living in a better time than that of our Patriarchs, and of the prophets. Look at Luke 10:24, and see what our Savior, JESUS CHRIST said: HE says, "for I tell you, that many prophets and kings have desired to see those things ye see, and have not seen them; and to hear the things which you hear, and have not heard them." For us, all that is required is to repent our sins through JESUS CHRIST who died for that very purpose. We can let JESUS, who paid the penalty of our sins and compensated for our sins with HIS Precious Blood, be our Identity, by acknowledging what HE did for us on the Cross at Calvary.

For indeed, though he was sinless and did not deserve to die, at the Cross, HE DIED for our sins. If it were not for our sins, He would not have died as He did. "For all have sinned and come short of GOD'S Glory; being justified freely by HIS Grace through the redemption that is in CHRIST JESUS: whom GOD hath set forth to be a propitiation through Faith in HIS Blood," Romans 3:22-23-26, 6:3-18.

All we need is to play our part, repenting our sin and giving it all to JESUS. When we give our sins to JESUS, HE will cleanse us, and get us back our lost identity. The identity HE gives us is clean. It makes us forget the old one. Actually, after that you will not tire of thanking GOD that you lost that old identity.

In addition, GOD will give you a new name that is written in the Name of HIS only begotten Son JESUS CHRIST, and you will not have to be ashamed again of your lost old ID.

The discouragement you have been going through will cease. Peace and Joy will fill you up. Then Mercy and Grace will follow you all the days of your life. If you obey the rules and regulations of GOD which are recorded in the Bible, GOD will turn all your misery unto Missiles of Blessings and Victory. Everyone will call you a blessed one, and you will be able to bless. You will be able to help turn many broken hearts into joyful ones for the Glory of God, Amen.

JESUS CHRIST the Son of the Most High GOD is faithful. Let HIM receive all the Glory for forgiving us our sins, and putting all our things right again with Our GOD the Father, Amen! If you are going through things that are making you feel ashamed or sorrowful, come to JESUS and HE will move your shame and sorrows far from you. For shame, HE shall bring fame, and for sorrow, joy unspeakable. In fact, HE did that for you and me over two thousand years ago. Prophet Isaiah in chapter 53:4-5 recorded that revelation he received from the LORD GOD over 800 years before CHRIST was born of Virgin Mary. Take HIS Yoke and give HIM yours: for HIS Yoke is light. HE is ready to carry away all your burdens and give you rest, Amen! Praise GOD Almighty! For HIS mercy and Grace for us! Yes, problems will come but they will not leave you crushed, neither are they going to leave you ashamed. If you feel guilty and you have been accused or you are accusing yourself, the Blood of JESUS CHRIST is still alive to wash you and make you feel newly created again. David after he got himself mixed up with sin, he repented sincerely and was washed and restored again, Psalms 51:1-16.

This man of GOD, "a man after GOD'S own heart" had sinned more than probably you have, but he prayed in Psalm 3, "I acknowledge my transgression and my sin is ever before me."

You see, after David had sinned with Uriah's wife, and got Uriah killed in the battle in order to hide his sin of adultery, David felt like he had lived in sin all through his life, 2 Samuel 11:1-27. All his anointing had been wiped away by the sin he had committed. But after repenting and saying to the LORD, "to You alone LORD, have I sinned and done this thing," and asking God to Please forgive him, The LORD GOD forgave him and blessed him restoring his monarchy and giving him a son by the name Solomon to carry on the dynasty.

In order for us to get the seed that will carry on our dynasty, we need to put things right with the owner of the monarchy that we belong to. That is the Kingdom of Heaven. Don't you know you are a child of the King; the King that rules over all the other kings and their kingdoms? If you know who you are and whose child you are, you will "count all these other things as nothing for Excellency of CHRIST JESUS who loves you," Philippians 3:7-10.

Let us go to Psalm 51, and see how the Psalmist overcame his guilt. You know, King David was wrong in his sinful actions. In other words, he had sinned grievously. He coveted, lacked love for his neighbor, was jealous of his neighbor for his beautiful wife, Stole his neighbor's wife, committed adultery with her, lied, and finally, killed. David desired to sleep with Uriah's wife without considering the consequences of sin, Romans 6:23, Ezekiel 18: 3-18. His selfish lust betrayed him, leading him to adultery and murder. All manner of sin simultaneously embraced King David. They were all born of covetousness. Covetousness brought lust and the rest of the sins followed in sequence.

Breaking one of the commandments, results to breaking all, and failure in keeping them. That is why we seriously need JESUS CHRIST. Previously, David had won over all the trials and temptations of vengeance and which had been brought his way when King Saul was after his life. Twice, Saul was delivered by GOD to David but David would not kill him. That was a tremendous passing of great tests, 1 Samuel 24, 26.

It was obvious that Saul had sinned by wanting to kill David, and so David could have taken it that GOD had given him a chance to kill Saul. But GOD gave him wisdom to know that it was temptation that he needed to overcome. At that time, while David was in the woods running away from King Saul, GOD ruled his life completely, 1 Samuel 23-30. Years later, however, after he had found respite from his enemies' attacks, his body's desire got to rule over him and he sinned terribly; the danger of comfort zone without prayerfully watching, 2 Samuel 11, 24. The resting period can be dangerous, and it's the time one need to pray more and be watchful.

The point of relaxation is where the devil waits for us, when all is well and we're fully rested from our troubles, Satan comes to show all the enticements that can keep us amused. That way we forget to worship our LORD and begin to worship ourselves. We need to remember we are commanded to pray without ceasing and never to serve other masters like master, "self".

Now, the best thing is, King David had known about the Savior and known that the Savior was a loving GOD. He also knew the secret and benefits of repentance and redemption. He knew that GOD being a just King and a loving Father, none of HIS children would ask for forgiveness and have HIM not give it lovingly. Therefore, King David humbly asked for forgiveness, and JESUS touched David's heart by the Power of the HOLY SPIRIT and caused David to go down on his knees and repent.

David humbled himself by reducing his status from that of a King to something worse than a slave. He slept on ashes in sack cloths, (2 Samuel 12:1-20). He did this so that he could approach the Holy Throne of his GOD with humility. David had to die to himself and become nothing before his GOD, forgetting his throne and kingship as a blessed king of Israel. At that moment, David knew that his throne did not matter anymore. There is only One Throne that matters all the time. This is the Throne above all thrones where everything originated and to which everyone will be answerable. That is the throne of the Most Supreme Master KING of Kings; the Supreme Master who made king Nebuchadnezzar to eat grass like a cow and live in the bush with beasts for seven years.

How many kings today, or even we who are not kings, can get out of their offices and go and sleep on ashes in presence of their subordinate staff in order to repent to GOD and show HIM respect; the respect of the Most High, the Greatest Master? King David challenges me so much that I am often gripped with a sense of unworthiness when I think of his actions. It is my sincere prayer that my GOD will continually create in me a new heart and give me a sweet mellow spirit; extremely humble before HIM. I also pray that HE will not let me fall into the sin of pride like King Saul did.

King David knew that if he did not obtain Mercy and Grace from GOD, his kingdom was gone and he would be forever forgotten. David took off his crown and his royal garments, leaving behind his throne, and he put on sack cloths to show GOD how much he revered HIM. Above all, that gesture displayed to GOD that King David acknowledged that all worthiness was HIS, that everything here on earth and in Heaven belongs to The Almighty GOD.

It is only our LORD GOD who can build us and make us something out of the nothing that we are. King David had personally known without GOD the Father and Savior JESUS CHRIST and the Anointing of the HOLY SPIRIT; he would be nothing and could not make it. David repented with all the humility and GOD restored him to his wealth and his kingdom. We too can be restored to God's goodness through repentance and humility.

It is important to remember this, that while King David was doing his repentance, his adversary Satan was not happy. Our enemy Satan is never happy when we repent because he knows we are getting closer to our GOD yet Satan's ultimate goal is to take us farther and further from our forever Heavenly Father's relationship.

I can imagine Satan enticing people to talk about David's sins as if they themselves had never sinned in their lives. Satan can make people feel holy when they are sinning with their tongues, by talking about others. In this way, he amasses victims out of one victim's situation. To the talkers, David's sins were more severe than their own sins. They did not know that David's sins had already been forgiven and that GOD had done away with them all. Hallelujah! The Almighty had turned King David's misery into missiles to destroy Satan's plans. The most amazing thing is; GOD does not examine the magnitude of our sins. Instead, HE looks at the brokenness of our hearts and the fullness of our repentance. Repentance is our turning point whereby we turn away from the sin; saying goodbye to it, never to go back to it.

It is sad when a person repents of a sin today and tomorrow falls into the same again, not caring what GOD is feeling when HE sees him getting into the same sin he repented of yesterday. It's terrible; we need to feel sad at such actions and pray for forgiveness like Nehemiah and Daniel in the Bible. Mark this: these two brethren had not sinned, but they had studied the Word of GOD and observed the action of their fellow Israelites from their fathers' generation to their own generation.

They had seen beside all the warnings that Israel and Judah received from the LORD through HIS erect the Prophets, they would repent and still go back to the same adultery and idolatry without minding what GOD is feeling about their actions. Sometimes they would be warn and not repent. But the Holy men of Israel continued to repent for the rest of their generation until GOD was touched by their prayer and heal the sins of their people.

CHAPTER 9

Habits

From Messes to Messages: and a messed up to a messenger:

If you are caught up by one of the sins that people often refer to as habits, repent on your own behalf and on behalf of others that are suffering from the sins that are called habits.

Look around and see in the community the people that are dying of sins (bad habits) like smoking, drinking alcohol, drugs and adultery. Pray for them earnestly as if it is your sin and your family's sin. Daniel and Nehemiah prayed; "we and our fathers and our fathers' fathers have all sinned against you. The whole of this generation and family of Israel has sinned against you dear LORD GOD. Forgive us and entreat us with your kindness." They fasted and prayed and cried to the LORD their GOD.

Let me ask this question, how many times have we fasted for other people that we do not associate with? It is high time we ask the HOLY SPIRIT to help us start fasting and praying for others.

We need to pray more and to fast more with a repenting heart for the sins that are going on around the world, no matter what label is attached to them.

Let us feel that the whole of this generation, ourselves, our children, our fathers and our father's fathers have sinned against GOD and that is why there are a lot of disasters and deaths of all kinds. It appears as if GOD does not care, but GOD cares. It is we who have neglected the responsibility of our duty. We are not doing our part but we want GOD whom we have abused so much to do HIS part faithfully while we do nothing to keep HIS relationship with us warm. A relationship works two ways. It is an impossible situation where GOD loves us to death, yet we do nothing to show him that we love him back. We must live in HIS obedience and serve HIM with all our might and with all our hearts. We must reciprocate. When GOD says, be you Holy for I AM HOLY; Leviticus 11:44, 20:26, and 1Peter 1: 15-20, HE means exactly that.

When the LORD GOD says, "Witness about my goodness to others, preach my Word throughout the world," HE means exactly that. But we cannot witness of HIS Saving Grace when we are not living to HIS Standard. Let s ask the HOLY SPIRIT to help us.

Help us LORD to know the evil we have done by neglecting our responsibility in the Godhood realm. Majority of the people in the whole world are worshiping the devil and adamantly rejecting the LORD. They do not care about this GOD, but they want GOD to care and get them out of their problems and watch over everything that belongs to them. We need to preach and not to soothe people: soothing is not loving! John the Baptist preached and never soothed, Elijah, Isaiah, Jeremiah, Ezekiel, name all the prophets before JESUS; they all preached and never soothed; they told the truth no matter how bitter people perceived it, they preached against sin to the WORD of Righteousness and Holiness.

When JESUS THE CHRIST came to HIS full ministry, HE preached and never soothed people. Today, churches are full of people getting appeased to continue in sin and not preached to stop sinning, lest they go away and leave unpaid church bills. What is more precious, their money or their souls? If true Gospel is preached GOD will enrich people, touch them to give. Let us pray and preach the Gospel. It does not matter the setup of the nation, GOD wants us to put HIM first by preaching HIS WORD.

Ann, the daughter of Dr. Bill Graham, answering to a question in a media interview asked, "If America has told GOD to get out of their schools, out of their court rooms and out of their public places, out of their country, how is it that Americans expect GOD to come to intervene when the enemy strikes?" She added, "GOD is a Gentleman, and he does not involve Himself where HE is not welcome."

That was the most incredible answer to that question the media had asked this wise lady. Even without the question, you can guess by the answer what the topic was. This was immediately after the 9/11/2001 terrorists' attacks in New York City, Pentagon, and Pennsylvania and most of the Americans plus the media were wondering why GOD didn't stop that cruel attack. At that moment, everybody turned to the Church of CHRIST, which was the most beautiful thing that a sad nation founded by GOD could do. But the saddest thing is, soon after the mourning was over, everyone went back to his normal routine and forgot that GOD wants our attention as a nation every day. GOD wants us to worship HIM every moment of our lives and that is why HE sacrificed HIS only begotten Son JESUS CHRIST so that we can know HIM properly through HIS Son by the power of the HOLY SPIRIT.

It is not complex, you just need to be humble before HIM as your creator, and HE will reveal HIMSELF wholly unto you. Our LORD GOD, help us. We need to pray and seek you more than ever before for we are living in the last days that are full of evil. The evil one is very angry that his time is almost over. Help us dear LORD so that we can see the urgency of unanimous prayers of repentance. Dear LORD, if we're not able to come together; all of us that love you; hear our individual cries and heal our land. Let us have the greatest harvest this year.

Let Matthew 9:37-39 be fulfilled in our time Dear JESUS and give us a message of your Word with power, knowledge, and understanding to preach and bring the harvest to you. Dear LORD, let every individual brother or sister that has a calling and is chosen for the Gospel preach more than ever before. Open the avenues and the doors that have been closed to preach your WORD. Supply us with money where we need money dear LORD for we cannot make it to preach without using the tool of money. Money belongs to you dear LORD and not to the liar Satan who has been holding it so that your children will have nothing to use to preach your Gospel. Silver and gold are yours Dear LORD and cattle upon a thousand hills are thine Dear LORD. Let us, your dear children that are ready to preach get enough to spend while we preach. Dear LORD, release the provision of money to us, your children, so that we can preach the Gospel far and wide. Also, give us more ways and methods to use as we preach this Gospel of our Eternal Kingdom more effectively. Let not the enemy poke his nose in the methods that you are going to give us to preach you Gospel, Dear LORD, as he has done in past.

Before I forget, the Media question that was put to Sister Ann Graham may sound like as if has only been asked in America. No! It was and it is a question asked all over the world and Ann Graham's answer was fit for all nations of the earth, especially those who have rejected God.

And do you know that such answer can be directed to an individual?

When an individual has engaged himself or herself with some activities that are not Godly, is that individual not telling GOD, I do not need you in my affairs? Proverbs 16:3, 3:7. Of course, yes! Actually, inside the Churches that we attend, have we not been taught that GOD is HOLY and our bodies are the temple of the HOLY SPIRIT? 1 Corinthians 6: 19-20 says, "What? Know you not that your body is the Temple of the HOLY GHOST, which is in you? You are not your own, for you were bought for a price: therefore glorify GOD in your body and in your spirit which are GOD'S." Unless we want to justify our sins, we need to repent and be sanctified from the evil one Satan. We need to be Holy like our Father GOD!

When we do that faithfully then we can expect GOD to turn our mess into messages and turn us into victorious messengers of HIS precious Word, and our victimization into victory. Amen!

If one holds onto sinful habits and calls them habits, never repenting, then one cannot expect the HOLY SPIRIT to dwell inside him or her. And instead of GOD turning you to a victorious messenger devil continues to make you his messed victim.

Only the liar Satan will dwell inside your dirty body, lying to you that "you are alright, GOD understands and HE cares. HE cannot leave you." That is a lie from hell, manufactured, polished, and released to confuse you so that you can die in a mess of sin and go to hell. Hell is as real as Heaven is real. Any habit that enslaves us is an idol. The worship of idols is forbidden in the Bible; therefore, bad habits are a sin and will lead you to miss your purpose in the only good habits of true prayer led by the HOLY SPIRIT. Fasting to pray, and worship, Praises unto the LORD GOD ALMIGHTY, that's the only good habit. GOD created you for a purpose and HE wants to fulfill your purpose in HIM while you are clean.

See Joseph in Egypt. He did not mix himself with sin. If Joseph had fallen into temptation and committed adultery of Potiphar's wife, he would have eventually fallen into the miserable habit of extra-marital sexual interaction; hence, sexual sin. Joseph would have been killed by his master for sleeping with his wife. What a disaster that would have been! But because he overcame that temptation, when he was put in the prison through false accusation, his GOD comforted him in that prison. Joseph knew, since GOD did not leave him in the pit, he could rest assured that no matter what the Egyptians would do to him, it would be for the Glory of his GOD.

Therefore, Joseph knew very well that his GOD is with him there in the prison, so he was as bold as a Lion, Proverbs 28:1. For the Bible says, "a righteous man is a bold as a lion." That is why he was able to interpret dreams for his fellow prisoners. See, even then as a prisoner, GOD gave him favor with the prison warden, who came to respect him as a great man of GOD. Joseph was never a little man, no matter where he found himself. Neither are you!

So long as you are in the Blood of JESUS CHRIST and you are covered in and out, you are not a little man. You are a mighty man of ALMIGHTY GOD! AMEN! Do we need GOD to intervene and help us out of bad habits? Yes! If you have bad habits, you really need GOD'S intervention!

This book will enlighten you in the things that you need to focus on in order to cement all the loopholes that the enemy can use to destroy you through for the lack of knowledge. When you do some things just because you see people do them, you put yourself into a big problem. For example, many smokers and alcoholics start because of the influence of friends. Especially, when they are young they find themselves falling into the traps of their peers. By the time one comes to realize that he or she has made a mistake, one is already addicted and cannot just stop.

Here is the solution, JESUS CHRIST; HE is the only one who can help you get out of that addiction. And I tell you, CHRIST is able; that is why HE is called CHRIST JESUS! CHRIST, meaning the anointed of GOD, JESUS or YESHUA, meaning savior or rescuer. He is also the Anointer of them that do believe in him. He will anoint you with HIS Power and you will experience a great change in your life if you humble yourself before HIM to get you out of your problems. If you totally surrender in the hands of JESUS and receive HIS full anointing sin will no longer reside in you.

I am a witness to that. I was addicted to the sin of range, and every small thing used to hurt me so much that I would feel dizzy with anger. When I surrendered to the anointing of our LORD JESUS, I do not know where that anger and range went to and now I have a testimony that JESUS can heal even anger and range. Well, let me say here, I know that my anger was taken back to Satan the author and the owner of anger and range, and all sins. It was a disease and because the devil knew about that, he made sure that people injured me daily by saying things or doing things that were going to hurt me. With great determination to win and be clean, I kicked that addiction of anger and range out of me by Worshipping my JESUS CHRIST. I worshipped inside me and outside me by the help of the Power of the HOLY SPIRIT. The LORD anointed me from the top of my head to the soles of my feet. And out of that Anointing, the LORD GOD birthed a ministry that has touched and changed the lives of many people here in America and internationally.

Now I only have holy anger, without range. I rejoice in the LORD to see how HE healed me.

Actually, I used not to rage or be angry for nothing. The devil used to make sure that someone did something very bad to me, so that even other people would look at it and see that it was bad.

The result was anger and rage every time, but I did not like being angry all the time, so I started seeking the LORD for a solution. I was never happy to quarrel with any one at all but no matter how hard I tried to be agreeable and to feel good about those around me, someone would rage at me and accuse me falsely. Sometimes I would feel like I could go and live in forest alone. But the LORD GOD saw my struggle to agree with people. He saw that I wanted to be happy about everyone and everything around me.

When I started seeking God about this sin I came to a revelation that it was a disease just like any other, I worked on it by praying and fasting just like I work on the healing of other diseases that devil brings my way; and JESUS CHRIST healed me at once. I said, if the LORD could heal me of Malaria, pneumonia, ulcers, asthma, appendicitis, and many other evils that devil has brought my way before; why not this anger and range? On the day I made this discovery, I worshiped like I have never worshiped the LORD my GOD before. This was a habit that had become a disease. The sin of anger and range started very slowly day by day, until I came to the sanctuary and repented: then the HOLY SPIRIT filled me afresh and taught me. There are many things we need to learn from the LORD GOD ALMIGHTY BY THE HELP OF THE HOLY SPIRIT AND HIS SON JESUS CHRIST OUR MEDIATOR AND INTERCESSOR, John 14:26-27 and Roman 8: 1-39

I thank GOD because out of that; after I repented and prayed, my LORD saved those who angered me and we are now brethren in deed. Our LORD is faithful; HE started a ministry for us to serve HIM through. Therefore, devil was a loser and a liar then, and even now he is a loser and a liar.

I have seen some people even ministers struggling with burden of wanting to stop smoking. The biggest mistake they make is to try on their own. They cannot make it. It takes a total surrender to the one who said, "come ye who are heavy laden and I will give you rest." JESUS IS THE ONLY SOLUTION TO THAT PROBLEM AND TO ANY OTHER PROBLEM, WHETHER ADDICTIVE OR NOT. HE IS THE ONLY WAY, THE TRUTH, AND THE LIFE.

My dear brethren, I feel for you and I do pray that you learn this secret.

Those of you believers that are struggling to stop abusive substances I know you have tried and you already feel that it is impossible to stop; you cannot stop it, yet you know very well that you are defiling the temple of the HOLY SPIRIT. Here you are, you're called to preach righteousness, yet you do not know how to preach without feeling condemned of your sinful habit of substance abuse. Let me tell you; for sure, JESUS CHRIST is able! If JESUS has done for others why do you think he cannot do it for you? You just need to put a little more effort and be determined to ask, pray and worship. And also, most important, trash those substances away from you to show Satan that you have valued yourself and you are no longer his slave.

Do not say you will "give it a try."

No! It is not a try; it is stopping it! Doing the stopping it serious business! Don't give it a try! It won't work! It has never worked. Just stop it! And stop it! Get out of that addiction! It is not your life! Come out of it! It's going to kill you and you do not need to die that way! It's GOD who should take you home when your time is full! See Psalm 91. Stop it! And worship the LORD your GOD. HE wants your worship now! You cannot die! You will live and proclaim the good works of the LORD Ps 118:7 who is going to help you get out of that killing problem. Anything that becomes your master other than your LORD GOD is an idol and a disease. Worship the LORD! If you have been going out to smoke, or whatever, go out at the same time you have been going out and worship The LORD GOD ALMIGHTY instead!

Hebrews 13:13-16 tells us, "Let us go forth therefore unto HIM without a camp, bearing HIS reproach. For here have we no continuing city, but we seek one to come. By HIM therefore let us offer the sacrifice of praises to GOD continually that is the fruit of our lips giving thanks to HIS name." Therefore, my advice to you is; learn a chorus of worship, carry a book, or even hymns on a smartphone or an MP3 player. That way you will get very powerful anointed recorded worship songs that are led by the anointed worshipers of GOD.

By the way, as you dip yourself in the Blood of JESUS CHRIST and you subject yourself into the will and the power of the HOLY SPIRIT, you will automatically learn how to worship the LORD your GOD without any book, or recorded songs' aid to help you. Songs of praise and worship will be flowing out of your belly as a flowing river, and with a lot of sweetness.

This book will teach you how to prevent yourself from the attack that will bring you miseries. It will make you know that: most of your miseries came because you let the enemy destroy you for lack of knowledge and apostasy; Hosea 4:6, Jeremiah 8:4-7, 8-9. The people of GOD during the time period of these two prophets had lacked the knowledge of whom, and whose children they were; and they mixed themselves with the rest of the world, which was full of bodily lusts just like it is today. Whatever the world says, Christians are agreeing with it in the fear of losing their jobs. Lies of Satan the devil!

If all Christians (if they were all strong believers of our LORD JESUS CHRIST) would say, we shall not work in any firm that does not want us to talk about our LORD JESUS CHRIST, would not many businesses be closed? Would they not be called to work within the next hour of their decree? But because of the love of the dollar, they would rather deny CHRIST, yet we look at Peter as if he was strange when he denied JESUS thrice before the cock crowed. Believers have become the pleasers of nonbelievers and that is why they no longer preach the Gospel of the Kingdom of GOD in the busses, and in open places where communities gather as they used to do before in 1970s and early 80s. Those of us who have been left doing it have been persecuted by even those who say they are Christians.

Growing up, I used to see brethren preach the Gospel and praise the LORD GOD wherever they happened to be: In the market places, by riversides, in busses, along the sea shore, and on the streets. When I got Baptized in the HOLY SPIRIT 1973, I thank GOD, HE put in me this same Spirit; I preach anywhere I find people, and I feel like a debtor if I would go to any public place and leave without witnessing JESUS CHRIST to the people I meet. From the time of my anointing I have always felt obliged to preach this Gospel of the Kingdom of my Father until CHRIST will come to take me home; Amen!

My motto is: to allow the HOLY SPIRIT in me to win as many souls as HE will to get to heaven. Why should people go to hell and yet the devil created nobody? GOD did not create hell for man; HE created hell for Satan and the one third of the demons that joined Lucifer, that Satan, that devil, as he fell out of the Kingdom of GOD my Father.

One morning at 5 am, My Heavenly Father told me, "I do not take men to hell. It is man who walks to take himself to hell, not ME." In other words, man takes himself to hell by his beliefs. The GOD of the 70s and there before is the same GOD today, tomorrow and forever; Hebrew 13:8. The commission HE gave over two thousand years ago is the same today, tomorrow, and until HE will come to get us home, Matthew 28: 18-20.

In this book, Our LORD GOD wants to teach us the duties of a true Believer in CHRIST.

Your duty as a believer in CHRIST JESUS is to do the will of our Father who is in Heaven; First, fulfill John 6:29 where JESUS said, "This is the work of GOD, that you believe on HIM whom HE has sent" and you earnestly "seek you first the Kingdom of GOD and HIS Righteousness and all other things shall be added unto you," Matthew 6:33-34. As you see in Matthew 7:21, the will of our Father in Heaven is when we fulfill the Great Duty that HE commissioned us to fulfill in Matthew 28: 18-20, Mark 16: 15-18. And at the same time we see JESUS CHRIST who came to physically teach us the will of our Father GOD in Matthew 7: 22 JESUS is telling us, "Many will say to me in that day, LORD, LORD, have we not prophesied in thy name? In thy name have cast out devils! And in thy name done many wonderful works! Verse 23 JESUS continues to tell us, "And then will I profess unto them, I never knew you: depart from me, ye that work iniquity." Verses 24-25 HE continues to teach us saying, "Therefore, whosever hears these saying of MINE, and doeth them, I will liken him unto a wise man, which built his house upon a rock: and when the rain descended and the flood came and winds blew, and beat upon that house and it fell not: for it was founded on a ROCK." JESUS CHRIST IS THE ROCK OF AGES: when your faith is founded on HIM nothing can fail you. Even when things look very dark, there is great hope in resurrection of that seems dead.

Verse 26-27 JESUS gives us the example of a foolish man that built on the sand and how his house fell heavily when the rain and the winds came and beat it up. It never stood the powers of the enemy. For it was founded on the soft sinking sand. It was built on the earthly materials. It was built on money, smocking, alcohol, adultery, and even good jobs and healthy food without CHRIST JESUS. Healthy food, exercises, good jobs with good money are all good and necessary when JESUS CHRIST is their Master and your Savior.

Our GOD has not given us many duties, but only to believe in HIM that HE sent; even JESUS CHRIST his only begotten Son; and to do HIS will. GOD has commissioned us to witness about HIS goodness and surely, is that too much work to do? All we need do is speak to others of how good GOD has been to us and to others; and to witness to people that he can be good to them too.

Do you know that preaching is nothing but witnessing of GOD'S own goodness to others? Well, where there is goodness, let us not forget there are rules and regulations that govern us so that the goodness can continue.

Our whole duty is to seek to know the will of GOD. In other words, to seek to know HIS rules and regulation that HE has kept for us so that we can be HIS completely.

In Genesis 1:28-29, Adam was blessed and commissioned to be fruitful, to multiply, to replenish the earth, and to subdue it. In chapter 2:16-17, the LORD GOD gave rules and regulations that would guide and direct the blessings and the commission HE gave to Adam. That is why JESUS CHRIST came to reinforce that blessing and commissioning, and so it is our duty as HIS children to keep it. And thanks be to our GOD, HE did not leave us helpless or powerless. HE gave unto us HIS HOLY SPIRIT so that HE can guide, direct, and help us to achieve the goals that he had for our lives here on earth.

Yes, GOD is all powerful, and all knowing, and all mighty, and all present. But HE gave you and me power and authority (dominion) over everything. We are in control of what happens to us, and unless we give HIM back the control over ourselves and over everything; HE cannot do it for us voluntarily. See Genesis 1:28-29, and 2:16-17. And then see what happened in Genesis 3:1-8; here, man gave the power he was given by GOD to the devil by yielding himself to the voice of Satan when he came to them in the garden through the snake; hence, man lost his legal identity to Satan.

Nevertheless, because GOD is all-loving to man, HE gave man a second chance. However, the second chance involves following formula in order to claim back the power that we lost at the Garden of Eden. GOD'S formula is simple; John 6:29, only believe in the ONE whom GOD sent; JESUS CHRIST, HIS only begotten son.

The purpose of Jesus walk through the Garden of Gethsemane to Calvary was to inspire us to draw the power back to ourselves. When we reclaim dominion over all things, we give our power back to our GOD so that he can now have the legal right to fight for us as HE ought to. When you read this book, you will have a clear deeper revelation of the two gardens, Eden, and Gethsemane. You will see the announcement and completion of the new life that, through JESUS CHRIST, was started at the garden of Gethsemane and announced complete on the Cross at Calvary.

CHAPTER 10

Back to the Habits

From Messes to Messages: and a messed up to a messenger:

Have you ever seen a habit kill or destroy someone? Your answer is probably yes, and I most certainly have! If you have answered no to that question, I urge you to look carefully around you, think of the people you have met over the years, and then re-examine your answer.

Nowadays sins are called habits and so no one is taking responsibility to instruct, restrain, correct, change or even more importantly, repent. To see why we should take responsibility, go to 2 Timothy 3:16-17. The law of the land that was based on GOD'S Law, which used to correct us, has been restrained from correcting by the law of the devil. No longer do people tell each other, "Stop doing that; it is wrong and sinful before GOD." The name GOD is now offensive to lawmakers all over the world; hence, sin has been let loose.

Today's law of the land does not allow us to reference sin to the wrongdoer. You cannot say, "Do not do that thing because that is a sin!" No! I understand that, even School-teachers have been instructed and obediently followed this law of the land; they cannot correct a child in the class using God's laws, but a teacher is allowed by the law of the land to stop a child from drawing a picture of JESUS CHRIST. A teacher can stop a child from saying, "I love you JESUS." In contrast, children can say anything else even if it is rude and never be corrected, for that is seen as the expression of feelings. Also, this is what I hear being said these later days, "You cannot say that! You cannot mention the word sin even if it is clearly sin. You will be Judging, and accusing! You are a bad person! You are hurting their feelings!" These sentiments are the result of the law according of this world, manufactured, packaged, and released to the hearts of mankind by the enemy of humanity, Satan.

Doing drugs, engaging in extra and pre-marital sexual interactions, abortions, homosexual, smoking, cursing, raging, and many other enslaving sins continuously defile GOD'S temple. Yet these sins are nicknamed and called habits, and procedures and have been termed clean and accepted to dwell in our communities. No one is taking the responsibility of repentance, and therefore, there is no reason to stop sinning any more. It's no longer called sin, and therefore, why worry about repenting when it is just a habit! There is no moral obligation any more. Communities have been set free to live immorally, and no one cares about the other. Everyone to himself, and GOD for us all! How can GOD be for us if we do not even care what HE feels when we sin against this body that HE created in HIS own Image and HIS Likeness?

I am not being judgmental, I am standing on the truth of GOD so that you and I, can have a common ground to reason out of love and not hate. I love everybody created by my Father GOD and I believe this is why the LORD GOD has put the burden of writing this book in my spirit to share it with everybody for our deliverance. GOD loves us so much and HE wants us to get away from anything that enslaves. GOD wants the best for us and HE is out to bless us in abundance if only we listen to what HE is telling us and do the right. Sin is enslaving, and deadly; read this in the Bible: "Know you not that ye are the Temple of GOD and that the SPIRIT of GOD dwells in you? If a man defiles the temple of GOD, him shall GOD destroy for the temple of GOD is Holy, which temple are you," 1Corithians 3:16-17. Here, Paul was counseling the Christians in Corinth for they had engaged themselves with many types of misconduct, as if they had not been born again. If you and I are born again, we have been regenerated to the new life in JESUS CHRIST and we cannot continue to live the old sinful life; Ephesians 4:22-32. "You are a new creature, and you are separated from death of sin to Eternal life of Righteousness, and Holiness."

To be born again is a serious business, but some take it lightly. We should always remember that, our re-birth cost JESUS his life. HE had to die without a sin so that HE can be able to carry away our sins. The blood of a sinner could not clean another sinner, but the Precious Blood of a sinless man, JESUS CHRIST, washes our sins away and leaves us newly clean when we repent.

Let me ask this; if you wash your clothes clean, and it happens that they fall on dirty ground and are now stained, would you call them clean again without washing them? I have heard some preachers preach that, "no matter what you do, GOD cannot cast you out of HIS House." They say, even if you sin you will still live with GOD in HIS presence here on earth and in heaven because you are HIS child. That preaching does not rhyme with the Word of GOD that guides us to eternal life. The Bible in the Old Testament and in the New Testament condemns sin as whole, and it is written for a warning, instructions, directions and guidance out of GOD'S love for mankind; 2Timothy 3:16-17. And the Bible says clearly in Ezekiel 18, "The soul that sins shall surely die." And in Romans 6:23, "for the wages of sin is death but the gift of GOD is eternal life through JESUS CHRIST OUR LORD." It does not matter whether it is me or you or who, whosoever sins is not of GOD and in the absence of GOD there is eternal death. We should observe to live a clean life as the Bible tells us. In the book of Romans 6 Apostle Paul was inspired of the HOLY SPIRIT to write asking: "And shall we continue in sin so that grace may abound?" The answer is: "GOD forbid," Romans 6:1-2. Romans 6 continue to say, "If we are really Baptized after repentance of our sins, which is the Baptism of our LORD JESUS CHRIST, we are baptized unto HIS death and HIS resurrection. We can no longer continue to live like the people that have not known HIM by HIS birthing us into HIS marvelous kingdom." GOD is righteous, and we must be as HOLY as HE is. If we let those things that contaminate our bodies take dominion over us, and call it a habit instead of condemning it as sin, then something is very wrong with our faith towards GOD. We need to do a thorough examination of our souls and ask ourselves, which temple are we, if we go for adultery, fornication, rage, bitterness, envy, malice, and hate, smoke, do drugs, drink alcohol, and all that defiles the body? Are we still the temple of the HOLY SPIRIT and is HE really dwelling in us when we have one of those sins residing inside us? The answer is NO, we aren't!

<u>Remember, he who breaks one of the commandments, breaks all.</u>

I have heard this saying, "the Prodigal son came back to his father and his father took him back." Yes, but on what condition could he come back? First, the Prodigal son had to do something; he had to recall the glory of his father's house. Secondly, he had to forfeit all the things he was doing to keep him dirty and out of his father's house. He had to leave those things behind before he got to his father's home. He knew his father was not a joke, and that even his servants were clean, holy, and righteous and well treated. The boy knew very well that he could not enter that home with any of the things that he was doing in that lost world where he had badly spent his life. Therefore, he had to do something to go back to his father's house, he had to <u>repent</u>, and leave all that he was doing and go home humbly. He decided to ask to be taken in as a servant not as a son. Since he looked dirty, and knowing that his Dad was a clean honorable man, he never thought he would be accepted back and be treated even well as a servant in that house; which would still have been far much better than his life with pigs. And so he went humbly. Thirdly, he made a move towards his father's house. Notice that it was not the father that went to look for him. Dirty as he was though; and that is why JESUS said, "Come as you are, I will wash you, cleanse you and make you whole and give you rest from all your defiling sins." CHRIST will not refuse us for being dirty when we are coming back home, but HE can never allow us live dirty in HIS Divine Presence. When we get close to HIM, before we enter inside HIS Holy Palace, in HIS Glory, in the Presence of GOD the Father the Son, and the HOLY SPIRIT, at the Throne of Mercy behind the veil, at the Ark of the Covenant, where the Blood of JESUS CHRIST is kept for our purification, HE cleans and cleanses us thoroughly through our repentance. The young man made a move to his father's house in great humility and asked the father to accept him back as a servant saying, "Father, I have sinned against heaven and in thy sight and I do not deserve to be called your son."

Hallelujah! Oh, I thank GOD when I remember that it took the HOLY SPIRIT to move me to this kind of repentance and humility. To get me out of where I was lost, it took JESUS CHRIST and HIS Blood and mercy. I thank GOD for giving me obedience to HIS WORD, for many are dying for lack of obedience. It is important to pray that GOD gives us obedience. Immediately we start coming Home to our Eternal Father, Our Father orders an immediate cleansing and purification. If you are washed and you desired to go out again to eat the swine's food, you will have to come afresh and repent so that you can be cleansed anew. You cannot come in as dirty as you are. The process must begin again for you to be accepted back in. Do not say, "But I go to Church every Sunday!" That is not a qualification to get into the Father's Eternal Home. By the way, what is a Church; a Church is supposed to be the Body of CHRIST, and not the building. The building you go into every Sunday is not the Church; the Church is those who are in JESUS CHRIST throughout the world. Each Individual gathering of the Church has a name that it calls itself, and it's officially known by that name. They will remain one part of the Church if they keep the Word or the Full Gospel. Let us go to Revelation chapters 1, 2 and 3; here, Apostle John is being informed by the LORD about the Churches according to their names and their actions of faith and beliefs. So the names are alright depending on the motive and ordination.

Back to the Prodigal Son, we see what other step was taken, and by who. Now it is the Father who will take steps to take the son back home. The boy took his steps back home by Faith, and the Father is taking steps by Love. And so at that moment, while the prodigal son was far off, his father saw him and recognized him, GOD sees us from afar when we start coming home and because HE knows us, HE runs towards us. "So the father saw him and ran to meet him at the gate," and he cried with love to see his son come back home wrecked, he hugged and welcomed him back home. But before the boy entered through the gate to the compound to get into the house, the father ordered his servants to get him ready: to be washed, be cleansed and be given new clothes to put on, and also beautiful ornaments. Oh, Praise the LORD for his mercies that endures forever. The boy did not enter with the old clothes and old sin that is called <u>habit</u>. He was stinking and filthy, he would have not been able to sit on his father's couches, or at the table for the big meal that was prepared for him, Luke 15-24. You see that is what GOD does for us, HE keeps waiting for the day we will come back home. After HE sees us coming, HE cries with love to welcome us back home where we belonged before we were born into this world of sin. Perhaps you do not yet know it, but the truth is that we all originated from heaven, where GOD the Father, The Son, and The HOLY SPIRIT Created and kept us in HIS Mansion: and that is why our Father GOD says HE knew us before we were in the wombs of our mothers, Jeremiah 1:5. And so, when we get to the door, HE orders the Angels to wash us with the Precious Blood of HIS Son JESUS CHRIST and to dress us in royal garments and ornaments.

This is a supernatural washing while we are here on earth. Not when we die out of this body. No! It's when we realize and repent our sins that took us away from our father's home like the prodigal son. Immediately you stop calling those sins habits and you call them sins, and repent them in the Mighty Name of JESUS CHRIST, the Angels are charged to come and cleanse and clean you from the top of your head to the soles of your feet and dress you with the most spiritual cloths and ornaments.

Is smoking and drinking alcohol a sin? Yes it is! And allow me to explain this very vividly and precisely how smoking cigarettes and drinking alcohol is a sin. JESUS said, "And you shall know the truth and the truth shall set you free; John 8: 32, 36." You see, you and I can only be set free by knowing the truth in the Word of GOD, not by ignoring it, Proverbs 23:23-24. The Truth remains, Smoking, and drinking alcohol is as a sin as any other sin. If you smoke, do not feel bitter for this revelation, only feel Godly sorrow and let me explain. For "Godly sorrow works repentance:" if you learn, repent, and stop, you will save yourself.

Actually, addiction to cigarettes and that of adultery are equivalent (the same kind of sin) in this manner; in cigarette smoking, you defile, contaminate and kill innocent people when that smoke goes to the air into their lungs and to the blood system. You pollute the air and you have no control over that smoke once it gets out of your nostrils. Therefore, you help or Aid Satan to kill GOD'S people by using Tobacco that GOD created for other purposes. When you smoke and release that smoke to the air you damage others while you are also killing yourself silently and knowingly or ignorantly. And devil succeeds to make you an imperceptible murderer, and you know that "no murderer, publically known or not known inherits GOD'S KINGDOM." 1 John 3:15

You see, most smokers do not even care where they smoke and where they throw/drop the remaining cigarette butts. It is absurd that some dads and moms will smoke next to their kids. Others will kiss their babies with that cigarette smell. In fact, the research carried in early and mid-90s revealed that, inhalers of cigarette smoke are worse affected than smokers. No wonder there is increase in Asthmatic Attacks, Bronchitis, Hypertension, Heart Attacks resulting to cardiac failure and other health complications.

Now, that is the spread and the predisposing of illness caused by cigarette addicted smokers to themselves and others. See now the similarity with adultery; adulterers are two separately married people who engage themselves into extra marital sexual activity. They are not married to each other. One has a wife and the other a husband. While they are contaminating their souls they are also contaminating their bodies, hence, if one has a sexually transmitted disease, he will carry it to his innocent wife and the other to the husband. Now, if one of them has HIV or one of these incurable STDs, children in two or more families are going to be left orphans. Therefore, the adulterers kill others as well as themselves. And above all, they contaminate and defile the body that GOD created in HIS own Image. You and I do not own this body. We cannot do what we want with it. We have to keep it clean and undefiled from every sin of pollution and contamination whether it kills physically or not: for sin kills first spiritually then eventually, physically and to eternal torment in hell.

We do not want to die of what we can prevent or what we induce to our bodies.

GOD holds us responsibly accountable for any death we constitute.

As in John 8:3-11, the law of stoning and killing adulterers was removed by JESUS CHRIST because both the adulterer and the stone killer has committed murder sin. Now that man has increasingly grievously sinned, GOD has constituted another death, HIV, and the rest of incurable STDs. Also, with smokers the same, they do not attain to the fullness of their healthy lives and mostly die earlier than 60years or in their early 70s if they so reach.

Alcohol moves many people to evil they would not have done. It is money consuming, and it kills body cells, hardens blood vessels; hence, hypertension, liver cirrhosis and is responsible for many kind of diseases just like other drugs are. It's addictive and eventually, a full drunkard becomes alcoholic and can never do without it. So alcohol enslaves and entices which is a sinful life to live in.

GOD wants us sober and not intoxicated, so that we can serve HIM with our clean bodies. All substances that cause addiction were not created for food and that is why GOD is never happy when they are abused. No need of trying any of them if you have not, devil stays alert waiting for you to try one; and then he will make you try a second and a third, until you are finally an addict as he had planned for you to become. Any of those, adultery or cigarette, if you try one, the body quickly falls into thirst and hunger after them; and you quickly forget you did not like to do that. And Satan makes forget "blessed are they that hunger and thirst after righteousness," if you had read Matthew 5:6. Notice that blessed are NOT those who thirst and hunger after other things like; sexual immorality, alcohol, cigarette, other drugs, tea, coffee or bodily desires. NO! It is those who "Thirst and Hunger after Righteousness and Holiness:" for GOD fills them and adds other good useful things that they desire and need for this life.

Before I go on explaining, if you do one or two of those action sins that are of course conceived in the spirit first, then manifested in the physical. Have you ever quietly sat and asked yourself, "By the way, why on earth do I smoke?" And have you ever taken a moment to ask the LORD GOD ALMIGHTY your creator, "My LORD GOD, my Master, why do I smoke, and why have I let myself become a slave of this thing?", Are YOU happy about that addiction?

First, you know that cigarettes are drugs and that is why you cannot give them to your children as an appetizer before you give them food or as dessert after a meal. Cigarettes are not counted in any food category; they are in the list of poisons and habit forming substances. Cigarettes are more addictive than most drugs and very difficult to quit. Actually, alcohol may more easily be stopped than cigarettes. Health studies say that cigarettes are deadly, and are killing millions of people.

Now you might ask, "But there are very many other diseases that come by other means, why are you condemning cigarettes?" You are not responsible for any disease whose cause you cannot prevent, but that you know the cause of, you can medically prevent, or hygienically or emotionally prevent. Therefore, when you are inducing high blood pressure (hypertension) or a heart disease, you are committing a slow suicide. In other words, you are killing yourself slowly, but as we saw earlier, your body does not belong to you. It belongs to the ONE Who Created you. GOD gave you that body to cover you; and for his own indwelling place; 1 Corinthians 6: 15-20 tells us how we do not own this body we live into. The body belongs to the ONE WHO CREATED it, JEHOVAH GOD ALMIGHTY.

For GOD is a SPIRIT: and HE dwells in those who love HIM and who obey HIM. Do you want to tell me that the LORD GOD ALMIGHTY will leave HIS other clean environment to come and dwell in a filthy smoky or drugged or sexually defiled body? Never! GOD IS Clean, And Holy, and if you want to consider and know, look at the air we breathe in. If a small foreign particle enters into the air as you breathe in, you will start coughing there and then. Why? The reason is: your body is trying to reject the impurity. God made the air pure and clean, and that is the way your body needs it. The same goes for your blood: if you have anything foreign in your blood, such as germs, or toxins of whatever cause you will get sick immediately. Why? When GOD Created man in HIS Image and HIS Likeness, HE made blood pure and clean. You can't Air or smell it, the same GOD IS all over but you cannot see HIM or smell HIM unless you are Holy as HE IS. That is why you see the men and women that keep themselves Holy in GOD by JESUS CHRIST receiving different gifts of Anointing to serve GOD with signs and wonders of miracles following them; Mark 16:15-18. For They Behold The SON OF GOD!

Now, when you smoke cigarettes or take tobacco in whatever form, or do some of those addictive things, you are contaminating yourself. You are contaminating the air and the blood which was made pure and clean. You are calling GOD a liar to have created those two very important life containing matters pure and clean. You are helping the devil, who gave the idea of making cigarettes to men to kill others slowly. Satan will rejoice to see that he has successfully killed you while you are outside the Holy Spirit. You cannot defile and contaminate the Body where the Holy Spirit is supposed to dwell and expect HIM to dwell in that defiled, contaminated and dirty smoky environment. HE IS HOLY AND CLEANLY PURE. You and I can live a dirty life if we choose to follow Satan's ways, but HE, the HOLY SPIRIT cannot, HE has never lived in a dirty environment and HE can never accept it. We must determine ourselves clean in all areas of our lives after we are washed by the Blood of JESUS CHRIST. We must live a clean life and that way the HOLY SPIRIT will have an indwelling place in our bodies as in 1 Corinthians 3:16-19, 6: 15-20, Galatians 5: 22-23. Galatians 5:16-21 and Ephesians 4:21-31, 1Peter 1:13-16, Leviticus 11:44-45, has a lot of teaching and counsel to enlighten to what life GOD requires of us to live for HIS Divine Purpose.

Giving JESUS CHRIST a chance to change your mind and convert it into HIS mind will help you live a clean, desirable life, Colossians 3: 10, 16-17, Ephesians 4:30. The first Apostles that lived with JESUS CHRIST and saw him face to face learned from HIM directly. The HOLY SPIRIT inspired them to write down these teachings so that we could also learn from JESUS CHRIST. The result is what we know of today as the New Testament, New Covenant.

Therefore now, allow me to tell you why GOD purposed to create tobacco. Tobacco was created for producing insecticide, and not for food or drink intent. I studied this topic because I was keen to know why on earth GOD, so loving and kind, would create such plants as tobacco for eating and smoking if they were going to cause death to man! And indeed, I found out that there are very many other plants including tobacco that GOD created so that humanity could put them to many different uses and NOT Food. Like Pyrethrum and other such naturally occurring plants that are used for insecticides; GOD intended tobacco leaves for substances such as insecticides to kill insects like mosquitos and all harmful insects, not for human consumption at all!

See the description in the World English Dictionary: "Nicotine is a poisonous alkaloid: a toxic alkaloid found in tobacco and also used in liquid form as an insecticide. Formula: C10H1N2.

2. Tobacco: Tobacco products or the smoking of them is informal and can cause blood toxicity. Tobacco is responsible for many illnesses to people that smoke or use it for snuffing or eating. It is of the family of nicotiana flowering plant: a perennial or annual flowering plant with fragrant white, yellow, or purple flowers, of a genus that includes the tobacco plant and belongs to the nightshade family. Nightshade plants' flowers or leaves mostly are poisonous." Hence, they were not created for eating purpose, and misuse of tobacco has caused the world a lot of life destruction and economic distress.

Surely, if you are a child of the Most High GOD, the creator of the universe; why on earth do you want to destroy the temple of the HOLY SPIRIT and make excuses that it is a habit and not a sin.

And say, "I need not stop." "I can't stop, it's my habit!" Different bodies tolerate toxins differently but with time the body can't tolerate anymore; hence, death.

Let me give this short story of life experience: I had a work mate in medical circles who smoked her life away. I tried to preach to this friend and pray with her, but; it was not easy for her to let go smoking. She held onto her smoking tight despite all the complications she had gone through. Having known anatomy and physiology as professionals, we would discuss, and she would tell me for sure she knows she is smoking toxins and that is why she coughs nonstop. Her lungs and liver were enlarged, the heart became enlarged, and year after a year she was getting many complications. By the time she accepted to get saved and stop smoking, her liver had filled her abdomen. She accepted repentance only when she was about to die. She got saved to surrender for heaven. She was expecting GOD to heal her after prayers because she had seen many people get healed of cancer, heart diseases, and all chronic diseases. But these were not self-induced diseases. Or the victims had not received the WORD before and hardened their hearts or despise the WORD OF GOD as she used to do. Or don't you know when you hear the WORD OF GOD and refuse to hearken and surrender yourself to HIM you openly show GOD despise? That's the truth and the real truth. It does not matter the excuses you give to yourself. The real truth and most important for you to look at is that you just openly despise GOD and HIS GREAT WORD OF LIFE. Unknowingly, you have no LOVE and you hate GOD, yourself and everybody else.

When I went to see her in her house, she asked me, "Why am I not getting healed and I have repented, and accepted JESUS?" It was the most testing question to be asked by a needy person who has just finished building a magnificent house for her early retirement at 55, and yet here she was, dying. I kept quiet for moment, praying inside, and told her; "Let's pray." She had told everyone how I had loved to preach to her that if she accepted to be saved she could have had the power to help her stop smoking. She talked of how I encouraged her daily to be saved, telling her that GOD loved her very much. And that is why JESUS CHRIST left heaven to come to live on this filthy earth, and to die, in order to save us from sins.

While we were praying, she was given a word of understanding by GOD, and looking astonished; she called me by my name, "Mary, I am grateful to GOD for accepting to save me despite all the disobedience that I carried as my treasure. Thank you for praying and preaching and loving me so much. I would have died a sinner at a very early age but now I'm above 55 years old. The LORD says, if I listened to you 18 years ago when we first met I would have been a very healthy person, and I would be preaching and praying for the sick as you do. I have seen all the mighty work that the LORD GOD has done using you in the hospitals and clinics as we worked. Your patients were very happy people with hope. I saw patients not wanting to be seen by other medics, because they preferred your counsel and encouragement as you treated them. I have seen, mostly, you did not even need to give them medicine as they came to believe, you just prayed for them and they got completely healed, and went home happy. Most of them live around my village and they give testimonies of GOD'S healing that HE worked using you." She ended, "I am not going to get healed, and the LORD says I would have been healed if I did not despise HIS Sweet Words that you presented to me over years. HE says, I should preach to as many as will come to visit me before HE takes me home. I should tell them how HE feels angry with those who defile their bodies because HE is A Holy

GOD and HE cannot dwell in an intoxicated body." Leviticus 11:44, 20:26, 1Peter 1:15-16 She went on saying, "GOD created our bodies as HIS house to live in here on earth, but we allow Satan to misuse our bodies by using the things that Satan has lied to people to misuse like cigarettes and alcohol." She said, "If I listened, and got saved early and stopped using alcohol and cigarettes I would be very healthy today."

Her daughter and another sister who were with me confirmed what she said. I had known the LORD was not going to heal her, but I really wanted HIM to speak to her. For we serve a GOD who speaks and can directly talk for HIMSELF when need arises. I had no doubts that she was going to be with the LORD, but my joy was; she was Born Again. She said, because she was very hard and naughty, GOD wanted to reject her and HE resisted her salvation even after confession, until she reminded GOD our everyday prayers as we worked together. She told us that she beseeched HIM saying, "Dear LORD, please remember the prayers of your servant Mary. She always asked YOU to have mercy on me and save me. Please LORD, save me before I die so that I can live with you." Then she said, the LORD answered her, "but you have enjoyed your life outside ME, why do you want ME now and MY eternal presence, seeing how you rejected ME when I could have used you?" 1 Samuel 15:22-26, 16:1 is a good example of GOD rejecting people when they reject HIM. She said that she pleaded day and night for several months. She reminded GOD that we prayed and asked HIM to look at those prayers kindly and save her. When JESUS CHRIST came and told her welcome home! She told us, she was so satisfied that, had she died that moment, she would not have cared about anything else on earth. She added, "You do not know the most painful thing on earth, it is not sickness: it's to be assured that when you die; you will go to hell directly."

However, she was happy as she waited for her day to come, so that she could go to her eternal home. Thank GOD! HE speaks and HE can talk to you now if you so desire. Every area of your life that you have ever questioned, ask the LORD about it in humility. You see, this lady of honor, GOD would not talk to her until HE brought her so low as to be able to hear HIM. You cannot hear GOD when you are so high; you have to come down very low to hear HIM. Salvation is life eternal, the most valuable in life, and it can only come through humility, total surrender and self-denial. Those intoxicating substances are used so that they can make people high, how can the Most High compete with the substances that HE created HIMSELF. Our Dear LORD GOD says we need to be drunk of HIS HOLY SPIRIT and not of alcohol. If you want to feel high, you just need to worship GOD in TRUTH and in SPIRIT and you will feel high, and higher than that caused by drugs and alcohol. Your body is supposed to be the temple of the HOLY SPIRIT and not the temple of alcohol or the drugs. Haven't you heard GOD saying, "I AM a jealousy GOD and I cannot share MY Glory with any other?" How do you expect HIM to share HIS Glory with substances of abuse? GOD BLESS YOU AS YOU READ THIS BOOK of GOD'S LOVE. KNOWING THAT HE LOVES YOU MOST AND THAT IS WHY HE IS ADDRESSING YOU!

Here, let's deal with sin of smoking cigarette only:

Let us reason together as people with GOD'S Wisdom who have love for one another and really understand what our GOD wants from us. With the description that the World English Dictionary has given us about tobacco and with the experience that you have gone through while you smoke it, do you really think it is appropriate for you to continue poisoning your body and eventually kill it with cigarettes, or snuff, or chewing tobacco? Do you think GOD wants you to do that to yourself? For sure it is not the appropriate appetizer, entrée or dessert for you, nor for your family. You do not want your children to smoke but you are smoking? **That stuff is too small to make you its slave. I look at people getting out of their offices at 10am just to** smoke and pollute the Air and feel pain and petty for them. Knowing clearly what is awaiting them and the end product of smoking cigarette. In 1 Corinthians 6: 12-13, Apostle Paul said, "All things are not expedient and I will not be put under the power of any. It is not necessary for me to eat things that can defile and enslave my body." Apostle Paul knew who he was in the kingdom of GOD and he would not want anything that would enslave him. We are supposed to be addicted and enslaved by The HOLY SPIRIT through our LORD JESUS CHRIST because HE died for us. HE bought us from the tortured miserable slavery of the devil that Satan, where we had sold ourselves into sin from the time of Adam and Eve.

I will repeat again, those of us who are Born Again, we only need to know who we are and our identity will remain safe even after the devil tries all the ways of killing our image. So long as we know whose image we are created into, and we do not assist Satan to destroy our bodies and image by using or doing his evil, then we shall not accept the negative lies of the devil. For we know that we are sons of GOD, John 1:12, Romans 8:1-

CHAPTER 11

In Whose Image and Likeness Are You?

Do you know whose image and likeness you were created in? Genesis 1:26-27-28, then GOD said, "let Us create man into Our Image and into Our Likeness; let them have dominion over everything under the sun that moves on the ground, in the sea and flies in the Air. And GOD created them into HIS Own Image, in the Image of GOD, HE created them male and female, and GOD blessed them." You can see that; we were created in GOD'S Own Image. Why should we then worry? Can really GOD destroy HIS image, and HIS likeness? Certainly, not! It's only man who destroys himself with sin and so the devil drives men to sin so that their sin separates them from GOD'S Presence, then the same sin eventually destroy the sinner; Isaiah 59:1-15. The devil knows that once he makes someone sin against GOD, there is no Divine Protection around that person. As long as the relationship has been cut off, Satan knows he can play about with that person in any way, without GOD'S Protection. But thank GOD for HIS Mercies are forever. HE still watches over HIS people even when they have been stolen by Satan with his lies and have rejected their HIS Way.

If you were Born Again and then went back to live in sin would that destroy you? How does sin destroy? Hebrew 6:4-8 says, "For it impossible for those who were once enlightened, and tasted of the heavenly gifts and were made partakers of the Holy Spirit and have tasted the Good Word of GOD and the Power of the world to come, if they shall fall away, to renew them again unto repentance: seeing they crucified to themselves the Son of GOD afresh, and put him to an open shame." verses 7-8 says that "those who hear the Word and continue to bear good fruits of the Kingdom are a blessing and receive blessings from the LORD. Those who receive the Word and keep not to it are likened with the trees that bear thorns and are rejected and cursed." I that not a clear answer from GOD HIMSELF; the WORD of GOD in the Bible it is JESUS CHRIST Written, John 1:1-5

When saved people have been driven by Satan towards the lusts of their bodies, they feel like they are in control of the situation. But wait until sin grows roots and they become accustomed to the sin and it takes full control over them, and the sin becomes what they call habit, of course, addiction. Sin is very addictive to the doer and the devil knows that the human body became less resistant to addiction when the first man sinned. Therefore, sin easily forms habits of anything sinful that it does repeatedly. Whatever kind of sin has enslaved a person, the devil uses it to bring sickness. It might be bitterness, from which come stress, depression and eventually death. It might be fear, uncertainty and eventually disbelief then lack of faith and confidence leading to emotional disturbance. This loss of faith may result in anxiety.

Anxiety has been linked to allergies, which in turn can lead to asthma. Anxiety can also lead to hyperacidity, causing stomach ulcers, or anxiety can result in hypertension, followed by cardiac arrest or CCF (CHF). Fear is the worst sin to fall into.

Fear can make you enter into any of these other sins, and can also be responsible for some types of mental illness. Remember, in the absence of Faith is fear; for fear is the counterfeit of Faith. Any time fear of failure, lack, or death encompasses you, pray seriously and worship the LORD your GOD in Spirit and in Truth. Do not let the enemy take away your gift by using the sin of fear. I have known this sin for many years. Even after overcoming by the Grace of GOD without a teacher to help me out of it, it still tries to creep back slowly. When Satan brings persistence problems my way, fear comes to tell me; "even here, do you think GOD is going to act?" You're going to go through disability financially, hence, be thrown out or sold!

I cast you out devil in JESUS HOLY name. My LORD GOD is not going to look at me getting into your problems and sinking into them! Go away in JESUS CHRIST HOLY NAME, you are defeated, and get out of my way. I am a child of GOD and I know who my Father is. HE IS THE KING OF kings and the LORD of lords. My Father commands the whole universe and also commands you. I bind you and cast you out with your lies Satan and there is nothing you are going to do to me. I am well protected and by faith, I have that money and the mortgage and rent are paid in full by my Father GOD of the entire universe, in JESUS HOLY NAME IT'S DONE! AMEN!

You have to overcome fear because if devil will not get you through all these other sins, he will bring fear so that he can get you to commit other sins, if it is possible for him to do so. Do you know even many women who go to whoredom do so as a result of fear? We have done thorough research about that; many will tell you they do not want to do what they do and they do not like that kind of job. It is the most dissatisfying career on earth. GOD Forbid those women maintain themselves that way. It's a job with numerous diseases including the killers Hepatitis B and HIV. These are the fruit of fear; hence, disobeying GOD, and sicknesses become the fruits of the sin. Then sin kills the bearer through the induced diseases that one could have stayed away from; for the soul that sins shall surely die, Ezekiel 18. First, the Image of GOD is killed, GOD'S Presence disappears and then the relationship is completely lost. Finally, the body dies slowly and sometimes suddenly.

Let us run away from sin and or the cunning devices of Satan and keep off from all his sinful nature: so that we can obtain favor with our GOD, Hebrews 4:12-16, and we learn that the WORD OF GOD is shaper than two edged sword and JESUS CHRIST who is that Word is our HIGH PRIEST that has passed into Heaven. And HE is touched by the feelings of our infirmities. Let us therefore have boldness to enter into Holiest by the Blood of JESUS CHRIST, keeping by faith our full assurance of our profession for HE is Faithful WHO has promised us; Hebrews 10:19-23.

Our GOD is A HOLY GOD. Let us strive to be Holy as HE is, Leviticus 11:44, 20:26, 21:8; here, the LORD GOD is emphasizing on us being Holy as HE is Holy. Deuteronomy 28:9 says, "The LORD will establish you as a holy person to Himself just as HE has sworn to you. Although in the Bible that verse 9 is talking to a plural Israel, the Word of GOD is Singular and plural because HE covers every one. Remember, Psalm 138:2, GOD has "exalted HIS Word above all HIS Names" such that HE "cannot lie," HE must do that which is righteous because HE Himself is that righteousness, and HE gives all that is Holy and good to be held. Palms 84:11 records, "for the LORD GOD is a sun, and shield: the LORD will give grace and glory: And no good thing will HE withhold from them that walk uprightly." Let me say this again, GOD is HIS Word, John 1:1-tells us, "In the beginning there was Word, and the Word was with GOD, and the Word was GOD." So if HE is HIS Word, then HE cannot lie. Whatever HE says HE will do, HE must do because HIS saying is HIS doing. When GOD says it will happen, it has to happen, for it has already happened in heaven waiting for you to receive Genesis 1:3-24.

Now you are Born Again or You Have Been So

This is the revelation the LORD is giving me from HIS Word about "HIS WORD."

GOD who is not like us human beings, when HE says something, that thing is done. We may not see it with our naked eyes, but it is done, and we need our spiritual eyes to see that which HE has said being accomplished. For GOD is not like us who will say something and we cannot accomplish it because we did not get time to put our hands on it to be done. For example, when I say, I will cook, unless I go to the kitchen and use my hands to take pans, put them on the cooker to cook, the food cannot be cooked and people would not have anything to eat. But when the LORD GOD ALMIGHTY says, "I will give you food," immediately, food is established for you and ready to eat. Are you asking me how do I know this? Luke 9:12-17, Mark 6:36-43, Matthew 14:13-21; In these Chapters, JESUS fed people with food cooked in heaven by the Word, HE just said to HIS disciples who even complained that there were too many people and they could not afford to feed such multitude, "give them food to eat," the next thing HE did after thanking the Father was to say, "get them to sit down in groups." After that the two fish and five loaves became plenty of food that fed 5 thousand men, besides women and children. Meaning, the number was greater than five thousand. Just imagine that in every collective congregation, one man is surrounded by about three women and those women most of them have more than three children with them. Therefore, that group of people could have numbered anything to thirty thousand or more.

1 Kings 17:4-6, 13-16 we see Elijah in those old days of the Old Testament was fed by Ravens for many days, may be more than one year. And after that, the flour was being manufactured by the widow's barrel while oil was being blend by the cruse of oil. GOD is Amazing and no one knows HIS ways of operation but HIM alone.

How about in the wilderness, when the company of Israel wanted to stone Moses for lack of food, GOD brought them Manna, and supernatural quail for meat, Exodus 16: 4-22. All those were extraordinary, supernatural provisions of foods which GOD chose to show HIMSELF mighty to HIS people. You are one of them because you are washed by the Supernatural Precious Blood of JESUS CHRIST. You will not lack, AMEN! King David prophesied for you over a thousand years before JESUS CHRIST was born of the Virgin Mary that; "My LORD is my Shepherd, I shall not want," Psalms 23:1. That is to say, David had known the children of the most HIGH GOD should not lack or be found wanting. King David continues to explain all the provision of the LORD to HIS dear children in which you are one of them, unless you do not believe in JESUS CHRIST as your LORD and Savior. In Psalms 37:25 King David says, "I was young but now I am old but I have never seen the righteous forsaken, nor his seed begging bread." Neither have I!

Oh JESUS our LORD and Savior, help us to stand on this Word and stand on your promises for they are; Yes and Amen! Let us not sit on GOD'S promises, but let us stand on them so that when the LORD says, move! We shall be able to move at once towards our miracles. LORD JESUS is our eternal Redeemer and Giver. HE came to save that which was lost and give life more abundantly, John 10:10. Here, JESUS says a very important Word from the mouth of our Savior, "The thief cometh not, but to steal, to kill and to destroy: I AM come that they might have life, and have it more abundantly." Who are they, we, you and I and all believers HE came so that we get life in plenty. 100% of life. Not sometime 50% or 30%, 20%, or 90%, NO! 100%.

You see, you and I as believers in JESUS CHRIST, we have more life and in abundance than those folks outside HIM. We are well established by our LORD GOD. John 10:9 says, "I AM the door," that JESUS CHRIST is the door to everything we need, Hallelujah! I love to hear that more and more! JESUS is my door for me to get everything I need! Amen! HE continues to say; "If any man enters by me, he shall be saved" I love this too! "He shall go in and out, and find pasture." Hallelujah! What a promise!

Glory! Glory to HIS HOLY NAME! AMEN! And Unto my Father LORD GOD ALMIGHTY, Glory: for bringing JESUS CHRIST to be everything that we needed. You should not live life without hope. The cure to devil's torments came more than two thousand years ago. On that day our LORD died on the Cross, HE said, I thirst you to be mine again, and it is finished, meaning, HE has completed the task of saving us and the work of Satan is completely destroyed and eradicated. When you look at the way things are going on in this world, it seems like devils' work is in full force, but it's all lies for that he does or says is a lie as far as the TRUTH of our GOD is, John 8:44. JESUS told us, all that devil says is nothing but lies. If what Satan says or does would be true, we would all be consumed. Why live in hell?

<u>Living in hell on Earth?</u>

The earth, without the presence of GOD the Father, the SON, and the HOLY SPIRIT can be a very nasty hell place to live in. But you can have a heaven here on earth by Faith: If you allow the Supremacy of the Trinity of GOD dwell in you and you in HIM, then you will have Joy, Peace and Love in the midst of crises; Galatians 5:22-23. As GOD the Father is in SON so are we in HIM by HIS Power and illumination of the HOLY SPIRIT, John 14: 20-21. When the Holy Spirit illuminates your life, you cannot remember problems again and you will be able to bear it by faith until the LORD GOD settles all your needs. Hebrews 11:1 says, "Faith is a substance," it is faith you hold when you are expecting GOD'S miracle. It is that faith you will keep on holding in your spiritual hands and even the physical hands. Because all that you Hope for cannot be seen by these naked eyes, only the spiritual eyes can see what GOD is doing to fulfill HIS promises to you.

That faith, which is a substance of the things hoped for, becomes the evidence of things that are not seen. It is that faith you can give to whoever wants to know why you are so happy when your children are sick or not doing very well in their lives. It is that faith you will hold and show to your enemy when he wants to blow you off with his doubts. You will be able to stand on the promises of the LORD and tell the devil, in the mighty name of JESUS CHRIST, I will get that thing you are refusing me to get. My children are going to be successful in the name of JESUS CHRIST and they are going to get out of all these problems you have put us into. By faith you will be able to stand on evil day and tell devil, I come to you in the Name of the LORD JESUS CHRIST MY SAVIOR and you will not kill me. Satan you can "come to me with your sword and a spear, but I come to you in the name of the LORD of Host of Israel," 1 Samuel 17:37. The testimony of victory comes before the battle is seen with the physical eyes over.

Hebrews 11:1-40 gives report of those who obtained mercy and grace from the LORD by faith. Chapter 12:2 says we should wait upon the LORD "looking unto JESUS CHRIST the author and the finisher of our faith." Isaiah 40:31says, "they that wait upon the LORD shall renew their strength, they shall mount up with wings like an eagle, they shall run and not be weary, they shall walk and not faint." How do you wait upon the LORD? Only by faith, and working that is serving HIM as a faithful waiter. Not folding your hands, NO! It is by serving your Master JESUS CHRIST by believing and testifying of your past victories in HIS Salvation. Therefore, the Key thing here is FAITH! Faith as the Substance that you hold onto and the Evidence that you present to show others the mightiness of your LORD GOD like King David what he held to demonstrate to King Saul and Goliath.

CHAPTER 12

By Faith All things are possible

The mountains will move by faith; Mark 11:22-24, Hebrews 10:8a, 2Cornthinians 5:7, Luke 17:5-6. The mountains are physically manifestations of the powers of evil spirits behind the mountains that are standing on your way like diseases, poverty, marital and substances abuse, and call it whatever problem devil has put on your way to make you unhappy. That problem is work of the devil and it is your mountain that you need to tell it, "Be thou removed" in JESUS HOLY NAME!

Hebrews 11:6 records, "And without faith, it is impossible to please GOD." And if you cannot please GOD then how are you not going to live, in hell down here on earth? GOD FORBID! Have faith in GOD! He is able, and you must please GOD with your faith. HE is not asking you to go to work for HIM in a certain place so that he can be happy with you. No! HE is only saying, "Have faith in ME, and trust ME and believe that

I am going to do it for you, and very soon you will behold your success." It is impossible to know how GOD does HIS things for us. "The ways of the LORD GOD are not like our ways," Isaiah 55: 8-9. And HIS methods of doing things are not like ours. So you can never comprehend the ways of GOD and know which step HE is going to take to deliver you from all your infirmities. Your infirmities may be financial like it is the case of believers today. Do not worry; GOD is going to fix every bill. Many people have failed in their lives because they could not believe GOD can do it without them being involved. GOD does not need you to accomplish HIS work for you and perform a financial miracle for you, or anywhere else where you have a need. Therefore, wait on HIM and again I say, wait on HIM. HE is a faithful GOD, and HE cannot fail. Sometimes, we get things done by faith, and when a bigger need comes, we forget that the one who fixed the other is faithful to do even this other one. Let's not doubt our GOD he is faithful. The GOD of Red Sea deliverance is the Same GOD of Jordan River and HE is the Same GOD who sank the wall of Jericho for Israel sake. And very much: is HE the GOD that killed the Bear and the Lion with the hands of a boy shepherd David before HE destroyed Goliath and Philistines for Israel with a sling and a stone in the hands of a 17 year David.

Read the Word of GOD as you wait upon HIM and worship HIM as you wait on HIM. AMEN!

"Hast thou not known? Hast thou not heard that the everlasting GOD, the LORD, the Creator of the ends of the earth, fainteth not, neither is weary? There is no searching of HIS understanding. HE giveth power to the faint; and to them that have no might HE increasth strength. Even the youth shall faint and be weary, and the young men shall utterly fall: But" (From here a song was formed,) "they that wait upon the LORD shall renew their strength; they shall mount up with wings as eagles; they shall run, and not be weary; and they shall work and not faint," Isaiah 40:28-31. And one person in the power of the Holy Spirit ended up this song by singing, "teach me LORD, Oh teach me LORD, to wait." And you know it is not by might nor by power but by HIS SPIRIT; thus says the LORD, IN Zechariah 4:6

Why did this servant of the LORD ask the LORD to teach him or her to wait? Because the waiting time is the most difficult and trying time! It is not easy to wait when you are pressed by a severe need and do not know the duration of your waiting. How long are you going to wait? How do you know if it will ever come? Are you sure it is GOD you are waiting for or you are just deceiving yourself? Are you sure of what you are doing? How do you wait? Are you going to be in bed or sitting on your couch waiting? Or are you going to pick up your phone and call all your friends to tell them how you are feeling, your frustrations, and struggles and praying? Or are you going to go about your other business as you wait upon the LORD?

All these questions and many more will come to your mind, but if you sing and pray those words, "teach me LORD, Oh teach me LORD how to wait" indeed, GOD will teach you how to wait upon HIM without anxiety. HE shall surely come, and come with help and a provision to solve all your troubles. The waiting time sometimes may be longer than you thought, but HE will surely come at the best of HIS time. GOD'S time is the best, but it is not the easiest of all. It was not easy for Joseph in Egypt to wait in prison for 13 years. Although Joseph had left his father's home at 17 year old via a pit to slavery, he kept on believing that he had dreamed and received from the LORD that he will be a leader, although he did not know how and when. While he served his time in prison, at times, he must have wondered if it was GOD who had given him the dreams or if it was all in his head. But he waited anyway! It was not easy, but he waited believing GOD that one day GOD would get him out of his captivity and make him that HE promised. It was not easy for Joseph in Egypt and even in that pit he was thrown, and also as he was being sold and carried away to a land he knew not. It was not easy, he wished every moment GOD would come and deliver him and take him back home to his family. That 13 year Journey was long for Joseph. But blessed are those who put their trust in the LORD their GOD as you and I do!

But the LORD GOD, the all-knowing GOD knew that if Joseph went back, his half-brothers will keep on trying to kill him. And, GOD wanted him to become a powerful king of two nations. GOD gives in double with more potions. GOD did not want Joseph to be a king to his people only and suffer the rejection of jealousy. GOD wanted to make him a leader whereby even his half-brothers and the nation of Egypt would glorify the name of the LORD GOD Almighty. The wisdom of GOD is not our wisdom, and actually without GOD we have no wisdom. And "the ways of the LORD are not our ways;" neither GOD'S methods are our methods. Nor are his plans our plans. Furthermore, GOD'S thoughts are higher than our thoughts, Isaiah 55:8-9.

Secondly, a waiter need to know that the time looks too prolonged if one folds the hand to wait like a beggar. Immediately you become a child of GOD you are engaged in HIS services of faith.

One, believing on HIM and that HE IS GOD and that it is HE who sent HIS SON JESUS CHRIST; John 6:29 and that that Faith alone, it is working or doing the work of GOD YOR LORD. When you believe on someone, you do the things that person tells and teaches you. You are royal and you carry on with duties with no argument and therefore, whatever JESUS CHRIST says we do you will do it with full acceptance. As a waiter waiting on the KING of Kings you shall be a doer of the WORD and not a hearer only. You will her and do as a faithful servant. Joseph in the pit, he knew he was child of GOD who keeps HIS promises and so he worshiped HIM and prayed working or serving his GOD in the pit, in the slavery and in the prison.

Joseph must have heard the stories of his father's miracles and his Grandpa and Grandma's miracles of waiting for 20years without a baby and how his father and his uncle Esau were born by their Grandparents who waited for 20 years. And their Great-grandparents Abraham and Sarah got their Grandpa when Abraham was 100years and Sarah 90years and said in that pit; devil you are liar; I shall come out of this pit, slavery, and prison as a King. That was Faith at work.

Likewise, King David being anointed at a very early age of his life to be a King over Israel he waited for 13 years in the woods, caves, deserts, foreign country and mostly with no food, water, and shelter. The very basic things of life, but thank GOD he was used to live with animals in the bush when taking care of his father's sheep. He was a shepherd boy until at the age 17 when he was sent by his Dad to take food to his brothers at the Army Camp where he killed Goliath and later taken to King Saul's palace. Entering that palace was like entering hell. For 13 years, this 17 year old shepherd was put on death sentence for no offence at all. King Saul decided he is going to David so that he does not become a King after him. Satan gave Saul the evil discernment to see that GOD'S Favor is upon David. King Saul was filled with jealousy after David killed Goliath the enemy that had subdued Israel. David was chased all over Israel by his King, Saul the King of Israel. For 13 years GOD covered him in the Secrete place of the Most High where he abode under the Shadow of the Almighty. And under HIS Wings, David trusted and found refuge until he became the King of Israel and thereafter as he wrote Psalm 91. If you read all the books of Psalms you will see a man called David the Great Worshiper. He also waited and went a long journey to be a King in Israel.

Therefore, let's wait upon the LORD prayerfully knowing that HE is A GOD who is ever loving and keeps HIS promises, working for HIM without doubt and anxiety. Only take the time to learn how to ask HIM for what you need: Matthew 7:7-12, Luke 11:2-13, CHRIST JESUS gave us directions on how to ask and how to pray. Our Lord's Prayer is longer than it is recorded in the Bible. JESUS was only formatting for us how to pray to our Heavenly Father. For instance, the beginning of this prayer brings us to a worship session and to the Throne Room of the KING of Kings, the CREATOR of everything we see and we can't see. "Our Father, Who art In Heaven, Hallowed be thy name!" With that alone, you can get right to the beginning of worship and you can worship the FATHER LORD GOD Almighty Hallowing HIM in all HIS Mighty Names and Identities and in HIS Mighty Works. Can you imagine how sweet GOD feels when you address HIM, Our Father, and HE allows you to go ahead and use all the exalting words that you can give HIM? HE feels loved and needed.

I learned this secret of adoring my GOD with all good words from my earthly Dad. My dad was a man of very few words but mighty works of providing as a father, a husband and the head of our family. And because he never used to make jokes and had no sense of humor, people thought he was the meanest person, yet he paid school fees for many other people's kids; some of whom grew up to become great men in the nation. He also gave food to very many families, and he gave away his own land to poor families who needed a place to live. He was the most instrumental supporter of modern education in that region, having given a big piece of land to build the Church and a community school. Besides all that, there was no disaster or a problem in the community that could be settled without him. When community financial needs arose, the community would wait for his decision and mostly the giving would be determined by how much he had given from his pocket. If he gave little, people would give less and whatever was to be accomplished would not be accomplished. Therefore, GOD had to teach him how to approach those matters of public family. And because of those tasks my earthly Dad accomplished for family and community, I learned that he was a very important person; and yet only one man in the whole community used to tell him of his worth.

The man who praised him became a great acquaintance of my Dad. I was also a very great friend of my Dad because I became the second person to tell him how great he was to us and to the community. Every time I talked to my dad, I used to start with adoration. I would first tell him how great and wonderful he was.

I would say, dad I am very happy that I am your child and not a child of anyone else because you do everything wonderfully. Which was true anyway, I never exaggerated to him anything for I knew my Dad was a no nonsense person, you could not go talking stupid things before him. So I would tell him, I love you Dad, and I want you to know that yesterday I was so happy when you did this and that for us. Not that my Dad loved to be praised but no one hates to be appreciated for a well done job.

You know Dad, you are great man! Sometimes, I would tell him of his goodness until I forget I had a need. Then after his virtuous smile and a few good words, he would ask me, what do you want me to do for you today, or before I go, did you want me to do something for you today? Then I would say, yes and dad, this and this today, and that and that tomorrow, but so and so also needed this and that. After giving me what I needed, he would tell me to go and tell that so and so and others to come to him and get what they wanted. Or sometimes, he would tell me, they will come to him to ask whenever they want, and I should not remind them. And mostly, because I knew how some members of the family feared and felt about him, I would use very polite words to mediate for them and he would look at me with a very wide smile and ask me, "Did they send you to me?" I would say, well yes, or no...but. Nevertheless, he would give me the thing and tell me to tell whoever I mediated for to reward me for being their advocate. You see, my Dad at his time was a lawyer/ financial advisor by profession and a Judge of African Asian Court of Appeal, so he knew the duties of an advocate.

In June 1986 during My Dad's well-represented and attended funeral, the then Member of Parliament (Position of USA Senator and Congress man put together) and Kenya Government Old Embu District Cabinet Minister in praise for my Dad, he said, "This man you see laying here was a great man in the Kenya Colonial Government. And even after his retirement at 70 (for that was the then Government retirement age and GCM knew it well) he has continued to be greater in actions to his community and outside community. Whatever counsel we needed, we have been consulting him." GCM added, "This man here, carried many offices in his office. The then Government used him as Judge, Accountant, his own secretary and clack to the Court that he managed as a judge and the Government Advocate." GCM said, "Besides, He has been our Attorney advising many on Law matters. Coming to the individual help," GCM added, "This man has been the instrument of our education system. He initiated the opening of many schools and paid school fees for many children including myself when I was going to Makerere University in Uganda. My Dad could not afford to pay Ksh. 40.00 equivalent 400,000/- today-1986. So my Dad shared his dilemma with this Mzee who was his friend and he gave him the Ksh. 40.00/- to pay my further education fee, so I pay my education tribute to this great man we are burying today," said GCM.

Allow me to use these inspiring moment I had with my earthly Dad to show you the value of Father-Child Relationship. Mostly, I used to make my Dad happy when around him and if he was not happy, I would feel very sad and fearful and ask him if I had wronged him. I believe that is the same way we should feel and look at our Heavenly DAD. My earthly Dad would ask my Mom, "Why does this child think if I do not show happiness it's because she has wronged me?" the time I persistently say, I am sorry dad; for you do not look happy today. Please forgive me or forgive us if we wronged you. I hate to see you unhappy Dad. My Mom would answer, "I do not know, just ask her." Then Dad would tell me, all right, go and do this and that. When you are done call your mom to see or when I get time I will come to see it. Alright! Yes dad! Then I would run to do it and do it very well until he approves it. I believe our Heavenly Father wants us to behave with that courtesy to HIM.

As I grew in the Christian Walk, I learned my Heavenly Father was more important and more graciously precious to me. I learned that he was all powerful and all Mighty; and greater than my earthly father was. I learned to approach HIS Throne of Mercy in a mighty way as I worship HIM. I exalt HIS Holy Name above all and make everything else nothing that would want to exalt itself above my GOD.

My Heavenly Father is all important because, I cannot breathe and live this life and enter into the life to come without HIM. Much as my earthly father loved me, and I too loved him, he was not able to give me all the necessities of this life. My earthly father could not supply me with air to breath, or with strength to breathe it and above all, salvation to eternal life.

If JESUS CHRIST is in you and you in HIM as he recorded in John 15: 7 that: "if you abide in ME and My Words abide in you, you shall ask what you will, and it shall be done unto you." But verse 5B says clearly, without the LORD JESUS we can do nothing. When I consider my life and these Words of my Savior JESUS CHRIST I see a great truth. There is nothing we can do for ourselves without HIM and that is why some times we face a lot of hells here on **earth when we try to go it on our own. As soon**

as a true Christian starts doing things on her/ his own, hell is set loose, and Heaven is shut tight. If we be sincere to ourselves, unless it's time of tribulation, most of the time we have set hell on ourselves by hurrying to do things before GOD's time, or doing it without asking permission from the Creator of the universe. How can we possibly start arranging to do things without hearing from GOD? May GOD really help us to be attentive in listening to HIS voice, and avoid the curse of disobedience that befell King Saul. We are living on very tricky days. Days full of uncertainty, hurt, discouragement, and misery. These days were predicted by the prophets and even JESUS CHRIST warned about them. In Luke 18:8B Our LORD asked, "Even though our heavenly Father will avenge those who cry to him speedily, When HE cometh, the Son of Man, shall HE find faith on earth?"

The reason I feel happy here is, my Savior promised neither to leave, nor forsake us. Also, HE has added that Our GOD will avenge HIS elect, who cry day and night unto him, though HE bears long with them that offend HIS elect, Luke 18:7. CHRIST HIMSELF is the Faith that we need, if you have JESUS CHRIST, the anointed atonement of Israel JESUS the Messiah, you have all that you need. You have faith, love, peace, and joy. Fear is gone because JESUS takes away fear and replaces it with faith. Fear is counterfeit of faith. Without faith it is impossible to please GOD; because in the absence of faith there is fear of unknown, and the presence of GOD cannot dwell in presence of fear (of unknown); Hebrews 11:6. Why should I say, fear of unknown? Because if you know what is causing fear in you, you can either have faith that GOD is going to remove the problem for you or you can remove that problem by yourself if you can or call some of your friends to remove it for you. Otherwise, anything that causes fear in you and leaves you helpless is probably unknown to you. But if you check in a Godly Spiritual carefulness, you will understand that fear is the element of the devil trying to confuses you and put you into fear so that you do not please GOD.

Again let me say, the devil knows the Word of GOD and practices it opposite of what GOD wants. And because the devil knows that he knows the Word more than we do, and that we do not stay in the Word as we ought to; as JESUS emphasized to us, that we should eat and drink HIM constantly; John 6:32-58 he knows how to confuse us with small matters and with his lies, he builds a mountain out of a molehill. "For if you drink and eat CHRIST JESUS the Anointed of GOD and HE will dwell in you and you in HIM." HE says; HE is the true bread, and the true drink. That means; HIS Word that we read in HIS Holy Book, the Bible is the drink and the bread. Of course, by faith, in the Holy Communion, we drink supernaturally HIS Blood in the form of unfermented wine, and eat HIS Body inform of the bread, but for it to have positive effect in our lives, it has to be accepted by faith and the believe that it is all done in a supernatural way. But on the other hand, JESUS meant that you can drink HIS Word and eat it and dwell inside it, and feel CHRIST JESUS in you. HE is the sweetest, most comforting, and satisfying Word or Reading that I ever came across. And every one who reads the Bible guided by the HOLY SPIRIT experiences a lot of encouraging sweetness and comfort in the Word. When we have CHRIST JESUS in us, we have faith because HE IS Our Faith. What do I mean by saying JESUS is our Faith? You see, when JESUS was telling HIS Disciples that they did not need mighty faith; they needed faith the size of a small mustard seed, HE meant several important implications in this statement.

Small Faith versus Little Faith:

When JESUS Said in Matthew 8:26 the Disciples had little faith and in Luke 17:6 what they needed was Faith as small as a mustard seed HE meant several things:

First, HE wanted to show the Disciples that they had no faith even the smallest to believe that HE is The Almighty GOD who is able to do all things. Many times, they doubted especially if a problem like storms came, instead of praying calling upon HIM, Master, especially when HE was not with them in the physical body, they were panicky and cried to one another. They never thought HE saw them and HE knew what was happening and HE could not let them suffer. The disciples did not see JESUS as by faith as GOD Omnipresent whom they needed to trust even when HE was not physically in the sea or in the house with them. At the time of the storm when HE was sleeping on the boat, HE had to make them remember HE was on the ship. And instead them of approaching JESUS as the LORD of all, and telling HIM their problem (about the storm): they went to HIM with this common thoughtless question, don't you care if we perish? CHRIST must have looked at them just as HE looks at us when we become silly, and said, "You, of little faith! Little faith is equal to nothing." Meaning, their faith was not substantial. It was a reduced faith. Mostly, the Disciples looked at JESUS as one of the prophets performing miracles like Elijah. That is why HE told them they had little faith. And a reduced faith is dead; it believes only in what it holds in the hand and not in what is in the supernatural realm. I have explained the difference between mustard seed faith that is small faith but full of life; and little faith with lifeless: for Faith full of

Substance and Life, and faith with less substance and with no life in it is manifested by patience and great hope.

Secondly, they were not aware of JESUS being inside there, HE is the Master of everything and even if that ship capsized they had the Master of the water and of the storms with them. They had seen JESUS heal sickness and perform miracles, but human fear had not left them, and their faith was reduced every time a problem came around them.

You see these men were followers of JESUS CHRIST, and they somehow knew JESUS was more peculiar than any other Prophet that had lived, but HE had not yet died for them to be saved. So their faith had not completely transformed and integrated with the Word since the Word had not been glorified by the Power of the Holy Spirit. Today, if we let the body come closer to us and we forget that we are living at a time when JESUS who is the Word has already been glorified, fear can easily creep in on us and encompass us, reducing our faith to the little faith that is not substantial. We are not supposed to let the presence of GOD and the Power of the Holy Spirit depart from us at any time because without the HOLY SPIRIT in us, we will operate with our carnal mind and our faith will be reduced to nothing. GOD forbid: that the believer would reach the point of little faith, better small faith that can grow. Actually, little faith is equal to no faith, it is dangerous.

Faith is the substance of the things hoped for evidence of the things not seen, Hebrews 11:1. If you can hold onto that faith JESUS gave us while on the Cross, and when HE resurrected, you will always have something to show the enemy and tell him, "Devil you cannot defeat me, and you will not hold onto anything that is mine, for you have no power over me. My LORD JESUS died for me, and HE paid all the penalties for me. I owe you nothing Satan, and you're a liar that is defeated. You cannot hold back my blessings for they do not come from you. I have very good evidence that nothing comes from you Satan. All came from my Heavenly Father and all belongs to HIM, and all is mine according to the Power of GOD who works in me by JESUS CHRIST my LORD and my Savior amen! My faith is the evidence that you cannot challenge because my faith is built on JESUS CHRIST the Solid Rock who died for me and defeated you devil! I cast you out of my ways now in JESUS HOLY NAME! GO and be forgotten in JESUS HOLY NAME! Thank you LORD JESUS CHRIST: FOR GIVING ME FAITH TO DEFEAT MY enemy Satan and his dirty kingdom of darkness.

Thank you LORD JESUS because you love me and your love for me is beyond the measure. Thank you because you love me so much that I have something to saw the enemy. Your love for me is enough LORD JESUS CHRIST MY LORD. I will not fret, but rejoice in you at all times because I know you said in your Words, it is over and this problem is over. Thank you LORD JESUS because I cannot quit being your child because you bought me with a great price of very Precious Blood.

How wonderful it is to be a child of GOD. It is enough evidence to show the devil that JESUS: You cared for me by Your Mighty Hand that Satan cannot separate me from. To be born again and stay born again is enough substance for me to hold onto and show that I am a child of the KING of all Kings.

All praise and worship is for my Heavenly Father LORD GOD ALMIGHTY. LORD I worship you, JESUS I give you glory and honor, I adore you, and I gave you praise and all the preeminence is yours my dear LORD JESUS CHRIST for dying for me. I worship you, I bow before you dear LORD and I say you are worthy, worthy, worthy Oh LORD, You are worthy, worthy, worthy, to receive you the Glory and honor and Power. I worship, I adore you, I give you glory, I bow before you, I love you, I cherish you, I lift You up above all, Oh LORD I Worship you my LORD, you are the Greatest and the only one I need and that I needed. I Thank you LORD for being there for me always, and I thank you for being there for me yesterday, today, tomorrow and forever; AMEN!

Do not die for fear of the unknown. Your hidden enemy Satan has put fear in you to counterfeit your faith. Refuse all his prescriptions and keep to JESUS CHRIST prescriptions. Isaiah 53:5, the chastisement of your peace was upon HIM and with HIS Stripes you are healed. What better prescription do you need than that? JESUS was chastised for your peace, so peace is assured when JESUS CHRIST is in you, but if you let the enemy tamper with your faith, then the Power of CHRIST is will have no effect on you. The Bible says, "They receive not for they pray amiss" "for without faith it is impossible to please GOD." You do not want to be praying without faith. Just believe, all things are possible and you will see it as long as you put your faith into practice. You cannot put faith into practice without the WORD. You must study the WORD and learn even to preach HIM to the people around you by giving them your testimony. Tell the people around you, "I will not die but live to proclaim the good works of the LORD!" That is a good testimony and it is a testimony of old that has evidence. King David used that testimony to defeat his spiritual and physical enemies and in deed, he defeated all of them. They died and they left him to become a King and a man after GOD'S OWN HEART. What a wonderful thing! Praise GOD! For you to be called a man or a woman after GOD'S Own heart, after the devil thought he was going to walk all over you and completely finish you. The people he has been using will be surprised. They will not know what has happened when they see you in a good shape financially and physically stable and renewed as an eagle. When they see that they cannot put you in a fix financially anymore and you are not their slave anymore! Oh, praise JESUS! What a wonderful thing it is to be a child of GOD and A GOD who cares. He is the owner of all knowledge and wisdom and understanding, Power and Glory.

We have said that our Lord's Prayer is full of worship. After Hallowing our Heavenly Father, We ask Him to give us HIS Kingdom here on earth as it is there in Heaven. You know very well in heaven there is no sickness, there is no poverty; hence, no unpaid bills, or debts. There is no envy, jealousy, nor the great enemy of man called fear, no killing, no death, no hunger and no anger and bitterness. In The Kingdom of heaven there is plenty of everything Good. There is a lot of Peace, Joy and Love that you cannot exhaust. So that is what it means when we want the Kingdom of GOD on earth. And that can only come in the Presence of GOD. The LORD says, HE "dwells in the Praises of HIS people." Have you ever attended a Christian conference full of worship? That is where the presence of the LORD Dwells. We need more of those conferences and really we do. After work, we need to feed and go to a place of worship where GOD is praised and praised more and more. Surely, you can have a conference with HIS Trinity. And you will be surprised, instead of growing old; you will be growing younger day by day. And you will live a healthy life all through. For David to live healthy when surrounded by his enemies and be able to enjoy life in full, he had to know the secret of worship. He was able to say, I shall not die but live to declare the Good works of the LORD, Psalm 118:17. 2 Samuel 6: 14a says, "And David danced before the LORD with all his might;" This is evidence and a substance that GOD will neither leave nor forsake HIS children. David would have been killed by King Saul in his youth, but he grew up in the midst of all that enmity and became a King after Saul.

You may be having many enemies, some that you even don't know, but when GOD is on your side, you will be alright, Romans 8:31. Just praise GOD for all things and keep on praising and praising and praising; and I tell you, you will not wait long before GOD shows HIMSELF mighty unto your enemies. You are a child of the KING of all kings. Remember, before the hatred you see on earth come to you it started in the air with the devil. Your enemy is Satan, and he is the one who causes people to harm you. It is the spirit behind them, not their own will. It is the powers of the darkness and that is why you need to forgive them because they are victims and are under the captivity of the devil like Cain. And in order for you to live and not die in early age, you need to forgive those who do you harm. The spirit of the devil is behind their actions: for if there was anything wrong with you that they knew, they would have called you and told you about it and cleared it with you instead of going behind you to hurt you and to make you sorrowful. Thank GOD for JESUS CHRIST who died for us at the Cross of Calvary! We can rejoice that we have a Savior and a KING of all Kings and a LORD of all Lords. Amen!

CHAPTER 13

Why should you die?

You "will not die! "But live to proclaim the good Works of the LORD" thy GOD; Psalms 118:17, 18: 3, 46

When King David wrote Psalms 118, he had already seen the greatness and the mightiness of his GOD, JEHOVAH, and known that there is no lack in HIM who lives forever. And mighty is the Power of his GOD to keep him alive until he gives the testimony like the one he gave in Psalms 37:25 that; "I have been young, and now I am old; yet I have not seen the righteous forsaken, nor his seed begging bread. And David concludes by saying, "The righteous is ever merciful and lends; and his seed is blessed." When David was writing these poems he had observed and looked at his GOD with an eye of GOD'S Wisdom. He had seen GOD being a Victor and not a victim. And he had known devil is a victim of his own making and he wants human beings to join him. David had known devil is a liar and he lies to people who do not know that he does exist; who think that it is GOD who does people evil. David had learned not to yield to the devil's devices from when he was a shepherd boy, and as he lead the nation of Israel, even before he took over the kingdom of Israel, David was very careful not to heed devilish suggestions; I Samuel 30: 22-25. And so David, with that knowledge, wrote, "I shall not die but live to give testimonies of GOD'S Victory and how GOD makes HIS people win battles after battles." Amen!

It is important for you and me now my friend that we look at our GOD like King David did and get to know HIM more and more. We have CHRIST JESUS who is our good role model, but above us, and we cannot emulate HIM, HE is GOD in the form of SON, but the LORD of Lords and the KING of kings. HE modeled for us how to live in the righteousness and Holiness of GOD: for HE was tried in all manner of temptation but HE never fell into sins. JESUS was demonstrating and teaching us that we can live a holy and righteous life with all the temptations, trials and tribulations we get here on earth. HE lived here on earth like us and with all of them, without a sin. And HE knows how to take us through those mountains of temptations safely as HE went through all of them. He went all the way to death in order to teach us how to live a successful, righteous life. The Devil is a liar. Do not fall into his lies! Let all the miseries that the devil has brought to your life be missiles. You will then be able to say like David that: "Let GOD Arise and HIS enemies be scattered," Psalms 68:1a.

RAISE A STANDARD

Isaiah 59:19b tells you

The spirit of the LIVING GOD will "raise a Standard against" Satan. Thus says the LORD GOD ALMIGHTY Whom I serve.

"When Satan comes in ranging like a flood, the SPIRIT OF THE LIVING GOD WILL RAISE A STANDARD AGAINST HIM"

You see, JESUS CHRIST did not leave us without a **COMFORTER** and the Comforter knows how to take us out of every temptation and every calamity of the devil. HE knows how to fix every broken heart and every broken part of our body. We just need to stay in the LORD JESUS CHRIST so that the HOLY SPIRIT will have a place in our lives. "Blessed is the man that believes yet he has not seen." "For faith is the substance of things hoped for; evidence of things not seen." You're created in the image of GOD and in his likeness were you made and that is why you and I need to hold unto that first Faith and Love that we received when we first believed. GOD is faithful, HE cannot lie, and HE must accomplish that which HE started in us as HE purposed. GOD created you for HIS divine reasons that HE cannot change or alter. And therefore, you must believe that JESUS died for you so that you may have life and have it more abundantly. And by faith HIS purpose for you must be accomplished, so live by HIS Faith and not by your faith. Jesus Christ said, "If you have Faith as small as a mustard seed, you will tell that mountain which is troubling you to move and go to the middle of the see and it'll go."

So JESUS was telling HIS disciples, "If you know that I am the same GOD of Abraham you believe in that HE dried the Red Sea for your forefathers, then you would trust ME for everything about yourselves. But because your faith in ME that I AM GOD; is little, it cannot keep you to the standard of remembrance of what I did yesterdays for you to discern ME and MY ability. Yesterday and the other past days, in your presence, I healed the sick, I rebuked the devils out and cleansed those who were possessed by demons of every kind, and I raised the dead. I fed the multitude of over five thousand men; besides children and women without a kitchen to have food prepared, without pots, plates and utilities, and without a store to go to buy that food. Twice, you have seen me use very small amount of food and multiply it to a lot food to feed multitudes of people." Again, JESUS was saying, you have not believed that I AM and the same who fed your fathers in the wilderness with Manna, and the ROCK that followed you with Water: for if you would know "you have seen me do all that, but you still do not believe in ME that; if you call upon My Name at the time of need I will come for your help and save you?"

The faith that you have now, it is for the physical and nothing supernatural. You only believe if you can see, but if you cannot see, you are still skeptical, you have to seem to believe that the ship will not capsizing. You do not need to see me with your physical eyes; you need to see me with your spiritual eyes that I am the LORD that keeps you alive and I have a great purpose in your lives. I have a great job for you and that is why I chose you. You have not chosen ME but I have chosen you" John 15:16. "I did all that to show you that I am the same GOD who gave your fathers Manner in the wilderness. And I am the Same GOD that kept them from being sick for over 430 years in Egypt the land of their captivity. And in the land of Canaan when I delivered them from the powers of Egyptians, I kept them in the wilderness for 40 years without a physician. Over 450 years, in this land I brought them, I kept them without the diseases of Egypt: until your fathers grievously sinning against ME then I left them to be carried into captivity, and all the diseases of Egypt was set loose on them." The saying of JESUS to his disciples that they had little faith had a deeper meaning than what we can imagine about a little thing and what the dictionary defines the little as being the adjective of small or young.

Here, the concept of small is that the thing may look small, but it is full, mature, complete, and whole. May not need to be added anything to be what it is. For example, a small human in size, can be a mother or a father. A small seed like a mustard seed, when planted it grows to a very big tree.

The concept of little: a human cut a little piece of himself even if he was a 6ft, 450lb human, can never become a human again or be a father or a mother. That is piece of a human that is not even alive. In other words, something little may not be alive if we look at it in this concept of JESUS CHRIST. As I have put it earlier, a seed of a corn divided in the size of a mustard seed will never grow to a corn stock even if you water it for ten years. In the first place, it will not even germinate from the ground. It will only rot and become a part of the soil. After 1 month, you cannot locate where you had planted it if you did not mark the place at the time of planting, it is mixed with soil and looks like soil. While a mustard seed, or any other smallest seed, full of substance and life, if you plant and water it, it will grow to a big tree. Therefore, in CHRIST'S meaning; anything little may not carry any life in it. And I believe this is what our Savior was teaching that we need a faith that is alive; that is faith with works: for faith without works is dead, James 2: 17-20-26. I love the way James has described faith; here, he says in James, 2: 20, "for wilt not know, O vain man faith without works is dead?" Faith with works is the faith that waits upon the LORD without seeing only holding on GOD'S promise. Abraham was told he would get a son and he would be a father of great nation when he was 75 years old. And he did not get that son until he was a 100 years old. It was a big job to wait while believing that inspite of all appearances to the contrary, what he had been told by God was true. It is not easy to wait for what you need so much for one, two, three years until you stop counting, and say, I will not count any more: but you continue waiting, believing that the one who promised you is faithful, HE will fulfill what HE said, even though you do not see it for over ten years.

QUALITIES AND QUANTITIES OF A SMALL FAITH:

According to our LORD JESUS, who is the Supreme Authority of every Word; we need just a small faith like a mustard seed, and we shall be alright. After I have done the definition of little faith, I have seen how many times I have operated with little faith and how dangerous it is to have little faith. A small faith holds firm to what she believes, and a little faith can easily be shaken and drop down what she was holding onto. Mostly, when I have been very successful in many mighty things that GOD has helped me to achieve, it is the SMALL Faith that has worked. When I have failed in getting what I believed to get by faith, either, I was entangled in the laws of this world, and I started doubting what I was doing in the move of the HOLY SPIRIT, and the little faith Crept in and moved away the SMALL Faith. But any time I have looked beyond the laws of this world, (I mean rules and regulations set by men) and worked by GODLY Faith in the law of the HOLY SPIRIT that moves mountains, I have achieved things where a **normal person cannot** achieve. Sometimes, you have to be out of your mind and get into the Mind of JESUS CHRIST and be **supernormal to get supernatural** things done by small faith attitude. And that is how I operate on everything

I have achieved in this world. It has been very hard for me to live without supernatural power and operate supernaturally. That is a great quality of A Small Faith. Small faith is never shaken it remains firm even during storms. Small faith is never movable even when its earth is removed. Small faith is steadfast in all ways always growing stronger in threatening situations and unbecoming circumstances. Small faith is never corrupted by the surroundings. In the midst of overwhelming seas and deserts, small faith says, move forward, backwards never!

I am sure those who know me well, will attest what I am talking about. But those who only get to know me from those who just meet me in their meetings, they better be careful before they say a thing about me. You may engage in false accusations and false talking, even though you know that you are breaking one of the Ten Commandments. To accuse someone falsely, it is as sinful as killing. Because of this, many people can call me what they want to, but I am still matching forward towards the mark of my calling in my Savior's perfection. I have to operate supernaturally, and most of the time to get things done I have to be in the supernormal Mind of my Savior and operate from there. One day JESUS is coming for me and I will just walk in there with HIM. If I feel like I am operating in little faith, I fall on my knees to repent unto my Father GOD in the Name of His Son Jesus Christ, Yeshua Ha-Messaiah.

CHAPTER 14

Small Faith Accounts

Small faith: let us define more the word small in the Wisdom of JESUS CHRIST: Small may look tiny in inform of any size of something, but it is substantially whole and complete. That

Small FAITH you feel like you have in you, it is from GOD and is the substance that you hold as the evidence that you are a child of GOD the ALMGHTY YAHWE and if you are a child of GOD, then you are a joint heir with CHIRST JESUS. Go to Hebrews 11:1, and Romans 8:17, and see the concept of faith's substance and evidence and joint heir with CHRIST. Therefore, that is the thing for you to hold onto and to tell the devil that he is a liar, and that you are Child of GOD; the evil one has no part in your life. While you are busy in the Power of the ALMIGHTY GOD: telling the devil off, and casting him away from you in the name of JESUS CHRIST, the HOLY SPIRIT is very busy raising a standard against Satan. And very soon, you will see the change in what you called the biggest problem. Very soon, you will see the overcoming power of GOD in your life. You will see the provision of material and financial supply to every need that was in your family. At times, we may not see when Our GOD is working for us, but it is true HE is working. If we stand still, we shall behold and see it as it parts like the Red Sea and becomes the road for us to cross on the other side of victory. The children of Israel did not see the act of the HOLY SPIRIT in the Red Sea when the sea started to part, but suddenly before them was the road they were going to use. They saw a dry road and were told to walk on it and go across to the other side of the sea.

If you would have asked Aaron and all Israel what made the sea separate, and how that sea-road was made smooth, they would have not known how to explain what had happened. All they could see was a road in the middle of the sea, cemented dry and leveled at the same level with the ground they walked on. That road had no bumps that could have prevented small children and mothers from walking smoothly. Amazingly, that crowd of the children of Israel was not small. It was a whole nation. We are talking of a people more than two million with their big and small animals, ducks, turkeys, chicken walking into this marvelous road in the midst of the Red Sea, which was created without them participating in the construction. The waters on both sides as a thick glass wall holding every sea creature inside the water. They had just finished murmuring and cursing Moses harshly for fear of the unknown. Yet, to our Father GOD those were HIS chosen children. Some wicked, and rude, others following HIS servant Moses' word, with GOD loving all equally, expecting them to learn how to handle themselves before their Maker. We need to know that GOD is waiting to see how we handle our Faith in HIM. Do we really trust HIM for who HE is, and that HE can fix it?

Do we really see GOD as a careful Father, or do we just think of HIM as some of those fathers who forget their children and carry on with their business without caring at all. It would be extremely wrong to view our LORD GOD that way; HE is a Father who completely and marvelously cares more than anyone else. If you want to see how Our Heavenly Father cares and Who HE is to us, look at Psalms 121:1-8, and you will really understand HIM. Also look at Proverbs 3:11-12, and actually, Proverbs 3:1-35, has all the advice the son need from the Father who cares. Do you know, the book of Psalms is one of the best books in the Old Testament that brings us to the knowledge and understanding of the wisdom of the full good relationship with our heavenly Father? Proverbs has teaching for everyone, from children to adults; husbands to wives; mothers to fathers; kings to beggars; sons to daughters, Servants to Masters. Study those two books and you will gather wisdom and the anointing of the LORD as you continue to study the rest of the Bible for your daily devotion. In 2 Timothy 3:16-17 it is written, "all scripture is given by inspiration of GOD, and is profitable for doctrine, for reproof, for correction, for instruction in righteousness; That the man of GOD may be perfect, thoroughly furnished unto all good works." The book of John and the letters of John are also wonderful in lifting our Faith in GOD'S promises and giving good counsel to a believer. Indeed, the whole Bible is full of encouragement and teaching. It's Our Heavenly Father writing HIMSELF on stones and papers so that we may know HIM well by hearing and seeing. Our Heavenly Father loves us very much. HE does not want us to get lost. Let us not lose ourselves by carrying a little faith instead of Small Faith. The only thing that God requires from us is to have Small Faith and full trust in HIM that HE is going to fix all for us.

As I look at some of the fathers of this world, I get perplexed by their love for their children. Some fathers have children who have grown to adults without them knowing the size of their children's clothes since they were born, or even what they eat, or how their beds look like, even their toys for that matter. Others stop bothering with their children as early as they turn 10 and others at 15, and they have never known where they sleep or how they spend their day. Our Heavenly Father isn't that way, HE does not sleep nor slumber while watching over us; supplying our needs according to HIS riches in Glory by CHRIST JESUS, Philippians 4: 19.

Children do not need only material from the parent; they want that wonderful counsel and the comfort of the presence of both the father and mother.

In some homes, it's only the mother who provides counsel and comfort to the children, but they would also love to hear the counsel of their dad. In the homes of the Godly parent, the counseling should be Biblical so that when the children grow up they will not depart from that truth. When problems come, they will know that they have A Heavenly Father who fails not and with confidence by faith they can lean on HIM.

I thank GOD for being Our Heavenly Father. You see, HE knew that some of us will not have big brothers in our earthly homes and it's important to have one and so HE has already provided one: JESUS CHRIST Our first born Brother, the LORD of Lords; and if you call upon the name of the Father through our first Born BIG Brother, our father GOD answers very fast, John 14:14, Jeremiah 33:3. GOD knows how to provide everything.

Mostly, we think JUSUS came only to die and to save us from sin. Yes! But that is not all, JESUS CHRIST came on earth as a Wonderful Brother to give us First-Class Brotherly Love, and as the best friend that we should trust and count on in everything we need. These other friends we have here on earth can fail us even when they are willing to do all good. Therefore, if we counted on them we would be very frustrated because of human limitations. Jeremiah 17:5-6 GOD has given us a warning not to put trust on others even when they are so close to us and HE has provided unto us HIM for a trust. HE is a counselor who will never mislead you, and besides, HE is the Prince of Peace to counsel you peacefully, and wisely. When you are stranded with a need or in the midst of problems feeling threatened on all sides, JESUS CHRIST is a specialist of Miracles and HE is a miracle worker. A Healer, A Redeemer, A Deliverer, and A Savior who will never leave nor forsake us. Romans 10:13 says, "Whosoever shall call upon the name of the LORD shall be saved," and verse 11, "whosoever believes in HIM shall not be ashamed." Who else would you like to have in you and around you other than JESUS CHRIST THE KING of Kings and the LORD of Lords! I feel sad when I see my friends rejecting JESUS and doing their own things that are contrary to the Word of GOD. However, the Bible in Romans 10:17 says, "Faith comes by hearing and hearing by the Word of GOD." If we do not embrace to drink and eat the Word of GOD; John 6:35-53, we may not have the requisite Small Faith to maintain us to the will of GOD so that we can do the things pertaining to the Kingdom of GOD. How wonderful it is to dwell in the secrete place of the Word of GOD and abide and the shadow of HIS Word to achieve all that our GOD has promised us by faith, Psalm 1:1-6, 91, John 15. It is by faith we achieve first GOD'S GRACE and we need to pray a prayer of faith that the LORD GOD ALMIGHTY will keep us in HIS faith by the Power of HIS HOLY SPIRIT. Again, Faith comes by Hearing and hearing by the Word of GOD." "Without faith, it is impossible to please GOD" Hebrews 11:6.

All that we learn in the Bible, basically, is maintained and manifested in to our lives by faith.

If we have no Faith with GOD we cannot have faith in HIS Word and then we cannot achieve anything that comes from HIM. Same Hebrews 11:6 continues to say, "For he who comes to GOD must believe that HE IS, and that HE IS a rewarder of them that diligently seek HIM." "The prayer of faith shall save the sick, and the LORD shall raise him up; and if he has committed sin, it shall be forgiven him." "Confess your faults to one another and pray one for another, that ye may be healed. The effectual fervent prayer of a righteous man avails much," James 5:15-16.

CHAPTER 15

How Small is your Faith?

As small as mustard seed or as little as a broken piece of corn?

If you break a seed of a bean or a grain of corn into pieces, the pieces may be bigger than a mustard seed. Now, if you plant those broken pieces, even if you plant them in the best fertile soil, and water them daily, give them the best air, they can never germinate to grow out of the soil and yield other seeds. Instead, they will very soon rot and become part of the soil without growing. But the very small tiny mustard seed, it is a full seed with substance and full of life. Its life has not been destroyed by cutting; it is full, and substantial and not reduced to a piece like the divided corn, or bean. And so is our faith, if we divide our faith with doubts, then it can never grow and yield other seeds. Neither can it grow to a plant or a tree like the mustard seed. A mustard seed is possibly the smallest of seeds on earth, yet when planted, it grows to be probably one of the largest trees in the region of

Israel and Middle East. That is why our Savior YESHUA HA-MESSIAH (JESUS CHRIST) likened the desirable faith with a mustard faith. John 20:29 says, "Blessed are they that believe yet they have not seen"; that is what Our LORD JESUS told Thomas after HIS Resurrection: for Thomas had not believed the report of the Disciples that had seen JESUS first. Thomas had little faith or nothing. Nevertheless, little faith is dangerous, it can never germinate and grow to a plant, and it brings doubts and failures, Matthew 14:22-31, 32-33.

Mustard Seed Faith moves mountains!

JESUS TAUGHT: Yesterday's failure can make your faith little. If you remain with little faith you can never see GOD work in HIS Supernatural way. HIS WAYS ARE NOT LIKE OUR WAYS. The parable of the mustard seed is so much repeated and so much teaching to all open to learn Spirits; the teachable, Matthew 13:31, Mark 4:30, Luke 5:4-5-6, Luke 17: 5-6, 12-19; and Matthew 17:20, Faith as Small as a mustard seed moves mountains; meaning, small faith grows mighty to do great.

Faith has power and is stable, never moved.

Jesus is alive from the dead. He has the power of life to give back to man, whatever the man lost at the Garden of Eden when he took the devil's choice of accepting lies and ate forbidden fruit, Genesis 3:5, 3:22-24. When you have a mustard seed faith (Small), you will attract those who love GOD but are looking for HIS power and clarity. If you live by GOD'S Faith, there are people who will never understand you. Some will think you have a lot of money or you are secretly corrupt and others will think you pretend a lot. Finally, YOU WILL BE PAINTED ALL COLORS BY THOSE WHO Have faith like pieces of beans or little pieces of corn Faith; little faith. People of little faith are dangerous to hang around. They will destroy your faith and eventually destroy you. When you have small faith, you are like a woman pregnant and is expecting a precious delicate baby. You cannot hang around people who can stress you and cause abortion or a premature delivery to your precious baby.

BY FAITH, KNOW WHO YOU ARE!

You have new clothes on you, which are covered by the Blood of JESUS CHRIST, Genesis 3:20-21. Do you know who you are? And have you ever asked yourself who you are. It is dangerous to live without knowing who you are. For that is how Satan steals people's faith; hence, identity. By Faith you should know that you are a child of GOD THE MOST HIGH This is a true saying, know that you are child of GOD bought by the precious Blood of the Savior JESUS CHRIST THE SON OF THE MOST HIGH GOD, John 3:3-8. For lack of mall Faith, Many Born Again have lost their identity for lack of this knowledge. Faith being the substance and the evidence, it's the knowledge that gives to know who we are in the LORD and what JESUS CHRIST meant when HE said, "you must be Born again" What JESUS simply said was and it is up to today that, "the old man is sinful. And therefore, be born again into ME so that I can give you a new man full of Faith and have a new identity." For JESUS said, "I AM THE WAY, THE TRUTH, AND THE LIFE, no man comes unto the father but by ME," John 14:6. Hosea 4: 6 records, "My people are destroyed for the lack of knowledge: Because they have rejected the knowledge, I will reject them, and they will not have a priest from ME: seeing they have forgotten GOD'S law, I will also forget their children," says the LORD!

You and I cannot afford really to forget the law of the LORD that brings Faith in GOD to us. And when JESUS CHRIST our Eternal Redeemer and Our LORD says, we must be born again, we need to know that this is the new identity HE is calling us for. By Faith, the new birth will take away the old man, and put knew man in us who cannot be destroyed by the devil with his cunning lies. That liar Satan has lied to so many people that they are nothing and no one cares about them, and he has put them under the captivity of his lies; hence, no faith in GOD. And when no faith in GOD, No help left of course. But when you identify yourself with JESUS CHRIST and HIS Blood by the Power of the HOLY SPIRIT, you will experience victory as you continue to worship the LORD YOUR GOD IN SPIRIT AND IN TRUTH. Never forget; here, the Key is to Worship the LORD GOD in SPIRIT and in TRUTH. If you cannot worship, your Faith will lack works, and knowing your identity is almost impossible and you will not be effective.

The enemy cannot run away from you or stop telling you lies when you stay outside The WORD, The Faith and The Worship: for that is the only way to saw "Faith with Works which is not dead. Faith with Works is alive and powerful but faith without work, "little faith" is dead and can never move the devil away.

There must be something important in your life that will expel the presence of the devil away from you, and your surroundings. And that is only the Presence of the ALMIGHTY GOD that comes and is obtained by your Faith in HIM. For there is no power in you to expel the devil other than the Blood of JESUS CHRIST in you: By Faith, The Blood of JESUS CHRIST brings the presence of GOD and carries the Power of the HOLY SPIRIT that brings the truth of GOD, which is in JESUS CHRIST our LORD. The HOLY SPIRIT is the illuminator and the completion of the whole GODLINESS. Therefore, when you worship GOD in the Spirit, your spirit hooks and enters into the SPIRIT OF THE ALMIGHTY GOD THROUGH THE PRECIOUS BLOOD OF JESUS CHRIST; Bringing Your Faith to Great Works and Manifestations.

GOD'S Truth starts manifesting in your life by GOD giving you new revelations on how to overcome. During worship, the Truth of GOD will reveal to you the strategies of the enemy and all his plans, the schemes and the assignments that he has targeted toward you.

And while worshiping the LORD, he will open your mouth through the HOLY SPIRIT and give you powerful words to use against the enemy Satan and his demons, so as to expel them and destroy all their plans.

FAITH BRINGS THE KNOWLEDGE:

Do you know that you are very precious in the eye of GOD, and are devil's target and Satan cannot rest looking for how he can devour you? Why is this? When an enemy is aware of his opponent's strength, he targets his adversary's small children and because you are child of GOD who is Satan's enemy, then you are Satan's target. I believe you know that from the time Lucifer fell out of GOD'S favor for his sin, GOD became the devil's enemy. Satan hates our GOD so much that he looks for every opportunity to frustrate LORD Almighty. But devil is a liar; he can do nothing to our Father. Satan has no faith in GOD only fear that his days are almost over. Therefore, you and I need to live in our LORD GOD'S Full Faith to Enjoy HIS Presence; hence, Victory.

<u>For you and me knowledge is Power:</u>

Now, let's know the formula that Satan and his demons use to weaken our faith. Since devil knows our GOD is the strongest and all powerful, he looks for HIS weak vessels to use. If your enemy is stronger than you, and you may not be able to get him, or he is smarter than you, you can only get him through his children or his weak associates. Devil knows, he just need to get one of GOD'S children and he will successfully use that child to get our Father annoyed, and he thinks that way he can make GOD dismayed. That is what devil did in the Garden of Eden. Satan got hold of Eve to try to change GOD'S DIVINE PLAN for us human-beings. That is why it is important to know who you are and why you are what you are. Also, it is important to know your enemy and why he is your foe and so mad at you. Then by Faith you put a whole Armor of GOD and Stand to be able to fight and quench the enemy's fiery darts; Ephesians 6:10-17.

This is all about the Kingdoms! When I was young, I did not know the different between us in the family and the servants and especially those who stayed many years in our employ. Some I thought they were our uncles, aunties and older brothers until later when I grew up to understand. The Bible says, when a child is young he does not know his identity; hence, a servant is better positioned until the child will come to the knowledge of his position. If you do not know which Kingdom you belong to, and who are the enemies of your Kingdom then you can betray your Father's Kingdom to the enemy. Unless you know who your enemy is and why he is your enemy, you may not know when you entangle yourself with him. Your enemy is Satan the devil because he is the enemy of your Father and he hates your Father GOD very much. Look at Isaiah 14:12-15, and you will see how Satan, "Lucifer" is his name, lifted himself up wanting to overthrow the Kingdom of our GOD and be the most high, and what was done to him by our LORD GOD ALMIGHTY because HE is the only Creator and the Most Supreme GOD. Isaiah 14:12 -15 records, "How art thou fallen from heaven O Lucifer, son of morning! How art thou cut down to the ground, which did weaken the nations! For thou hast said in thine heart, I will ascend unto heavens, I will exalt my throne above the stars of GOD: I will sit also upon the mountain of the north: I will ascend above the heights of the clouds; I will be like the most High. Yet thou shalt be brought down to hell, to the sides of the pit." How do you overcome this proud spirit of Lucifer? Revelation12:11 tells us it's only by the Blood of The LAMB JESUS CHRIST, and by the Word of your Testimony. For they that were before us "overcame by the Blood of the LAMB, and by the word of their testimony; and they loved not their lives unto death" Revelation 12:11.

By Faith, you must have a testimony and the BLOOD OF JESUS in you to overcome the devil; otherwise, life is not easy because Satan, that Lucifer and his demons must kick and kick, harden your life to see if he can overcome and get you to hell with him.

Lucifer feels that if he can get more people in hell than those who are in heaven, he will be a winner, but that is a lie he has lied himself. Our GOD'S Victory is not determined by how many people are in heaven. GOD is GOD the Creator and the Owner of everything even that evil devil was created by HIM for the day of destruction, Proverbs 16:4. The devil knows all that but he has no capacity to believe GOD'S truth for he lied to himself from the very beginning until he himself became that lie. Therefore, he has cheated himself! He can never be a winner! And he can never be GOD! GOD IS VICTORY AND HE IS NOT LOOKING FOR VICTORY FOR HE DOES NOT COMPETE WITH Satan at all! Only Satan who thinks he is competing with GOD ALMIGHTY.

The only safe thing Lucifer should have done was to humble himself before his Creator the LORD GOD ALMIGHTY and accept that he can never fight with GOD and ask for forgiveness and stay as a clean obeying Angels. The world would be so sweet without Satan! However, repentance is not in Lucifer's capacity or vocabulary so could not humble himself. His character is pride and self-exaltation, lifting himself up to humiliate GOD and those who live a righteous life. What Satan forgets is that he is too little to humiliate GOD, and too powerless for GOD. Satan has really lied to himself with a big lie! It's only people he lies to.

Do you know what humiliates that liar Satan? When you live a righteous life!

Righteous life is the Satan's poison, great venom to him and all his demons, and an absolute disaster, while righteousness is OUR LORD GOD'S character and HIS Joy. That is why Satan hates those who are righteous, but who cares? I don't care! I want him to hate me 100%.

I know that the devil always wants to humiliate you and me so that he can frustrate GOD through us but GOD has already turned our humiliation into HIS humility so that we can enjoy HIS Peace, Love and Joy in the HOLY GHOST and be overcomers.

So he thinks that when he hurts us, then he has frustrated our Father GOD but what a lie, Satan, to yourself! A very big lie devil! And you are defeated in JESUS HOLY NAME! AMEN!

When you are feeling very frustrated, devil feels very good. If you start worshiping and praising GOD; because you will automatically be happy and excited, Satan gets very frustrated, dizzy and he will try all that is within his reach to make you not worship and praise GOD. Therefore, praise and worship the LORD in the midst of all heartaches. The devil knows that when you praise and worship GOD you will be drunk with Love, Joy and Peace of Heavenly Wine and feel good and his miseries becomes missiles to him.

Worshiping GOD makes Satan feel very bad and angry and the more you worship the more he goes far from you. You better start worshiping so that Satan can flee away from you. Another weapon to defeat Satan and make him flee away is by giving testimonies of victories that your LORD Father GOD has won for you.

That drives the devil crazier. When you testify about the mightiness and goodness of your LORD GOD, you get more equipped with greater missiles to overcome Satan.

When you are going through a terrible trial, know that JESUS CHRIST has given an encouraging Testimony about you and to you HE says, "Behold, I come quickly: blessed is he that keeps the saying of the prophecy of this book, Revelation 22:7.

WHO AM I?

Here below: my testimony on the revelation of who I am; August 14, 1977

I want to give you my living testimony of when I came to know who I am in the LORD and how my GOD loves me. Over years, that knowledge has really helped me to turn my miseries in to missiles. Every time Satan has come to oppress me, the HOLY SPIRIT who lives in me and I in HIM and I stay tuned into, prompts me to remember who I am in JESUS CHRIST my LORD and my Savior.

It was on a Sunday afternoon, when I had a real encounter of face to face fighting with the devils that I did not know they exist. This was after I had been openly and strongly saved and Baptized in the HOLY SPIRIT for five years. To make it clearer, before I got declared strongly saved and confirmed into the Power of the HOLY SPIRIT in 1973, 31st August, devil had brought to me so many problems that had developed into anxiety and anxiety had borne or attracted a spirit of allergy that developed into a stronger spirit of Asthma. Those who have suffered asthmatic attacks know how severely that demon can attack. Actually, even in the medical field it is called an asthmatic attack. So if you want to argue that it is not an evil spirit it is a disease, I can ask you, what is a disease? A disease is anything that inflicts the human body, the society, animals, or plants, with pain or with any kind of disorder; and therefore, it's not sweet, it's evil.

Where do those histamines, substances that cause allergies or germs that cause infections come from, only to inflict? From GOD? For what purpose would GOD bring diseases in HIS creation that HE Created in HIS Image and HIS likeness? Genesis 1:26, James 1: 13. And what are they in reality? Exodus 15:26, 23:25, 1-33.

In 1975, I cried to GOD and enquired to know why my colleagues in the medical field are too hardened to be saved. Most of them you would preach to them and they would just intimidate you with what they thought they knew. But when my Father would come in HIS power of HIS Might, they would also feel intimidated. When JESUS CHRIST would come and heal a desperate patient of a terminal disease like cancer, severe congested heart disease (failure) and the patient goes home alive and well; actually, healthier and younger looking than before, some of those colleagues would feel very bad instead of rejoicing because someone is healed. While I was preaching as we worked on a patient, and while I gave my patient hope of live that is in JESUS CHRIST MY LORD AND SAVIOR, some of my colleagues would not want to hear that language of Heaven. Thank GOD the law in Kenya is open to the Gospel and that way; many, regardless their religions' faiths, creeds and believes were receiving healing as they believe in our LORD JESUS CHRIST'S DIVINE HEALING and GO home rejoicing, Mark 16:15-18, John 14:12-14, Act 3:1.

And because of that I did not care whether some of Nurses and Doctors wanted to hear me encourage and give hope of life to desperate patients or not. Heavenly language is a true language and that is the Language I am well taught to speak. I speak of salvation in JESUS CHRIST; healing; restoration, rebuilding, provision, overcoming, joy; peace; love, and faith.

While sharing, some of my colleagues would get mad at me and ask me, do you know anything else that you can talk of? Laughingly, I would ask them, anything else such as what? Like how many people are being killed and how people are doing evil to get rich quick or like what? Anyway, I would not argue with them but those who wanted us to reason we would reason out and my GOD would make them know the truth; that diseases are spirits of the devil and he releases them from hell with their fake names to come and steal peoples' lives, kill and destroy. Those of us who have lived in the LORD GOD ALMIGHTY without wavering have known this and it is a true saying. But majority of people in medical fields and even outside medical circles will not be allowed by their master Satan to reason out, lest they come to know the knowledge of the True GOD, be saved, and turn away from their wicked ways.

Since 1982, the spirit asthma had tormented me for five years, and on this day of August 14th, 1978 that spirit of Asthma came unwaveringly to attack me. We had just relocated because; we had found out that I get attacked when I am in a certain area we had lived in for 8 years. It was in the afternoon, and I was in the kitchen organizing what to cook for dinner. Usually a strange smell would precede an attack but on this day I had not smelt anything strange, but the attack came anyway: irritation of the nose, the throat, and slight coughing, followed by sneezing, strong continuous coughing and finally wheezing and restlessness. Aha, I knew the devil has attacked me again despite being in a new place. Must I run to the hospital to get a shot? Oh LORD! I cried! I was tired of those intravenous injections to put in Aminophylline, and subcutaneous shots for adrenalines, Oh LORD MY GOD! I cried again.

I cried with self-pity. I said, we have just moved, and the children are happy that we are in a neighborhood with a good school and the whole family thinks that my problems are now behind me. Help me my Dear LORD, I proclaimed in through tears. The LORD had healed me of stomach ulcers 4 years before, when a brother who had been healed of lung cancer prayed for us in a group of people with chronic illnesses. And just a year after that, the ALMIGHTY GOD had literary operated on me! After I prayed a prayer of faith in desperate pain, GOD had removed a swollen appendix that was ready to perforate at any time. I had cried to him, "Oh LORD, operate on me the way YOU operated on Adam and removed Eve out of him. Take this sick appendix out of me and give a healthy one. Let me not go to the surgery room to be opened by a man when you were the first and the best surgeon dear LORD." As I prayed that prayer within my spirit, joy filled me, and I said, "LORD, You were the first Surgeon, the HOLY SPIRIT was the first doctor anesthetist and JESUS CHRIST our LORD performed the duties of the doctor in charge of the surgery room, operating on Adam to get Eve. You must have created that moment of first surgery to teach people about medical surgery. Indeed all the best treatment comes from you." As I meditated in that wonderful event in the Garden of Eden, on that material wonderful day when Eve was created out of Adam; Genesis 2:21-22, the LORD caused me to have a deep sleep and when I woke up, I was healed.

The events preceding this healing are a mystery to this day! Here is what happened, first, GOD allowed a more serious emergency to come to the hospital while I was being prepared for surgery. A man with a bust abdomen, all the intestines out, was brought to the emergency room. He had to be rushed to the only general surgical room. That patient should have been taken to a closer and better equipped hospital, but for some reason known only to my GOD he was brought to the hospital where I was being prepared for emergency appendectomy, *(surgery done to remove a sick appendix)*. I started fighting in me. Was this also a demon, or an evil spirit? Yes, because it was the work of Lucifer. He was the one who had infected my appendix, so that I would fail to sit for my second year exam to prevent me from finishing college at the right time or never finish. He had prevented my education from my youth, and he had punished me from my childhood. Let me tell you my discovery about the devil and his demoniac activities.

If Lucifer the devil knows that you have been given a gift that can win others out of his kingdom, he will do everything to kill you. But the good news is, Satan has no power over GOD'S plan and he cannot kill GOD'S Purpose. Devil may try and people may talk and be used by the devil in any way, but wait until the LORD GOD ALMIGHT starts manifesting HIMSELF in you. There is nothing the devil can do to stop GOD'S work in you. The LORD GOD must bring that which HE purposed in you into HIS accomplishment. Hallelujah! Praise GOD ALMIGHTY! AMEN! I feel good when I remember this instance, among others, when Satan was put to shame before my eyes and the eyes of surgeons, nurses and any other persons who were near that time. As my Jewish Surgeon wrote in my discharge form, "She has been healed by her GOD. Go and serve your GOD who has healed you." I thank GOD. The devil is a liar, and he is defeated in JESUS HOLY NAME! AMEN! It's in record 1976 MKS MTC Hospital, read it if you doubt.

Now, back to the testimony of healed asthma, the attack strongly started, and I am worried, and that demon loves worry. It is a worrying, stressing demon. One cannot stay close to other people because of the wheezing, and the constant coughing with a lot of mucus.

It is a stressful and restless condition. But on this day! Oh, my GOD is great! Oh! This very day, Satan was defeated! My LORD GOD asked me, do you know who you are? And do you know who asthma is? I said, yes LORD, I do. HE asked me again, then why do you let the devil stay in you? I was astonished by that question and up to today that question rings in my ears as clear as it did on that afternoon of August 14th 1977. I was facing a kitchen window which was tightly closed. We had moved from one district to another and entered in a newly built house; in a place called Silver Spring, in the city of Embu, Kenya. This house had been thoroughly cleaned. There was no smell of detergents or anything else that should have triggered the attacks I got in the old neighborhood of Siakago city.

As I said, "Yes LORD." The Spirit of the LORD'S knowledge overshadowed me and I felt great power and started telling the devil who I am and who he is. I said, "Satan! Listen! I am a child of GOD, Born Again in the Blood of JESUS CHRIST and Baptized in the power of the HOLY SPIRIT.

My body is the Temple of the HOLY SPIRIT! Get out devil! Now! Get out! There is no bargain between me and you devil. Get out! Now! I mean now! Not any other moment. Right now, Satan, you get out in JESUS HOLY NAME! Satan you have no place in me, get out in JESUS HOLY NAME! Devil you cannot dwell in this body; it belongs to my FATHER and you have no authority to live in me! You have no authority and you are an illegal in me so get out of my lungs in JESUS NAME! No one has given you permission to live in my lungs! My lungs belongs to the one who Created them and that is the LORD GOD ALMIGHTY, who created the whole of me; and you, Satan, cannot live in the same place with my GOD, so get out in JESUS HOLY NAME! Get out!! Get out in JESUS HOLY NAME, COME OUT NOW! IN JESUS NAME, I bind you, devil, from your roots and cast you out of my lungs right now in the Mighty NAME OF JESUS CHRIST, get out devil! Come out bound, devil, in JESUS HOLY NAME and go back to where you came from! In JESUS HOLY NAME I cast you out of my body now!! NOW! Get out! Come out! Come out! In the NAME OF JESUS CHRIST, COME OUT, devil! CHRIST DEFEATED YOU FOR ME OVER 2000 YEARS AGO, GET OUT, devil, in JESUS HOLY NAME!I am A Temple of the HOLY SPIRIT and indwelling place of A HOLY GOD! My body is Holy as my GOD is Holy! You have no place, you dirty devil, get out of me!" It was a real big battle.

After more than two hours of persistence casting and rebuking the demon of asthma, and resisting the devil, he flew like a tiny bird out of my mouth and I saw him fly out of the closed window. He did not break the window on his way out, but I saw him leave with my own two eyes, for during the battle I had kept my eyes open. Let me stress that this was a battle and not a prayer. And by the way, many times, when I am worshiping a worship which I am directing the devil to his place and letting him know how tiny he is before my Father; I do not close my eyes. No one told me nor taught me not to close my eyes except the HOLY SPIRIT. I say this because I have never consciously thought about keeping my eyes open; it just happens automatically that I fight with my eyes open. I think this is logical even physically; no one fights with closed eyes.

Although, with prayers we have spiritual eyes and we do not need our physical eyes open to prevent interruptions, this time both my physical and spiritual eyes were wide open. I saw with my physical eyes that asthma spirit flee and leave me through my mouth. It came out-coop-co-! And I saw it with my eyes! As the tiny, dark brown birdlike demon flew out the closed window, I screamed at it and told it to go to where it had come from and never to touch any one on its way in The Mighty Name of JESUS CHRIST! "You are defeated devil you will never come back to me I do not belong to you. I'm my Father's child and a temple of the HOLY SPIRIT; An indwelling place of A HOLY GOD!" It left and I was set free! "You shall know the truth and the truth shall set you free," John 8:32, Mark 16:15-18, Luke 10:19, John 14:12

When CHRIST JESUS told us that, we shall know the truth and the truth will set us free, HE meant exactly that. That day the truth of knowing my identity set me free indeed. Indeed, here, the application of truth was the one that did set me free from the asthmatic spirit completely. From that day and until my LORD JESUS CHRIST comes again to take me home that demon will never come back to me. I declared so as I cast it out; I directed it to the bottomless pit to stay there chained with chains of darkness until the Day of Judgment, Amen! I was set free from the spirit of Asthma completely.

Divine Healing is very much alive.

And it is very much here on earth but you have to get it in the way the LORD GOD has prescribed it for you. Asthma was my third divine healing of a major illness.

Although I had been healed of very many other diseases, but these three were very remarkable because no medicine was going to heal them, especially the two, asthma, and peptic ulcers. Although appendicitis is certainly curable through surgery, I was in danger of rapture due to the delay caused by surgery room availability. Thank GOD for the delays that come our way when there is an urgent matter. Most of the time when you see the delay, unless the HOLY SPIRIT orders you to pray against it, thank GOD for it and praise HIM because HE knows why. HE may be keeping you longer to teach you something after HE delivers you from an oncoming calamity. While you are going through suffering and many miseries until many questions come to fill your life, let your question be directed respectfully to your Heavenly Father and do not be like the wife of Job. (What did she do?)

Ask your LORD GOD respectfully why HE has let that devil Satan attack you. Enquire of GOD and he will let you know everything. Some brethren will tell you; 'Don't ask GOD anything for who are you to ask HIM." But I say, I have never seen a father whose children cannot approach and ask questions of anything that they are not satisfied or that they are not sure of. Sometime we may not need to ask because the answer is right there. If you do not know or you are not sure, ask HIM HE IS YOUR FATHER AND HE HAS THE ANSWER.

With thanks giving that HE has been your GOD, your Father, your Creator, and HE keeps you alive helping you in every area of your life: Approach HIM and ask HIM, "my father, I thank YOU for what you are to me: a good and loving Father you are to me, but I would like to know why this problem is so persistent in my life?" Is it because of my sins? Have I disobeyed you dear LORD? If so I repent in the name of JESUS CHRIST my LORD and my Savior; I ask you LORD, Kindly forgive me of my sins and heal me of this situation. It may be a disease; the LORD will heal you and make you healthy. It may be a financial problem; the LORD will heal your finances and bring an increase and a multiplication in double a hundred folds. Is it any other type of problem, family and all these things Satan comes to bring our way? Our LORD GOD is a specialist of healing. Nothing is impossible with our GOD to them that believe, Hebrew 4:14-16. In every situation the devil brought to me, I learned to give him my testimony and that makes the devil mad because he does not like hearing the Name of JESUS CHRIST and the Blood that cleanses us from the filthiness that he puts on us, Philippians 4:6-7.

Let Satan know who you are, you are not one of the sons of Sceva recorded in Acts 19:14-16, that did not know who they were in the LORD GOD because they were not Born Again.

And if you are not yet Born Again, accept the LORD JESUS CHRIST NOW! It's your time, my dear! HE is the only savior that can save and give you an identity as a child of GOD and give you power and authority over demons.

Do not stay any farther without knowing who you are or your nationality.

The nationality of this world is coming to an end, but JESUS CHRIST'S Nationality is forever. HE is the only one who has everlasting life, John 6:35-58 HE will give you all the equipment to fight the enemy with. Remember that your overcoming is HIS goal. 2 Timothy 3:16-17, 1 Samuel 16&17.

JESUS CHRIST Looks forward for you to overcome and so HE will strengthen you even when the battle is very severe, Isaiah 40:31. Give the devil your testimony so that you can defeat him; Amen! Triumph over the devil, for you are a victor not a victim, Amen!

THE TRUMPET:

our LORD GOD ALMIGHTY Says "Let the rain from heaven fall upon you. Let it refresh you. For, in the refreshing of that rain your spirit man will be quickened, your faith will be energized, and you will come to know and feel that MY glory is coming in a fresh and in a new way. There will be an abundance of new life within you. MY power will spring up, and the power of MY word will become the sword (Missile) by which you will defeat the enemy. Allow the rain of the Spirit to bring that which is needed. It is time for you, MY people, to ask for the rain, in the time of the rain, and this is that time. It is time for you to ask in faith that the water of heaven would fall upon you and bring you out into a bright place; into a place of glory; into a place of MY presence; into a place of healing; into a place of rebuilding, harvesting, restoring, restoration and renewal. Let the rain of the

Spirit become a living river of water of life that flows through and around you," John 7: 37-38.

SMALL STRAWS IN A SOFT WIND, the manifestation of Small Faith:

"To those of you who seem to be stuck and don't know what to do to get unstuck, you need to quiet the inside voice of worry and regret, and seek ME for wisdom. Do not rely on your own ideas that emanate from frustration and desperation, and refuse to allow emotional reactions to motivate you. I will show you the next step and the way out of your dilemma if you will truly listen," says the LORD GOD ALMIGHTY. *Proverbs 3:5-6* "Trust in the LORD with all your heart, and lean not on your own understanding; in all your ways acknowledge HIM, and HE shall direct your paths." Paths of prayers, and waiting upon GOD while you are diligently serving HIM in Spirit and Truth.

CHAPTER 16

GOD gave me missiles (Bombs) to Destroy Asthma

From those sicknesses, and the healing, I learned I had missiles to fight the enemy with. I do not care what other people say; I care what my LORD GOD Almighty the creator of heaven and earth says about me and what HE does for me, and with me. I care about how he uses me in HIS services for the other people that are not contaminated b Testimony y their religions. Please allow me to say this, religious people, and especially them that are in the Christian religions, have a hard time grasping the truth of the Gospel and the actions of JESUS CHRIST on their behalf. Also, I know some of my brethren who are so spiritual that they do not want to mention the name of Satan or rebuke him because they feel that by so doing they are worshiping him. I do not think that is the case; because no one rebukes anything that is right or good.

You cannot worship and rebuke at the same time. You rebuke and cast away what you hate most.

Some say that, the angels at the mountain of Moab with Moses' body did not rebuke the devil. Instead, they said, "May the LORD rebuke you." Yes, because they were angels and not Born Again sons of GOD and joint heirs with CHRIST JESUS, Romans 8:16-17. What those brethren need to know is that, we are very different from angels and we operate at very different levels and capacities. Angels are our Spiritual servants and if need be, physical servants and they are not joint heirs with CHRIST as we are. Romans 8:14-19.

We are sons of GOD and JESUS CHRIST gave us power and authority over the devil and all his demons, Luke 10:19. Power and authority not for laughing with the demons, but to cast them away, Mark 16:15-18 and to rebuke them away from us in HIS MIGHTY NAME; AMEN! The Bible tells us that we shall even judge the angels. Which angels? The fallen Lucifer, Satan and all his demons, 1 Corinthians 6:2-3.

All the angels were created before us together with Lucifer and the one third of angels that sinned with him. Lucifer was an arch angel before he sinned and judged forever.

We have other Arch angels like Michael, and Gabriel, that do the ministries of the LORD around the Throne of our Father and they are Holy and more powerful than Satan and his demons. By the way, one holy angel can chase away a billion demons. The Arch Angel Michael is in the Book of Daniel 10:12-13, 20-21, 12: 1-3, Jude 1:9 and Revelation 12:7-12 in charge of Security of Israel. I believe he also protects us, the true believers. Gabriel is sent where very Important messages have to be delivered like in Daniel 9:21, Luke 1:19, 26. So do not fear the devil, JESUS CHRIST announced his defeat over two thousand years ago at Calvary. Use the Power and authority that GOD gave you over Satan the day you repented and accepted CHRIST JESUS As your Savior. Luke 10:19 says, "I have given unto you power to tread on serpents, and scorpions, and over all the power of the enemy: and nothing shall by any means hurt you."

Why on earth would JESUS CHRIST the SON OF THE MOST HIGH GOD give us power to go to the woods to tread on snakes, and scorpions and over men or women that are our enemies? Do you think that this is the case? No, not at all!

The power JESUS gave us was to tread over the demons that will come to hurt us in the form of snakes, scorpions, and Satan with all his powers. We have the power to tread upon them by faith spiritually. Remember demons are spirits just like the clean Holy Angels and we can only use words as missiles on them, we cannot use bullets, arrows, bombs, and guns and such like weapons. The way you use your words to Satan it is what will mater. If you just fearfully with doubts tell him to go he will not go. Devil is a terror, and can only understand terrorism not beseeching or comforting words. How can you comfort Satan when he is discomforting you? No! I believe that is why HOLY SPIRIT Used our Brother Apostle Paul to write many places that, "Brethren, I would not have you ignorant."

You have to use HOLY SPIRIT Power and the Word of GOD to bind the devil and cast him away, Mark 16:15-20. If you have no power from on high, ask to be baptized by the HOLY SPIRIT OF GOD because that is HIS duty. To baptize you with the Power of the ALMIGHTY GOD, and give you power, Mathew 2:11, Mark 1:8, John 1: 33, Acts 1:4-8, 2:1-4.

John 16:13 JESUS says, "When the Spirit of truth is come HE will teach and guide you into all truth:" And 1 Corinthians 2:1-16 the Word of GOD by the mouth of Paul summarizes the work of the HOLY SPRIT in us, HE teaches us wisdom and knowledge with understanding so that when we speak we speak mysteries of GOD, which is in CHRIST JESUS. This is a great testimony for us all that are in CHRIST JESUS. That is why I boldly tell Satan who I am, and what I am in my LORD GOD'S Kingdom. I cannot let devil get hold of me as if I am his. No way! That I do refuse in JESUS HOLY NAME!

When Satan comes raging like a flood, the SPIRIT MY GOD raises a standard against him, and I have also to raise a standard against him using the POWER that was given to me by my LORD JESUS. According to HIS Word, Isaiah 59:19, and Daniel11: 32, and Ephesians 3:20; "according to the power that works in us." If the power of CHRIST is working in you, you will raise a standard against your enemy and do exploits with exceeding and the abundance of what you need, Amen and praise the LORD Our GOD! When Satan comes to discourage me using past failures that he brought me, I stand against him in the Mighty Name of JESUS CHRIST and I remind him of his past failure, the present failure and of his future failure: I remind him that his days are numbered, and that he will spend his eternity in hell.

If he tells me that I have previously sinned so grievously that I cannot be forgiven, I tell him, "You are a liar Satan! My sins were forgiven and cast in the sea of forgetfulness. And JESUS' Blood is ever ready and alive and waiting to wash out of me any sin that may come on my way." Satan is the only one who sinned without any possibility of remission of sins. Human beings, will be forgiven if they repent. Even Adam and Eve, if they had only asked for forgiveness, it would have been given unto them. Had they repented, today we would be reading in recorded history that they sinned, and after crying to GOD with repentance: they were forgiven. And today, the devil would have no power to take us through what he takes us through.

CHAPTER 17

The importance of a testimony

Your testimony will determine your victory.

Revelation 12:10-11 tells us, "And I heard a loud voice saying in heaven, Now is come salvation and strength, and the Kingdom of our GOD and the power of HIS CHRIST: for the accuser of Brethren is cast down, which accused them before our GOD day and night. And they overcame him by the Blood of the Lamb and by the word of their testimony; and they loved not their lives unto the death."

When devil accused those who lived before us, we see that they used the Blood of JESUS CHRIST in them to fight and overcome. That is the Blood that washed them from the sin and gave them power to testify about their Savior and power to become the sons of GOD.

And Power had to proceed through their mouth. This happened whenever they gave their life testimony about JESUS CHRIST being their LORD and Savior the Power covered them.

Today, that provision of the Power of Testimony is being killed by the devil speedily in the form of modernization of Christianity. People do not want to hear your testimony nor do they want to give their testimony. They would rather take quality time to talk about the stock market, their new clothes and shoes, and if they have children in school, they will spend good time talking about their children's progress in school than talking about what CHRIST is doing in their lives. Their so called "preaching through actions" is also not portraying 'Christ-like people.' They are as common as any other person on the street.

You can hardly tell who is a Christian today and a non-Christian by their talk and by their actions. It is pathetic and we need to examine ourselves. We hear much talk about TV preachers, but I tell you, better those Brethren because they are seen on TV preaching CHRIST and if you meet them, majority will give you that Christ-like look. They know we know them, and if they show another side it will be put on secular TV very fast. Thanks be to GOD for TV preachers if they keep the righteousness of Our GOD as they preach. Your Testimony is a very important Missile to destroy all the efforts of the devil and nullify his work of destruction upon your life.

You can never overcome the devil by good works alone, but you can challenge him through good works and good works must be followed by your testimony. Good works are very important in a Christian's life, but you know, it is not the good works that saved us. It is by the Grace of GOD and the Blood of JESUS CHRIST we received salvation by Faith and for Faith to take effect it has to be testified.

By Faith, Joseph Testified who he was to be, and his brothers were jealous, but they did not stop the testimony to be fulfilled. Actually, they enhanced his testimony when they sold him Egypt, where GOD was planning to use Israel for the Testimony of HIS Glory. You see, GOD would want us to go through some undesirable problems like Joseph and later Israel in order to glorify HIMSELF when HE delivers us through many tribulations, Psalm 34:19. Sometimes, we get our lives messed up by things that we cannot avoid, but our GOD knows how to deliver us from such messes and turn them to messages Psalm 34:18-22.

Therefore, hold onto your faithful testimony of your salvation, and give it out of season and in season. Testimonies preach the Word, and do not need a pulpit. Testimony about what CHRIST Has done in your life and about how great HE is in our life will give witness about Our Savior, and make HIM known by those who did not know HIM. Remember, HE told us to be HIS witnesses, but how can you witness about HIM when you cannot testify about HIM. It is impossible to talk about The Power of Our LORD JESUS CHRIST, THE FATHER, AND THE HOLY SPIRIT, ALL IN ONE GOD, and as the supreme authority without giving your testimony about HIM. You must say, and testify about your relationship with HIM, and about HIS power that has made you believe and live in HIM.

Testimony is practiced by speaking the righteousness and the Power of our LORD GOD that is in you by JESUS CHRIST.

As you work out your salvation with fear and trembling, striving to live a righteous life and reach the mark of GOD'S perfection, which is in CHRIST JESUS: "for it is not of your good works that you are saved," but of HIS Grace and Mercy by HIS SPIRIT that you are saved. In other words, when GOD'S Grace saves you, the same Grace enables you to do the good works of the LORD and you will find out that your testimony is growing as big as a mustard tree that grows from a mustard seed. And I believe that is the Faith our Savior JESUS was always telling the First Disciples to testify of to the situations like the storm in the Sea of Galilee and to sicknesses. In order for them to overcome, they needed to testify to the situation about the miracle working Power in CHRIST that they have witnessed. They should tell that situation, "As it has been done to that sickness that possessed that person and we have witnessed the healing, so shall it be unto you storms, go away and you sea be calm now in JESUS MIGHTY NAME!" And storms would have calmed! And instead of them fearing and seeing death, it was their opportunity to see victory. Likewise, every storm we go through should be an opportunity for victory. JESUS wanted them to practice their testimonies through what they have seen HIM doing. And so are we.

Personal testimony on JESUS CHRSIT'S work in your life is very important. It will edify and teach the Church how JESUS is Powerful, and give a witness to them that are not yet in HIM. If it is about healing or provision of finances, or clothing, housing and above all, keeping you saved and healthy it's an encouragement to others and yourself. It is good to let people know what GOD has done for you spiritually and physically. How would we have known about the woman who had the issue of blood for 12 years if she had not given GOD Glory through her testimony? How would we have known about the blind man who was made to testify by his parent when they feared the Pharisees? If that man did not testify and say; John 9:25 "all I know is that I was blind, but now I can see." How would we have known about Noah and his righteousness and the building of the Ark? And about the rebellion at Babel and the confusion of languages if there was no testimony about men progress on earth? Testimony made us know our Patriarch Abraham, and his Faith in YAHWEH. And how would we have known about Isaac born of Abraham at 100 years if there was no testimony given about him. Both works and words' testimonies enlighten the hearer and are good and important for edifying.

The Bible is full of testimonies of GOD YAHWEH telling us about HIMSELF and HIS actions and HIS mighty works for the human race. Also, about man with his successes, disobediences and his failures that started from the Garden of Eden to the Garden of Gethsemane and Calvary to crucifying JESUS CHRIST with all our problems on the Cross for JESUS to Resurrect with Victory. Testifying about GOD'S power that resurrected JESUS and the Power of the Cross that saved you is very important. Even outside the Church building, we are supposed to give our testimonies to non-believers as we interact with them.

We should not engage ourselves talking and discussing earthly events and activities with non-believers unless we are looking for an opportunity to testifying about our Savior. Else, we be entangled and enticed by their great empty words and start entertaining ourselves with emptiness and hence fall into their temptations. The WORD in 2 Corinthians 6:14 warns us "not to be unequally yoked together with unbelievers; for what fellowship do righteousness has with unrighteousness and what communion has light with darkness?"

Many wonderful Christians have lost their way in the LORD by entangling themselves with the world by entertaining their talks. Keep your testimony burning and walk it, and live it. Do not give a testimony of what you do not practice in your life. At times, we believers of CHRIST, we do give a testimony of the things "that are not as they are." If you do so by faith, please keep to that faith strongly and be faithful unto the one who makes things that are not faceable to be faceable in order for non-believer to see and marvel at the great things that our GOD does. GOD wants to Glorify HIMSELF by doing good things for us.

GOD is waiting for HIS believers to receive their miracles so that they can glorify HIM through their testimonies to non-believers. The more you testify the more you move GOD towards yourself and the less you testify the less victory. May GOD help us to keep to our testimonies, and to witness the power of our Savior JESUS CHRIST, Amen! Overcome the enemy by the "Blood of the LAMB and the Word of your testimony," Revelation 12:11

Now, do you have a testimony?

Yes, because you are child of GOD'S purpose you have a big one to give. The sick will get healed when they hear how GOD delivered you from that sickness. The poor will get rich when they hear how GOD delivered you from that poverty spirit that had sat in your house like a giant not ready to move out, and without any man to help you get it out of your house! But because you are chosen by GOD for HIS purpose, HIM who is the greatest of all, came and removed that poverty spirit at the twinkling of an eye, and replaced it with the abundance of wealth from a resource that you could not imagine. Amen!

"Greater is HE that is in us than the one who is in the world," 1 John 4:4.

When the devil strikes you with his spirit of poverty, and Our GOD allows it, it's only for a moment and HE will come in and remove all that lack and put you into an abundance of life with money and every necessary thing. Our LORD GOD says, we shall not be the borrowers but the lenders. And our GOD is faithful; HE does exactly what He says. What HE promises, HE must fulfill it, and HE must accomplish it.

The only thing we may need to learn about our GOD is that; HE never comes late neither does HE came earlier than HIS time, HE comes in HIS good time. Just in time in the very good time! While you are starting to think that all is gone wrong and nothing on your side shall ever be right again, here HE comes and brings abundance according to HIS promises. When you thought you are going to sink in the sea of poverty and be sold for the debts and devil is causing you to see only how you may be evicted from your apartment. Or your mortgage may be or has already been sent for collection, and your credit report is getting worse unless GOD intervenes. Keep on testifying positively that GOD is going to do something for you and you will not sink.

Stand still and see GOD'S salvation at that moment. Do not keep quiet and cry, talk and give GOD Glory with a testimony about you and about the victory to come. Say, "I have a miracle in my hands because faith is your miracle and it is your substance that you can hold at that moment, and the only evidence you can stand on and show the enemy." Until it is done, you can only testify by faith and say, "The LORD GOD ALMIGHTY has done it and HE has already given us."

Your testimony will scare the devil and he will free.

How can you resist the devil that is oppressing you? By giving the testimony of your GOD'S Victory on everything that you need HIM to do for you!

You see, until David came with a testimony of GOD'S Victory at the valley of Élah, Israel stayed tormented by the enemy Philistine and their giant Goliath.

All the mighty men of war did not remember the LORD GOD ALMIGHTY, who for their sake killed the Egyptians' firstborns, dried the red sea and in it destroyed the Egyptian army. They did not remember how their GOD flattened the wall of Jericho. Owe unto us if we forget where GOD has taken us from. Surely, can we afford to forget all the valleys, and mountains that HE has leveled for us in past? And even what HE did for Israel is enough for us to remember, and thank HIM and wait upon HIS Mercy and Grace.

Your testimony will build others and help them to wait upon the LORD. When in the Name of JESUS CHRIST, you tell the enemy that is standing there relaying with his lies of spear and javelin that he is defeated and destroyed; for you have come to him in the Mighty Name of the LORD JESUS your GOD the Captain of the LORD of Host and your confession works, you

Glorifies GOD and encourages a broken soul. You see, we are not fighting a physical Goliath; we are fighting the spiritual goliaths and the spiritual philistines.

Your purpose is great in the Eyes of GOD!

The reason GOD created you was for his own purpose and not for your own purpose. You did not know that you were created or were going to be created. You did not know that you would be born of the mother and the father who bore you; that is why you should believe that you were not created for yourself.

Can you imagine that none of us could have made a choice of when to be born? Further, we could not pick our parents and neither did they know if you were going to be formed in them. As a matter of fact, they did not even know it when you entered the womb.

No human being can arrange or organize for an ovum to be conceived. It is only GOD who makes it possible. I have heard and seen some couples who have tried to get pregnant even through the most modern test tube pregnancies. Eventually, they give up when they get tired of trying and not succeeding no matter how they trusted their gynecologists. The Doctors try and end up saying; they are not able to do anything helpful for the fertilized ovum to embed in the uterus of the mother. Or other ovum refuses to unite with the spermatozoon for fertilization to take place. Some ova even break and die in the process of embedding in the mother's uterus. But GOD of life brings conception when all fail.

Why do all these things happen?

For GOD to prove man wrong and to show him that; "it is not by might nor by power but by MY SPIRIT;" thus says the LORD," Zechariah 4:6. God can reveal an invention to man but as soon as man decides to make himself a god, the real GOD the Creator withdraws HIS power and knowledge from the man and the man becomes a failure in his methods. Man has to know that GOD created everything plus us human. And every one of us who is born on earth comes to this world for GOD'S purpose not for the purpose of man, nor for the devil. That deceiver Satan has deceived many by designing lies and succeeded with the help of man.1 Corinthians 6: 19-20, starts with a big question, "What? Know ye not that your body is the temple of the Holy Spirit which is in you, which you have of GOD, and you are not your own?" Meaning, every good inventive helpful knowledge in man it's GOD who puts in him to help man serve GOD well. Not for evil uses that man is practicing today like in medical circles, music and financial industries.

The WORD continues to tell us, "For you are bought with a price: therefore, glorify GOD in your body, and in your spirit, which are of GOD." GOD wants us to serve HIM and be successful in every area of this life. But the devil has blinded many of the believers in such a way that they are doing things just like the way the world has been doing in worship to their master the devil. We who are in the LORD JESUS CHRIST, we need to do our things in such a way that our GOD will receive Glory by our actions and our speech. Give thanks unto our GOD for all things and praise HIM in everything. In Philippians 4: 6-7, the Word tells us, "be careful for nothing, but in everything by prayer and supplication with thanks giving let your request be made known unto GOD. And the Peace of GOD, which passes all understanding, shall keep your hearts and minds through CHRIST JESUS." When GOD allowed you to come on this earth by the means that HE used, you were very important to HIM and you need only to realize how much HE loves you. Now, you are about to ask me this question: "if GOD loves so much as you say, then why do I go through so many troubles?" Well, my answer is; first, I too used to ask that same question.

Whenever I saw other people looking happy and prosperous, while I looked and felt miserable and rejected, I used to suffer from self-pity and a lot of pain in my heart and I would wonder, "LORD; I work so hard, when shall I be happy and have prosperity like the other people I see? Some work only one job, but I am working almost round the clock to make ends meet, what am I going to do?"

"Until I entered into the sanctuary of my LORD GOD"; Psalm 73, 17, and searched myself in the LORD and found first, I was entered by the spirit of wanting after I had gone through a lot of challenges during my youth. Praise the LORD that "the name of the LORD is a strong tower. The righteous run into it and are safe." First, look at your past life and see the people you lived with, and what they taught you about yourself. Secondly, did you get a chance to learn how to enjoy the little you have so that you can be able to enjoy the much when GOD gives it to you? And do you know that in this world there is an evil spirit that fights our joy day and night and it is called the enemy of peace, Satan?

Again, have you ever given yourself to true worship of the LORD for you to give HIM glory or do you only ask and ask, without giving back?

Well, your question is good, and the answer is both broad and narrow. Learn how to give GOD glory for all things, and then approach HIS Throne of mercy with thanksgiving and you will see results. You will start getting rich even when you have no money in your pocket. Your bills will be paid without you having to struggle. Immediately you start struggling, you should remember, you are under attack from the enemy. The devil is tempting you, and if you lack worship or you forgot to live the life of worship, then you may give him a chance to win. Or if you are worshiping and it happens that you are surrounded by problems, you are being attacked so that you can give up and stop worshipping your GOD.

Again remember, Psalm 128: 1-2 says, "Blessed is every one that fears the LORD and walks in HIS ways. Thou shall eat the labor of thine hands and happy shall you be and it shall be well with you." It is not devil's good pleasure to see you worship the LORD your GOD and walk in HIS ways. When you worship and walk in the ways of the LORD, you demonstrate the full fear of the LORD and the real hate to devil and his kingdom. Do you know the day when you exactly annoyed the devil and all his demons? It was on the day you declared yourself born again! As you walk and keep on walking in the fear of the LORD your GOD, the devil gets ever bitterer with you. His only hope rests on his belief that you will never stand up for what you believe. Satan believes that he can still take you back to his kingdom. Let GOD help you to walk carefully and never to stop worshiping, and praising your

GOD in Spirit and in Truth. Do not stop, continue to worship and tell Satan that you will continue to worship your Father GOD until JESUS CHRIST comes for you. "From the time of John the Baptist the Kingdom of GOD suffers violence: and the violent take it by force" that way, you will resist Satan and he will flee, and leave you for a while. By the way, the devil never gives up, because he like counterfeiting our Father GOD, so you are also supposed not to give up. Devil knows he has no much power to get you unless he tricks you like Eve but he still persists to get you for his destructions. Nevertheless, our Father GOD will never give up on you and HE can never let Satan "tempt you beyond what you can bear." Luke 4:13 says, "And when the devil ended all the temptation he departed from HIM for a season." If he left our Savior JESUS CHRIST only for a season; meaning for short time, how about us humanity? But there is assurance from our GOD that HE cannot leave us nor forsake us.

GOD will always put a new Spirit in you to be able to bear the pain and the trouble you are going through until HE puts Satan under your feet and make him to go away a shamed. Do you know how heavenly Kingdom rejoices when you have overcome the evil without falling? Please, let us pray that GOD will continue to strengthen us at the time of temptation so that we can rejoice with HIM and the angels as they rejoice over our victory. Your victory is recorded in Heaven and celebrated there: therefore, let us give GOD glory for your victory.

And all your miseries are being turned into missiles and your miserable moments will be turned to Merry. And all your messes into messages; Amen!

There is one thing we need to remember, the group of people you associate with will either bring you to your victory, or to victimization.

I believe by now you know that, the people you associate with determine your entire walk with CHRIST, your success, more than you determine it yourself. If you live with people who do murmur and complain all the time, you will find yourself doing the same even if you never used to. If you live with people who only gossip, you will be a gossiper even if you did not like it before. If you live with people who talk the things of the world only, that will become your talk too. And we do know that, all those things are sinful before GOD and will not bring blessings. Romans 3: 10-14 says, "As it is written, there is none righteous, no, not one: there is none that understands, there is none that seeks after GOD. They have all gone out of the way, they are together become unprofitable; there is none that doeth good, no, not one. Their throat is an open sepulcher; with their tongues they have used deceit; the person of asps is under their lips: whose mouth is full of cursing and bitterness." Who are these human beings the Word is referring to in Romans 3:10-14?

It is very important to deliberate not to entertain anything evil in your talking and in your hearing and in your looking. But that will be determined by how you handle those who are in your company, and it matters a lot how you present yourself to those you associate with. If you have been buried in CHRIST, then you have died into HIS death and raised with HIM into eternal life.

Romans 6:11-14, "Likewise, reckon you also yourselves to be dead indeed unto sin, but alive unto GOD through JESUS CHRIST our LORD. Let not sin therefore reign in your mortal body, that you should obey it in the lusts thereof. Neither yield you your members as instruments of unrighteousness unto sin, but yield yourselves unto GOD, as those that are alive from the dead, and your members as instrument of righteousness unto GOD. For sin shall not have dominion over you: for you are not under the law, but under Grace."

Therefore now, do not entertain anything that is not Godly, so that the LORD GOD of all Grace may abide in you and HIS Blessing may follow you everywhere you will be and in everything that you do, Proverb 3:5, Psalm 34:1-2,8-10,11-15,16-22

As I write this I am also learning from the HOLY SPIRIT what HE wants out of us and I have prayerfully worked very hard on myself to keep my members away from company that can defile my body with their tongues. Psalm 34:12-13, asks, "Who is he that desires life and loves many days that he may see good? Keep thy tongue from evil and thy lips from speaking guile," The summary of keeping ourselves righteous is concluded in Psalm 34:11-14, and19:7-14. It is very possible to have your whole body defiled by what you hear and how you respond to what you hear and see. You can tell who watches secular TV constantly, from one Harry Porter movie to Batman, by their conversation. Your testimony has to be strengthened by the things you converse about. James 2:14-26

This has reminded me of 1977, when I had just graduated from college, and was started working in a hospital. Every time we finished procedures and the patients were calm, the nurses and other staff in my pediatric ward would sit in a circle for a chat.

I was the youngest in the whole group and the only Born again. Mostly, the discussion would start around how to improve patient health. After about 10 minutes, they would engage in other talks like who was the best soccer player. At this point it was still a healthy discussion, but as they continued soon the talk would start touching other people's personal affairs and so on and so forth. While they talked, I would try to enter a Word of GOD but after a short time, I found out that; the Word and I were not welcome there. I discovered the HOLY SPIRIT was getting grieved and HE was not interested in me trying to impose HIM on that group. First and foremost, they knew about my salvation and that alone would make them ridicule me. Some would say that they had once thought themselves saved until they found out that there was nothing like salvation. Others would say that everyone is saved in his own way, and others would say there is nothing like being born again it is all pretense.

I would answer with few words. I would say, "When JESUS CHRIST appears in the air, every eye shall see HIM, and every knee shall bow and every tongue confess that JESUS CHRIST is the LORD to the glory of GOD. But the righteous; those who did not doubt the word of GOD; they will have been taken up to heaven."

I want to be taken up with HIM when HE comes, it does not matter what everyone has to say about Salvation and being born again. Personally, I know it is real and the truth of GOD and life eternal: for I know what my LORD GOD has done in my life and the changes JESUS CHRIST has put in me since I was properly Born Again.

As the other staff continued to talk, I would excuse myself from the group and choose to go to read my Bible then I would go round the ward, praying and encouraging every child. At the visiting hour, when their parents came I had enough time to pray with them and encourage them. Actually, after a few months of working in that ward, GOD turned things around for me and for the patients. It became a sanctuary, and I was filled with joy. No longer did I sit in a circle discussing empty topics.

I found a better job to do with my patients, and their relatives. I invested my time better, in the Word of GOD and in prayer for the sick, which increased my mustard seed faith to grow large enough to cover what I do today. I hate to waste the time GOD has given me here on earth with empty talk. I felt that my ministry to patients was better compensation than the salary I was getting every month.

I still remember most of my young patients that the LORD GOD healed of terminal diseases. I met some of them just before I left the country to come to the U.S. What a blessing to see them in their teenage and others in their early 20s. Whenever I would meet them in the market place or elsewhere with their parents; their parents would introduce them to me with great joy. And I would really thank GOD to meet any of them now that they are grown to adults after my CHRIST JESUS delivered them from the killer diseases where medicine had no hope. I remember in 1981, two babies died. The Doctor certified each one dead, but GOD brought them back life. One had died of epileptic complications and the body was cold and stiff, but GOD had given those mothers confidence that when I prayed, HE did something good to their kids. We had previously prayed several days for healing but the severe attack continued.

I would go off duty come and pray for the healing for each child and many would get healed and go home well but this one child was not healed. One day I reported on duty at 7am 30minutes earlier than usual, when the mother of this one baby boy saw me enter into the ward; quickly she went and picked the body of her son where it had been laid waiting for the undertaker to come and take the body to the morgue. This mother in tears threw the body to me like a ball saying," If you didn't go, Gitonga would not have died!" I held the baby's body and cried to my Father GOD Almighty in the Mighty Name of JESUS CHRIST with a lot of feeling. I felt much stuck not knowing what to do since I saw the mother run way outside screaming saying, "My baby! My baby!" Oh, LORD! I remember that day as if it is today. I cried with a loud voice like I was in a place I cannot tell, and called upon the name of the LORD. GOD is gracious and merciful; HE saw the situation that Mama had put me into. The boy forcefully sneezed out the packing cotton out of his nostrils. The nurses who were with me there run and removed the cotton packs out of the mouth and from every orifice. Immediately the boy cried out like a new born baby.

When I saw that the baby was alive again, I was astonished, and I was like, LORD! YOU MEAN YOU HAVE DONE IT SO FAST? I shouted a big Hallelujah and everyone else answered Hallelujah! Praise JESUS CHRIST! I had seen supernatural healing of all kinds of diseases but apart from my brother who my mother had prayed for when he was dead of measles when I was about 5 and he rose up also sneezing blood clots, I had not seen any other dead come to life. I was thrilled and amazed of the LORD. Some nurses went running looking for the mother and found her at the bus stop where she was desperately waiting for a bus to go home. She came in fearfully not knowing what to say as she took her baby thanking GOD. And we were all very grateful to GOD.

After several months, another one; the 8 months baby died of a very severe Bronchopneumonia. His mother had learned; for the few days she had been in that ward, whenever I am working I call the mothers and we pray for the children and I was also going round praying for each kid as we treat them. These wards are open halls with beds and on each bed there would be about two to three babies with their mothers sitting on bedsides.

I believe things have not changed in the 12 years I have been out of that country. In this particular case, the mother of this boy run away from the ward when she saw the Doctor and the Nurses removing out of the boy the fluids, oxygen, and other life support equipment that were put on him. I was coming in for the evening shift. When I saw her running away, I knew the baby may not be alive. I run to the ward and indeed, they were preparing the boy for the last office. They had done the one hour resuscitation but in vain, and waited for one more hour with no life coming back. I saw and felt my legs and the whole body moved towards this boy's body and all what I remember is kneeling there beside that bed and I cried, "O LORD! Please, LORD! Master JESUS CHRIST let him come back." I cannot remember all that came out of my mouth but all what I know and the others witnessed was the boy came back and cried like a new born baby sneezing and coughing up all the congestion in his throat. The mother who had run away to kill herself was brought back and took her baby happily.

In April 1998, just before I came to the U.S., a young man of 16 years was introduced to me by his mother and he gave to me and others around his testimony about his relationship with JESUS CHRIST. He said that his mother had told him that JESUS CHRIST had brought him back to life. I encouraged him to live a life worthy and full of JESUS CHRIST so that he can fulfill the purpose of GOD bringing him back to life. When after prayer the LORD heals or brings back to life, it is not that person who is praying who prays; it is the HOLY SPIRIT who prays and uses the mouth of that faithful believer; James 5: 15-20. For indeed, I cannot tell you what happens that moment when the HOLY SPIRIT is about to heal or on bring life back! When GOD is going to use you in HIS Mighty Work; one really moves in a movement that is not of real human. At times, I have prayed when it is me praying in human compassion and mostly the healing may not come instantly and sometime it may never come. But when it is the HOLY SPIRIT, I am caught up in the power that moves me to speak and do things in an extraordinarily way such that I do not recall myself. I am no longer there. I love that moment of abundance of great anointing of the SPIRIT OF GOD.

Early 1997, in a different hospital not far from the other, (actually, in my hospital Sunrise Hospital in Embu, Kenya) I remember a mother insisting that I pray for her daughter to come back to life. But I was feeling, no, there is no confirmation of the HOLY SPIRIT. And I could not tell her I can't do it. She had already been told about a 68 year brother that I had prayed for when I found he had died and his wife sitting miserably sad beside his hospital bed. It was about three to four months when this mother now came with her daughter who had died on their way to the hospital. She knew the brother and she had been told how he came to life; she could not let me go away without praying her daughter back to life. It was a very frustrating moment. I tried to pray and both prayed but I could perceive in my spirit we are doing a zero job. I thank GOD FOR THE HOLY SPIRIT and for HIS Wisdom. I had to pray for the mother to be given understanding and I talked to her kindly explaining slowly that it is the work of GOD the Father to heal through HIS SON JESUS CHRIST. And unless the HOLY SPIRIT moves me towards it, I have no power of my own to do anything. There is nothing one can do without the HOLY SPIRIT helping and moving one towards GOD'S manifestations of HIS only begotten Son JESUS CHRIST. It has to be GOD and one has to be fully dependent of the HOLY SPIRIY to be completely moved in there, and be completely separated from everything else. Only do that ministry as the LORD moves you to it. It can be very frustrating if you think every sick and dead person GOD is going to heal or bring back to life. HE knows why and when death or sickness is coming since nothing happens behind his back. Though Satan brings diseases and calamities, GOD allows them to come. Some to make us learn and HIS Name be glorified and others to take us home those who are Born Again. Those who are living like the good rich man in Luke 16:19-31, they die and join the rich man in hell. I am sorry, but I have to say this even though I feel for them and pray for myself to live a righteous life until my savior comes for me, and those who have not made up their mind to commit their lives to JESUS CHRIST to be rescued from dying in sin and go to hell.

I have given those four cases as an example of what GOD can do with us when we separate ourselves from the world. I am not saying I was better than those others in that hospital. No! By all means that is not what I am saying. What I am saying is, GOD is ready to bless and use us, but we cannot be blessed and be used if our talk is about things of this world and we walk the worldly walk. We have to be separated from this world both physically, and spiritually. We have to exalt the name of the LORD as the only Most Supreme, and make HIM the only ONE we need.

There are times you will have to separate yourself and be alone with the LORD your GOD only for you to see GOD move and do miracles. For months, or a year or more I became like an outcast in that hospital, but loving all the staff and hating nobody. And my GOD was at my side with signs and wonders of numerous miracles to patients, even some to the staff, and to me too. It was after that separation (sanctifying and not hatred) the LORD had mercy on me and I got promoted to a position I did not deserve. My GOD moved me form that hospital to a place nearer to our house and in a better position as an in-charge to start a new health institution fully government sponsored. If I say, I saw GOD'S favor in my early life of Salvation I would be telling the truth. Whenever the enemy of my Father who is also my enemy Satan, tried to displace me using whoever he wants, my LORD GOD would raise a standard against HIM and do an extra-ordinarily new thing. I remember, after the LORD GOD moved with healing in those two children's wards, between '78 and '81, the SPIRIT OF THE LORD convinced many and GOD started saving some nurses and other employees who were very stubborn in that hospital. And those who were saved before started getting encouraged. I write this with great humility. There, I was nobody and even now I am nobody but a child of MOST HIGH GOD who lives mostly in a lot of humiliation but in GOD'S Grace and Mercy.

When we love our GOD, we must feel jealousy when the world is ridiculing HIS Word and HIS Work. Why should we stay there to hear them talk bad about our Father? Our uncontaminated testimony is very important. It is our best missile at the time of need. If you let your testimony be defiled by the company you associate with, you are weakening your missile, and this is very dangerous for you. Your testimony will save you at the time when no one is on your side, and even when beloved ones cannot help you: it is your testimony and the Blood of the Lamb JESUS CHRIST that will save you. You know, you cannot have the Blood of JESUS without the testimony of HIS Blood and his saving grace.

Further, you cannot be under the Grace without the Blood; and all are attested by the testimony you give. In the book of Daniel 3:16-18 &19-22&23-30 the testimony of the three young men moved mountains out of the king's heart. It is written that after seeing the power of GOD of the three young men he threw into the furnace fire, King Nebuchadnezzar ordered that all the people should only worship the GOD of Shadrach, Meshach and Abednego.

In addition, the three received promotions after their testimony of who they are before the LORD GOD Almighty. This all came about as a result of their refusal to bow before the idol that Nebuchadnezzar had raised to be worshiped. The three gave a testimony about their GOD and said they could never worship an image. The King ordered them burned to death. Not fearing death, they went into the fire worshiping their True GOD, and JESUS CHRIST THE SON OF THE MOST HIGH GOD entered into that fire before them to quench it for HIS Beloved Sons; for HE is greater fire. Beholding the might of their God, Nebuchadnezzar's faith was changed and so was that of his people. The same case happened with Daniel in Daniel 2:1-49 when King Nebuchadnezzar dreamed a dream he could not remember or understand; Daniel was given the dream and its interpretation by GOD as he prayed in agreement with Shadrach, Meshach, and Abednego. King Nebuchadnezzar spired the lives of his advisers including Daniel and promoted Daniel. Read the book of Daniel 2:1-49, if you are not familiar to that Word of life and your testimony will increase power if you believe the same can happen to you. GOD can use you in the same or greater mighty way as Daniel and these other three Brethren. Also, King Darius, in Daniel 6:1-28, was made to order Daniel to be thrown into the den of lions. After Daniel slept a whole night with hungry lions in the same den and found alive the following day, Daniel was highly promoted because he stood by his testimony. When you give a clean testimony, the enemy will try it but do not worry, stand by it for it is the Word of GOD and HE cannot fail it, and HE can never let Satan disapprove it. We have heard and seen very many healing testimonies: but know this; the Word of GOD is tried, 2 Samuel 21:31

CHAPTER 18

Financial testimonies

Let us hear the testimony of GOD'S financial provision.

I have seen my GOD standing on HIS Word of being a provider, a giving and a supplying Father at a time when things looked very bad financially. Whenever Satan comes in like a flood to defraud my finances and leave me with bills and debts, my GOD knows how to raise a standard against HIM. And HE provides miraculously. I have learned that being gloomy with self-pity causes me to murmur and get nothing from my GOD. Now I have a new way of approaching my financial situation, and I believe that this is what majority of successful brethren do: I stand on my Father's promises and proclaim my blessing upon every need that I have. Sometimes, it forces me to rebuke the enemy and cast him away from my spiritual and physical areas so that I can be able to have a breakthrough.

Remember, the devil is a spirit and he can be anywhere any time unless you forbid him. That is why JESUS in Luke 10:19

pronounced that HE had given us power over the scorpions, the snakes, and over all the powers of the enemy. JESUS knew and knows that Satan appears anywhere anytime and in any invisible form of spiritual deadly things like snakes and scorpions. You will not see Satan with your naked eyes, but spiritually you will experience some funny feeling especially sadness and fear of the unknown. Know at that time the devil is biting or stinging you through situations and circumstances, and he is preventing you from making a breakthrough in your worship. When you try to say prayer words inside you or by mouth that brings you to a real energetic spiritual worship you start feeling tired or lazy, or dumb or get a headache or feel miserable, sad, lethargic, discouraged, or sleepy or interrupted by things you can't tell where they coming from. I mean, you cannot even give an account of what made you not to get time to pray and worship JESUS THE LORD. If you had not done anything to exhaust you physically or taken some medication that makes you feel drowsy, then know the enemy is trying to keep you from Worshiping so that you do not overcome him and get your breakthrough blessings.

Satan will try heard to make sure that you don't defeat him and be victorious. But JESUS CHRIST CAME so that HE may give life full of victory, Amen!

Therefore, at that moment, you need to stand strong spiritually and cast the devil away, Mark 16: 17, in the Name of JESUS CHRIST! And tell him, he has no power over you and he cannot control your life neither does he have any control over your worship to your Father GOD. Start giving GOD thanks and all the glory, honor, and all the power and adoration and worship HIM in all ways. Tell Satan you must worship the one who died for you. Tell JESUS of HIS worth and that all the power and the glory are HIS, for HE is a righteous and Holy GOD. HE accepted to come to die for you and became your Savior, healer, deliverer, redeemer, mediator, best companion, overcomer, your sleep and your waking up, your life, all that you needed, and need now to eternity, the KING of all Kings, and the LORD of all Lords.

The LORD who cares for HIS servants and Father who cares most for his children, and who will never leave neither forsake you. Tell HIM, "LORD, I bow before you, I worship you dear LORD Sweet JESUS. My LORD, I Love You so much! Ooh! Hallelujah! I Praise You JESUS! I Love you my LORD and my GOD, I Love You and I praise YOU! Jehovah Jireh, Jehovah Raphah, Jehovah Sabaoth, Jehovah El-shaddai! Jehovah Nissi, Jehovah Abba-father, I Worship YOU! O LORD GOD ALMIGHTY, THERE IS NO ONE LIKE YOU! CHRIST JESUS, You accepted the crown of thorns so that I can have a beautiful crown of life with stars of gold and diamonds! Praise, Honor and Power is to your HOLY NAME MY SAVIOR!" When you reverence your LORD that way, HE feels good and releases all the power and the blessings you need. Amen!

CHAPTER 19

The Instrument of Praise is the best Missile

GIVING GOD PAISES AND HONOR; Things are done quickly:

Our Father who is in Heaven loves to hear our voices rising unto HIM in worship and praises. And if we can learn to keep our line connected unto HIM in the rule of 24x7x12: "not 7-11" that is 24 hours 7 days a week, 12months a year, until JESUS CHRIST will come to take us home, then we can be sure of quick Heavenly Kingdom supplies.

Sometimes, we need money or some other things that can or cannot be bought with money very urgently and we may not be aware about it, but our heavenly Father knows all about it because

HE is the Omniscience GOD. Even before we open our mouth to pray, HE knows what we need. However, we must pray and ask to receive. WORSHIPING GOD is the only Missile that devil cannot stand. Immediately you start worshiping GOD in Spirit and in Truth, demons start fleeing one by one speedily. Demons of frustration flee and ones that held your finances flee. The ones that held your prosperity flee, as you continue to worship The LORD GOD ALMIGHTY IN THE NAME OF JESUS CHRIST, the demons that were standing holding your healing away from you flee. And those that held your joy captive; those who took away your peace and love; as well as others who sat on your faith, they all flee, and you start experiencing a tremendous surge of joy, love and peace in you. A great faith encompasses you, letting you know that everything is going to be alright. Your faith in GOD grows stronger and you start feeling a lot of Love for your GOD. The HOLY SPIRIT will keep on reminding you that your father has done all that you have previously asked him to do for you, and so is HE doing the rest for you now and tomorrow.

You will gain the strength to wait upon and receive from GOD the Father. Wisdom, knowledge and understanding of Godliness start flowing in you and you start receiving your gifts as your LORD GOD gives you. It is important to learn how to worship the LORD GOD with your entire heart and with all your might. The only hindrance to this may be the limitation of the Power of the HOLY SPIRIT in you. If you have not been endured or baptized with Power as Our LORD JESUS CHRIST commanded the disciples before HE ascended, it may be difficult to worship in the Spirit and in Truth in that tremendous way that I am talking about. Read here: Luke 24:49-53,Acts 1: 8, 2:1-4, 14-21, Joel 2:28 to see the promises of our LORD GOD and the instructions of the fullness of GOD'S MERCY In the provision of HIS Power IN THE HOLY SPIRIT. You need to pray and start praising and worshiping the LORD desire and asking for that gift of the Power of the HOLY SPIRIT, it is yours for the asking, Matthew 7:7-11, Luke 11: 9-13. This is not a religious teaching, this is a relationship teaching. If you have not: I am teaching you to get to the real relationship with JESUS CHRIST; the one who died for you and to get you out of the bonds of religion. It takes full commitment and enthusiasm to be able to wait praying, and praising worshiping GOD for the baptism in the HOLY SPIRIT. You wait thanking HIM as you have received, yet you are asking.

Every one of us we are born into a religion because from the fall of Adam and Eve, man became a religious being. The spirit of religion is rebellious and idolatrous. That is why there are very many religions on earth. Even before CHRIST came, there were very many religions competing with *each other*. Relationship does not compete; relationship has her unique Character of true love, peace, joy, and faithfulness to the winning of the soul of each other for heaven not for self. Religions look for multitudes and fame, not for the truth. Whether people in their congregations are living according to the Biblical Moral Principles and Ethics or not, it's not the business of religious leaders; because it's not a big deal to them for one to die and go to hell. Provided their number is growing in their circles, it is alright. Relationship seeks for the people as many as are led by the SPIRIT OF GOD to heaven. Relationship knows very well that we have no a permanent dwelling place here on earth, and we need to preach the Gospel of repentance in CHRIST JESUS to receive HIS Divine love in order to get to Heaven one day. Relationship knows very well that we do not know the hour of JESUS coming and we cannot waste time with many things that are not taking people to heaven. Amen!

We need to preach and encourage each other, so that we can stay in the kingdom and not go out. I am talking about our relationship with JESUS CHRIST and not a religion. The Baptism of the HOLY SPIRIT is one of the promises of LORD JESUS and it is as old as the Old Testament is. Moses experienced the same, Joshua, and David, Daniel and his 3 companion brethren, Elijah, Elisha and all the Prophets, and Joel Prophesied about our time from the time JESUS CHRIST was Glorified: the Power followed, John 14: 16, 15:26, 16:13, Acts 1:8, Acts 2:1-4. You cannot be able to preach effectively without receiving the Power and the Fire of the HOLY SPIRIT, Matthew 3:11, John 1: 33 to consume the carnal mind which is enmity to the SPIRIT OF GOD; Roman 8:1-8.

Every Christian needs the Power of the HOLY SPIRIT for it is our promise from our Father GOD Almighty. And I say this, I have observed and seen, many Christians receive the Power, but because in their denominational circles there is no teaching of HOLY SPIRIT Baptism, they fail to acknowledge that they have been baptized in the Power of GOD; therefore, they hinder the manifestations. Salvation is a gift from the LORD GOD Almighty and no one else can give it to you. The gifts of the Holy Spirit are also received by faith and individually. Wake up and receive the gift of the LORD, and do not let people cause you to stumble, for you will face the journey alone when the time comes. Only JESUS CHRIST will be there with you when you go to heaven, if you believe in HIM. If you don't believe in JESUS CHRIST as your LORD and Savior, then you will not go to heaven, hell awaits you, I am sorry, I am here to tell you the Truth for only the Truth can "set you free" and free indeed; John 8:32. Accept CHRIST JESUS, HE is easy and ready for you; for HE alone can save you and baptize you as you wait willingly on HIM.

Those other brethren who went before will not be there. Even if your Mum and Dad are very saved; they won't come to help you get into heaven. When your time to get out of this earth comes, or if the trumpet of the LORD is sounded by an Archangel at the appearing of OUR LORD JESUS CHRIST, YOUR PARENTS WON'T BE THERE TO HELP YOU TRANSFORM AND BE LIKE THE LORD JESUS AND BE ABLE TO MEET HIM IN THE AIR; 1 Thessalonians 4:14-18,1Corinthians 15: 49-54. If they truly were born again, they will transform each one separately or independently; no one will be helping one another. So do not be fooled! Don't follow people's ideas. Follow JESUS CHRIST'S teaching and that of HIS Apostles. Follow all that is in the Holy Scripture, 2 Timothy 3:16-17. Anything that JESUS promised in the Old Testament, and to the early believers and it's recorded in the Old and New Testament, it is ours also, and it is our right to ask for and get it, Amen.

I would not have let anyone talk me out of following my Savior JESUS CHRIST to the river, for baptism with much water. I knew it is my right because it is there in the Bible. I did not need consent from my parents or anyone! No! They were not there when JESUS CHRIST AND I MET. And when JESUS CHRIST made the HOLY SPIRIT convince me that I am a sinner! Even if they were seated next to me, they are my parents; yes, I agree and I love them but they would not have known that the LORD JESUS was saving me at that moment. My Mum had tried to preach to me, but she had not convinced me that I was a sinner until that day the Word she had used many years before touched my Soul and I made up my mind to accept that; I am truly a sinner, and I need JESUS CHRIST to save me in order to be able to live a sinless happy life.

Therefore, I did not need to go to ask them if I needed to be baptized. The word of GOD tells me expressly, it is after repentance of the sin that I am supposed to be baptized. It is not after going through Catechism or denominational classes. Those classes are good, for teaching people the Bible, if they are taught as the Word is written in the Bible and not in a distorted manner to block the truth. So, I had read the Word in the Bible, and I was convinced that, besides the Biblical name I received, and the verbal denominational confession I made; I need total repentance to let CHRIST in me. Then after I really confessed my sins, those I knew and that I did not know, and accepted CHRIST in my life; now, I needed to be baptized like my Savior JESUS CHRIST, although my Savior had not sinned. HE was Holy and needed not to die. HE did all for me: to teach me how to fulfill all righteousness of the LORD after repentance of my sin and the washing of the Blood, Matthew 3:15, Mark 1:2-9, Luke 3:16 read vs 2-23, John 1: 29-33

Repentance or confession of the sins brings washing of sins in the Blood and that is the First Baptism; one is supernaturally immersed in the Blood for cleansing of the sins and it is best to live supernaturally inside there in the Blood. The second Baptism is of inside the water to be physically immersed into the deep water and come out of water signifying that the old man died to CHRIST when you entered into the Blood of JESUS CHRIST. And now you have buried that old man with CHRIST inside the water and you have risen with HIM as a new man in CHRIST to the newness of life, 1 John 5:4-8! Also, read Matthew 3:13-17, Mark 1:10-11, Acts 8:26-39, Acts 44-48; actually, you can read Acts 10:1-48, it is full of GOD'S mysteries. Immersion or baptism means to be buried in the Greek translation.

The biggest problem we are having today in the body of CHRIST is that the devil came to divide us by revising the Bible, removing some of the powerful words and works of the LORD. Also, Christians being too busy to read the Bible and meditate every Word they read as an Important Word of GOD to them they only listen the radio or TV Preachers. Some of these deeds in the Bible are quite clear, such as JESUS' baptism by John on the river Jordan. You might hear a religious preacher today say that JESUS CHRIST went to Jordan to have a little water poured on HIS forehead by John! Surely, the Bible says clearly, "when HE came out of the Water," Matthew 3:16-17, Mark 1:10-11, John 3:22-29. I thank my GOD that I learned my early Bible lessons at school with great interest; and from the Anglican Church where I grew up, I read from the original Bible. The original Bible has since been revised several times removing most of the Word that would help a learning Christian feel the Power of the HOLY SPIRIT IN THE WORD.

The original Bible, no matter what language it was written in, had the Power of the Word. Today's Christian needs to read the Word from the original Bible as they grow in the Word and be able to get the real meaning and the taste of the Word before they read revised Bibles. I am not condemning revised Bibles, no! I am just saying it has some omissions or removal of GOD'S Word; diluting the Power of the Word leaving it not as emphatic as the original

King James Version or other old versions that were copied from the original Hebrew languages of the Bible. King James Language is very sweet for worshipping and it leads the reader to feel the Power there is in the Word. However, please do not mistake me, the WORD of GOD IS STRONG IN WHATERVER VERSION IT IS, IT REMAINS THE WORD OF GOD! Get to the word and worship. All these preachers you see very successful in their ministries nationwide and internationally are all worshipers of GOD IN SPIRIT AND IN TRUTH. I mean the true preachers of the Gospel; those who preach the Word under the Power and Anointed Authority of the HOLY SPIRIT, and not those who are using some other powers like alcohol, some drugs to feel high and some magnetic devices to confuse GOD'S people. NO! I don't mean those kind of money preachers! The SPIRIT TEACHES. Therefore, worship in the Power of GOD'S Spirit and HIS Truth and you will really enjoy your worship, Amen!

When I speak of Worshiping in the Power of the Spirit of GOD, I do not mean worshiping in one kind of physical like worship while shaking the body or shouting and howling, and crying, No! That is not what I mean. Neither am I condemning vigorous movement nor shouting nor crying, no! It depends on what the HOLY SPIRIT is moving you to do, so long as it's the SPIRIT of GOD and not personal emotions used by the enemy. Some of you may know what I mean. You can whisper or look focused on the LORD with no words heard by others, but you are inside there feeling the presence of the LORD GOD mightily in you and around you and in your worship receiving love, joy, peace, and anything you are praying for by faith. Some brethren have been born and baptized with power as they worship and they have not known about it because somehow, they feared to be seen speaking in new heavenly tongues. Or they did not recognize when they were baptized in the HOLY SPIRIT to receive the sign of tongues that brings the breakthrough.

If you can worship while focused and be able to glorify GOD in your worship for several hours without being distracted by other thoughts or interruptions, you must be living in the power of the HOLY SPIRIT. All what you need to do my sister, my brother is to ask the LORD to manifest HIMSELF in you by the breakthrough of speaking in New Heavenly Tongues. If you cannot Worship even for 10 minutes or you do not know how to worship Glorifying GOD, even for a minute; all what you are able to say are some words of asking and a few thanks giving words or sometimes you just say, "GOD we/ I thank you for this and give me/us this and that we/I need this and that and amen." Well, that is a good prayer, but that is not really what real Worship is! Worship consists of deep-felt thanksgiving, and praises, as you enter in the Gates of GOD'S throne; the gate of HIS Heart with thanksgiving in your heart to activate the opening of HIS door for you to enter into HIS Courts to praise HIM: The Psalmist sang, in Psalm 100:4 "I will enter HIS Gates with thanks giving in my heart, I will enter HIS Courts with praise, and I will say this is the day that the LORD has made, I will rejoice for HE has made me glad" let us sing it and rejoice now for HE has made us glad.

CHAPTER 20

CHRIST JESUS My Financier

What do you do when you cannot pay your bills and you have no idea where the next penny is going to come from for you to buy even food to put in your belly? You cannot drive to go to look for a job because you do not have money for gas, and you do not know what to do next? You have spent all what you had saved in previous jobs and now jobs are not available? Will you sleep and die or what are you going to do? Let me tell you what I did, and what I do whenever that moment comes in my life. I have been a victim of devil stealing the money GOD gives me so many times such that I have learned to live without sufficient money for a long time. Sometimes I live without any money but you wouldn't know unless I tell you. Sometimes I tell someone who may come to ask me for some money, or I may not tell if I do not need to.

By the way, before I tell you what I do, let me also tell you that GOD gave me a gift of giving. I can really give and not money only; even time; especially for GOD'S Work, but I thank GOD for that is banking where moths and thieves cannot reach. In Malachi 3:8 says, "Will a man rob GOD? Yet you have robbed me. But you say, wherein have we robbed Thee?" The LORD answers, "In tithe and offerings." Verse 9 continues to say, "ye are cursed with a curse: for you have robbed me, *even* this whole nation.' Verse 10 says and in a command from the Master, the Creator, "Bring ye all the tithes into the storehouse, that there will be meat in my house, and you will prove me now wherewith, says the LORD of hosts, if I will not open you the windows of heaven and pour you blessings, that there shall not *be room* enough *to receive it*." Verse 11, "And I will rebuke the devourer for your sakes, and he shall not destroy the fruits of your ground; neither shall vine cast her fruit before the time in the field, says the LORD of hosts."

Do you hear what the Master of all masters has said; HE wants our tenth of everything that we have. Sometimes it is not possible to give the tenth of everything that comes your way, and that is why I love and pray for GOD to help me when I have money not to be carried away by needs. I love doubling my tithe or tripling it as the LORD gives me so that if I get any money or any gift, it is **already covered by my willingness to give. First, you must know it is the** willingness for giving that helps you and not the giving. You must be willing to give in order for you to receive. Over the years, I have gone through a lot of financial problems and many other kinds of problems in this world so much that I wonder if they are temptations or tortures. But any way, it is for my learning so that I can be able to relate with those who may get in such difficulties. Also, be able to help others when they go through financial problems and all those other afflictions that the enemy brings to humanity. I thank GOD for every problem and trouble I have gone through. I really thank GOD so much to have let **me learn all that I have learned in the past and to help me in such** hard times as we are in today to stand on HIS promises that will never fail; Psalm 119:71.

Sometimes it is so hard that I do not know what I am going to do the next minute, and I do not feel like I can be able to wait another second in that situation. But let me tell you, for sure, I do not know neither do I understand how GOD takes me through such times, and how HE saves me. What I know is, I do not crush, or die, or go crazy nor am I left to drift away from the **LORD**; Oh praise the **LORD GOD ALMIGHTY. HE is a wonderful MIGHTY LOVING GOD! At such times, I find myself very** composed, strong, worshiping **GOD. Well, there are times I do cry and feel like I am down-trodden, or I may fall, but in my tears, the HOLY SPIRIT holds my hands and HE tells me, "Worship the LORD, for that is your duty, your duty is not to cry and fall into the sin of self-pity." The whole duty of man is defined as to "fear GOD and keep HIS commandments;" Ecclesiastes 12:13. In which in the Ten Commandments, the LORD meant that we need to worship HIM alone and without focusing on our problems.**

Sometimes, I have found myself worshiping problems because the devil comes to magnify them. Right now, just a few minutes before I resumed this writing, I was telling a friend how I found myself murmuring and grumbling because I have not paid some pressing bills, and I do not know where to get a coin from. That Satan the devil started magnifying his problems and focusing me only on the money problems, so

that I do not see and count the blessings of my Father. Devil did not want me to remember that my Father has healed my daughter from the deadly poison that she was given and that had put her into unconsciousness for more than a week. Devil is a liar but a defeated one!

When we were praying for her healing and interceding that the LORD may bring her up, the enemy was saying, she will never come out of this condition; she is going to die, and if she lives she will never be normal. Thank GOD she came out of that poison Satan had given her through his agent. She regained consciousness normal, with a sound mind, saved and sanctified; the LORD JESUS CHIRST increasing in her. Everything that the enemy was saying was a lie for he is a liar from the beginning, and the father of all lies. But, my LORD said; Genesis 15:1, "if I am your shield, your great reward, and your provider, then know my banks are never closed day and night! And all those other problems are all going to end and leave you standing if only you can stand on my promises." Is that not very sweet to hear a voice like that of assurance from your Heavenly Father? Wherefore, whenever HE tells me to worship HIM, I just wake up wherever I happen to be and not matter what I am doing, I start worshiping my LORD GOD.

Mostly, I have learned to stay in worship even when I am working in the office or in the kitchen, and when I am talking with people; I love to talk things that will give GOD glory. When I am driving, I thank GOD for giving me a car; I really worship as I drive and the driving becomes so sweet, and safe. I worship speaking and singing in all the languages that I know and even in the heavenly Tongues until I feel all the Kingdom of heaven in me and with me. You can draw the throne of GOD where you are because, GOD HIMSELF is HIS Throne. For where HE is, that is where everything is; yet, HE is all over and HIS throne is established within HIMSELF. It is difficult to explain some of these revelations. I enter HIS gates with thanksgiving in my heart, and HIS courts with Praise. So, whenever I start thanking HIM, HIS gates open, then I go in and start praising HIM so as to get to HIS Courts.

When you are at HIS Courts, then you can go farther and farther as you go closer approaching HIM to get you into HIS inner court at the MERCY Seat behind the veil near to the Ark of the Covenant at the throne of Mercy where sin and devil can never enter.

Where is that?

In the Holy OF Holies of the Most Holy Royal Throne of the KING of all Kings. When you worship with thanksgiving and praises, the worship takes you to GOD'S Kingdom, by GOD bringing HIS Kingdom to you. In Isaiah 46: 9 the LORD says, "for I am GOD, and there is no other; I am GOD none like ME." When CHRIST JESUS taught us to ask our Father who Art in Heaven, to let HIS Kingdom come on earth, I believe that is what he was exactly telling us; Matthew 6: 8-13. And the Scripture says; "GOD dwells in the praises of HIS people," so the more you worship, the more you get GOD to dwell in you. And the more you murmur, the more you send GOD away from you. LORD GOD ALMIGHTY, HELP US THAT WE LEARN TO WORSHIP AND NOT TO MURMUR, AND GRUMBLE; we ask this in JESUS Holy Name! Amen!

As I worship, first, my LORD makes me forget all the lack that the devil has brought around me and I start seeing HIS riches in glory becoming mine, and I start seeing HIM supplying all my needs, and then mostly, HE reminds me that HE paid all my debts on the cross and none was left unpaid. Therefore, whenever Satan brings to me his debt; I tell him, "It is paid: and devil! You should not worry me with your lies! There is no mountain that my Father cannot level and HE climbs all and 'makes all the crocked ways straight and breaks all the bars of iron and brass for me to give me even the treasures of the dark places and hidden riches of secrete places, that you may know that I, the LORD which called thee by thy name I AM GOD of Israel,'" Isaiah 45:2-3. The best Worship is when you use the same words that the LORD has used in promising you blessings. Refer to the Word for the WORD of GOD is GOD HIMSELF and nothing was made and can be made without GOD and without HIS WORD, John 1:1-4, and Genesis 1:3-24, 25-31. "The earth is the LORD'S and the fullness therein" Psalms 24.

Secondly, the LORD at that time of worship, HE reminds me about some provision of money some place that I had forgotten, or he shows me how to use what I have until it is enough. I believe that God can multiply even money that is in your bank account as HE did with the five loaves and two fish. Actually, sometimes I do not know how I pay bills with the money I had, and how we eat. It has been an amazing thing to me most of the time. Whenever I forget to worship, problems start creeping in, I have to live that way and I ask my GOD to help me live a life of worshiping HIM until CHRIST will come to take me home. It is a life of all riches and a life lacking nothing, Psalm 23.

There are moments that Satan comes raging like a flood with things from very close members of the family that I cannot ignore. If I forget to worship, and start acting naturally, I start sinking like Peter in the sea of those problems. Do you know problems can become a deeper sea than the Sea of Galilee? Yes, one can sink there into the sea of problems until no one knows where you are. It is the deepest sea that the devil created for the children of GOD. A sea called lack of this and lack of that and I do not have, and I am not getting this. Whatever it is, there is nothing our GOD cannot give. And what HE has not provided today, HE will give you tomorrow. If HE is not giving you, it is because you do not need it. Our GOD knows what we need and what is best for us. Sometimes, I see sisters getting sick for lack of husbands. That has been one of the biggest problems for sisters in these last days. Worship the LORD Sister and let JESUS be your eternal Husband. Making JESUS your only Husband means getting things done. JESUS will never tell you, "I do not have money to pay that bill." Or tell you, "You need to look for a job now. I cannot be the only one to bring money in this house." No! HE is the entire provider even for those men. Well, I am not saying a husband is bad, no; by all means it is good to have one. But if the LORD GOD ALMIGHTY has not brought one yet, why have a headache, get depressed, and all the stress that the devil can provide, when JESUS came to give you HIS life and more abundantly?

To conclude this section, let me say, I have applied the method of worshipping my GOD and worshiping off the bills, debts, and many financial problems over years, and it works. Some of these bills are false bills, and false debts, but our GOD knows when Satan is bringing his false bills to us and those false debts. GOD pays them in the most miraculous ways. Of course, everything from our GOD is the Best.

FROM VICTIM TO VICTOR

Are you a victim? Very Soon, You will be a victor. In JESUS HOLY NAME!

Before you complete reading this book, by faith you will have become a victor and come out of all your suffering; Amen! In Matthew 9: 28-29, Before JESUS healed the two blind men HE asked them, "Do you believe I am able to do this?" "And they said to HIM, Yes, LORD!" "Then HE touched their eyes, saying, "According to your faith, let it be to you" And in verse 20-22, the woman with the issue of the blood, "JESUS turned around and when he saw her HE said, 'Be of good cheer daughter, your faith has made you whole.'" That means, JESUS knew this lady and had already seen her come as a daughter coming to the Father knowing that there is no other who could help her. JESUS knew she was a reject in the community and she had spent all her money on physicians. She had given the gynecologist all that belonged to her, but they could not get a chemical or a kind of surgery that could stop her bleeding. She could have suffered hormonal imbalance or fibroids that had grown over the years slowly until they became advanced, or slow cancer of cervix that was culminating into cancer of uterus. She was a woman with a very big problem more than what I have heard many preachers describe. Some preachers out of ignorance say, she had gonorrhea, others say any kind of S.T.D. Gonorrhea cannot have made her bleed for 12 years.

By the way, commonly, any abnormal or persistent women bleeding does not come as result of Sexual Transmitted Diseases (STD); some STDs may causes light PV bleeding due to mucus membrane inflammation causing irritation into the bladder. One type or two of STDs cause urethral painful bleeding but most of them cause no bleeding at all. There are other causative factors with signs and symptoms signifying such sicknesses that we may not discuss here. Actually, her problem must have been a very severe gynecological condition. **Nevertheless, on that day, she met with her Father, her Lover, her Healer and her Comforter, YESHUA HA-MESSIAH (JESUS CHRIST).** She seems not to have had a husband, or a relative to accompany her. Maybe she did not even have children. Whatever had caused the bleeding may have kept her from childbearing; who knows, hence divorce. So she had no escort to the LORD like the palsy man with the four friends who carried him to MESSIAH, and whose faith made him whole. Here, we see faith is very important. Most of the people that CHRIST healed they were told, either their faith or the faith of their loving relatives or friends had made them whole.

The society may reject you, but YOUR FATHER, who Art in Heaven will never leave you nor forsake you. You may feel a victim of so many things that the devil has brought your way. For example, sickness, financial crisis, and betrayal by your best friend whom you trusted very much or rejection by the people you love. Even the community may reject you for lack of what the majority has. But remember, you have JESUS CHRIST. Hiih! The MESSIAH to tell you, “Daughter, your faith has made you whole.” Therefore, be faithful to HIM until you touch HIS heart, and unto the end of it you will receive a positive answer and the crown of a daughter of the KING of Kings! JESUS CHRIST is the Word of life and the Power of GOD. John 1:1-5 says, "In the beginning was the Word, and the Word was with GOD, and the Word was GOD. The same was in the beginning with GOD. All things were made by HIM, and without HIM there was nothing made that was made." Genesis 1:3, "And GOD said let there be Light: and there was light." THIS SAME GOD WHO MADE THINGS USING HIS WORD, IS THE SAME GOD WHO IS GOING TO TURN ALL THINGS THAT HAVE BROUGHT YOU MISERY TO BE YOUR MISSILES TO DESTROY the efforts and the plans of the enemy Satan that he has imposed on You!

Do not forget that devil is a liar and he is defeated in JESUS HOLY NAME! AMEN! Yes he is a liar and the father of lies. In John 8:44 JESUS tells the Pharisee, "Ye are of your father the devil, and the lusts of your father ye will do. He was a murderer from the beginning, and abode not in the truth, because there is no truth in him. When he speaks a lie, he speaketh of his own for he is a liar and the father of it all."

That description JESUS gave us about Satan is enough to tell what sort of spirits we deal with. All those problems he heaps on us through his people bringing us exaggerated bills, false promises of things that are not there, and all his demons of sickness are nothing but lies. The devil makes his lies look like they are real and true, but they are all lies. And there is nothing Satan does that is real. It is a lie, false and it is illegal in your body as it is illegal in heaven. So he brings his lies to you to cause the kind of fear that he carries to discourage you, but remember devil's 'fear' is "False evidence appearing real" (F=false, E=evidence, A=appearing, R=real) and not real. As there is nothing of the devil that can stay in heaven; and therefore, we should not let his lie stay in our bodies, and in our homes. I have been refusing his imposed lies in my life and my family. My children are not going to live in the lies of the devil. I refuse it in JESUS HOLY NAME and I believe my FATHER even as I write this book, HE is bringing great total deliverance into my children and my entire family and in my life and Amen. It is good enough for us to learn how to handle our enemy Satan's lies.

Also, I believe GOD for every person who will read this book that, the LORD GOD ALMIGHTY will meet all their needs, supply them in everything that they need, performing miracles in their lives such that they will never forget GOD YAHWEH'S name and the power of HIS provision. And they will give YOU GOD all the Glory and Honor for YOU really deserves it all. LORD give the readers of this book the money they need for their use and for YOUR service, and heal the sick, deliver them that are under captivity of sickness and any other kind of captivity that Satan has put in their lives in JESUS HOLY NAME I pray and believe! AMEN! GOD is ready to take away your captivity and you will be a victor from your victimizing opponent Satan. He has been too stout on you but your GOD has been waiting for HE knows that it is a great opportunity to put him to great shame, Exo.14:25-31. Our loving Father GOD is really going to shame that devil-Satan; and we Glorify JEHOVAH GOD!

Learn what you need to do in the last days of last days: TODAY, GOD SHOULD BE FIRST IN OUR LIVES AS HE WAS IN APOSTLE PAUL'S ENTIRE LIFE. In Apostle Paul's Personal Mission Statement he said, "I want to know CHIRST and the power of HIS resurrection and the fellowship of HIS sufferings, becoming like HIM in HIS death, and so to attain to the resurrection of the dead," Philippians 3:10-11. In his declaration Apostle Paul says, "It's no longer I that lives but CHRIST LIVES IN me, Galatians 2:20"

We hear a lot these days about planning and goal setting. Proponents of planning say, "If you aim at nothing, chances are you will probably hit it." They say that to wander aimlessly through life is like sailing a boat without a sail and rudder. You end up wherever the wind takes you. Paul understood his personal GOD mission, which should be the personal mission of every believer in JESUS CHRIST.

It is the one summary statement that best describes the purpose of our existence here on earth and the goal of our Christian (CHRIST LIKE) experience. It can be divided into three important characteristics. 1. To know CHRIST, 2. To experience the power of HIS resurrection, 3. To identify with HIS sufferings. All that flows from these three objectives becomes by-products. Salvation is a by-product. Miracles are by-product. Christ-likeness is a by-product. Paul's focus was on relationship. He understood that the deeper the relationship, the more power he would experience. Apostle Paul also understood that as he grew in this relationship, there would be suffering. Whenever the Kingdom of Light confronts the kingdom of darkness, there is a battle, and this often results in casualties. CHRIST confronted these earthly kingdoms and suffered for it. If we are living at HIS level of obedience in HIS service; we too, will face similar battles. We cannot be exceptional, see John 15: 16, JESUS CHRIST told us that we did not chose HIM but HE chose us and ordained us to bring forth fruits that remains. And in 15:17-19, 16:1-11, Our

LORD JESUS is describing HIS relationship with the world and said that should be our relationship with the world too. That is why in chapter 17 CHRIST prays for us, and that simply comes with the Territory of Your FATHER'S KINGDOM of Righteousness in the HOLY SPIRIT.

And therefore, when you attack devils' territories of darkness by repenting your sins and living a righteous life and you start teaching others who have been registered in devil's immigration office and received status in Satan's land of darkness you have violated his home affairs law. Thus, devil becomes your adversary for three reasons: first, you quitted his kingdom of darkness. Secondly, you are attacking his kingdom and treading teaching against him in his territories. Thirdly, you are proving to be a very great threat to his work and his kingdom. He sees he cannot thrive because of you. So he must fight back, but you must stand firm like David of 17 years. When he killed Goliath the Philistine, and proved to devil that he does not recognize his kingdom, the whole universe rejoiced. You too must prove to him that you do not fear his battles because they are forever defeated battles by your Mighty Captain JESUS CHRIST. "The Captain of the LORD'S Host," In HIS Blood, defeated devil, that Satan and his demons and it was announced on the Cross at Calvary.

But remember, while firmly and courageously fighting, you must suffer the pain and apprehension of the battle. Be equipped with perseverance that brings confidence knowing your Master is never defeated and HE is also your Father who can never let you lose; Ephesians 6: 10-17. And putting the whole armor of GOD; knowing that you are in a mission of a conqueror that is ready to pursue and fellowship in his Savior's sufferings in order to enjoy the power and the glory of HIS resurrection. Does this sound like your personal GOD mission statement? Is your focus in life centered on knowing CHRIST JESUS and the power of HIS resurrection? If not, you better pray and ask GOD to give desire to press into HIM today in order to begin experiencing CHRIST more intimately and allow HIM to be your vision and mission statement.

"Now Samuel did not yet know the LORD: Neither was the word of the LORD had yet been revealed to him," 1 Samuel 3:7. Samuel was born to Hannah, a woman who had a deep commitment to GOD. She was 'barren', but she cried out to GOD for a son. The Lord gave her Samuel, whom she completely gave back to the LORD for His service. After weaning him, she took him to the house of the LORD to be reared by the priests. Eli was the priest of Israel at that time, but he was not as Godly in his leadership, he was just religious. He had allowed much corruption, including the sins of his sons, in GOD'S house. GOD was not pleased with Eli and later judged him and his household. Samuel grew up in the temple serving GOD. He also grew up seeing the hypocrisy of Eli's household, yet this did not change the young man, Samuel. GOD was with him. We learn that even though young Samuel had a belief in GOD, he had not yet experienced a personal relationship in HIM. GOD called to Samuel three times, but Samuel thought it was Eli the priest calling him. Finally, Eli told him to say, "Speak LORD, for your servant is listening" (1 Sam. 3:9).

This is what Samuel did, and GOD began telling Samuel important things to come. Many of us grew up in religious environments. We went to church every Sunday and even now, many go to religious Churches every Sunday. We have ahead knowledge of GOD, and know that there is a GOD that we go to pray every Sunday or Saturday or Friday or whatever day we found being worshiped as the Sabbath day. (For they worship the day not the LORD of Sabbath, Matthew 12:8, read vs 1-13 who created that day) People can learn and know, especially in Christian and Jewish gatherings a little of GOD'S Language like Eli, but refuse to follow and obey HIS voice. Well, to some extend it may look like it is all right and fulfilling. But it is not because when we do not learn how to hear and recognize GOD'S voice of command in our lives there is no danger of living in disobedience. Eli as old and experienced as he was could not hear the voice of the LORD HIS GOD, WHOM he was supposed to be serving. Samuel could hear but was too young to have known GOD does speak. There comes a time when we must recognize GOD'S voice for ourselves.

GOD does not want us to have a religion; He wants us to have a relationship with HIM. A relationship that allows us to have a-two-way conversation with HIM: whereby, we are not only talking and speaking our minds and our needs to HIM. It is important to hear GOD speak in our lives; otherwise, life can never be fulfilling. Samuel was never the same after his encounter with A HOLY GOD. From his first encounter with GOD as a child, Samuel would know GOD'S voice and would respond to Him in obedience. Do you know GOD'S voice? Can you recognize it when He speaks? In order to hear GOD'S voice, you must be clean before Him and ready to listen. Listen to GOD'S voice today and follow HIM to enter into His plans that HE has for you. Eli never obeyed GOD, so he lost the Godly eye sight and the Godly hearing capacity; hence, he fell into the worst disaster. Do not say, I am living in the time of grace, Romans 6:1-2 read vs 1-23. Grace of GOD: GOD'S love and favor that we do not deserve at all and that is the most abused by the today's Church again and again.

Actually, that is not why JESUS came on earth. HE did not come to bring us a message of disobedience to the Father Matthew 5:17. JESUS came to bring us to the fullness of HIS obedience. And therefore, we cannot keep on sinning and expect grace and mercy to fall on us. Eli was a high priest, and GOD'S mercy would have fallen on him and his family if positions did matter before GOD; "for be ye not deceived, GOD is not mocked" Galatians 6: 6-9, and "GOD is No Respecter of Persons;" Act 10:34, James 2:1-13, Deuteronomy 10:17, James 1:13, Galatians 2:6. Likewise, we are a peculiar people and royal priest-wood and joint heir with CHRIST JESUS. But in order for us to obtain, and maintain that Grace and Mercy in that position, we must stay Holy because the one who created, and died for us is Holy and Righteous all together, Matthew 5:6, 6:33-34, Leviticus 11:44, 20:26.

Mark 8:34, "if any man wants to come with me, he must deny himself, take up his cross and follow ME," says CHRIST JESUS. The Anointed and the Holy one of GOD of Israel is HOLY. Our LORD JESUS is the only Man that lived and walked on this earth as we do and never fell into any kind of sin. "He was tempted as we are, but never sinned," so HE became the very wise of GOD, even JESUS CHRIST Our LORD! I thank HIM very much because it is by HIM I am wise and I receive HIS wisdom, and knowledge of understanding even the secret things that are hidden to the mighty men of this world. How glorious it is to be a child of GOD and receive HIS wisdom that cannot be measured. Proverbs 9:10 says, "the fear of the LORD is the beginning of wisdom: and the knowledge of the Holy is his understanding." Psalms 53 says, "The fool hath said in his heart, there is no GOD. Corrupt are they, and have done iniquity: there is none that doeth good." And we can see King Solomon agreeing with his father King David in Proverbs 9:10. He emphasized on wisdom in most of his writings. King Solomon, in his later days, was encompassed by foolishness after GOD had blessed him for twenty years in his monarchy. He became proud and forgot all GOD'S commandments. 1Kings 11:1-13, King Solomon married many women and to make matters worse, strange women with their gods. Hence, he was made to worship idols, and forgot that he was of a peculiar nation that worships the Living Most High GOD only. Many Christians today do the same thing as King Solomon.

<u>In Humility:</u>

Humanity, need to pray a special prayer of mercy: when GOD brings blessings to them, they become so arrogant and start worshiping the wealth instead of The LORD GOD who gave them the wealth and the power to get it, Deuteronomy 8:12-18. Worshiping the resource; instead of worshiping the source. No wonder Solomon wrote in Proverbs 8: 1-36; here, King Solomon looks at the wisdom of GOD and how That Wisdom cried for him when he was lost in the palace sinning with all sort of women he could get. HE looked at the Wisdom of GOD and saw HIM being a person crying for him to come back to his Father GOD who his earthly Dad, King David respected and honored. Here, King Solomon saw someone Holy in heaven crying for him in all HIS wisdom, and spoke of JESUS CHRIST in a prophetic manner, calling HIM Wisdom. He says, "Wisdom cries." The poetry uses the feminine description of this Wisdom crying instead of masculine, and I believe it's because it is JESUS CHRIST who travailed for us from Gethsemane to Calvary and supernaturally bore us on the Cross with HIS Precious Blood; John 3:3. Also, it's female that travails to birth a child and too cries for her lost child as JESUS CHRIST did for us, John 10:7-18. When I look at the whole GODLINESS, I see a lot humility in HIM; hence, unmeasured Wisdom and Love.

<u>GOD Had to Come, Live with us to Bring Us Humility and Wisdom; Isa 7:14, Matt 1:23</u>

There is no other way that is more amazing than that of a virgin conceiving and bearing a son that lived on earth only for 33 years. And when JESUS was born, everything was wisely pre-arranged in such way that you and I would not know how to organize in such a way. The Augustus decree of registration, so that JESUS is born having his mother and the earthly foster father legally married for Joseph to be able to take full control of bringing up the Son of GOD as his own Son. Joseph was given a lot of humility. Wisdom and humility for Love right there. GOD coming so low to stretch HIS Right Hand of mercy for you and me.

Miracles for Joseph and Mary started from JESUS' conception to HIS Death and of course; I believe, there after GOD did not leave nor forsake those two precious people. Another miracle, next to the big miracle of Holy Conception was: for Joseph and Mary not to have been stoned and killed by the Jews for the sin of what they thought it happened "having sexual relationship before marriage," it was a great miracle. For sure, Mary and Joseph did not have sexual relationship or interaction before JESUS CHRIST was born. Read Matthew 1:18-25. But many would have assumed it for not acquainted with the Supernatural taking place to natural, and for not knowing GOD, or HIS Power, neither HIS Word nor HIS Voice.

How the community accepted them to go register in Bethlehem as a man and a wife; and being pregnant before the proper Jewish marriage that remains a mystery to them that know the Torah and the restriction of the commands that GOD gave to Moses as commandments to Israel. There, I took a big......breath! Did GOD Break HIS Commandment? NO! But to us that do know their GOD and know HE is a miraculous GOD, we know it was the power of GOD that was moving; commanding, manifesting and made the Jewish custom submit to HIS will and Authority.

GOD being the owner of those Commandments, HE has the power to do what HE sees is best for us and for HIS glory, and HE will do it and make man quietly forget the law or be powerless like high Priests and Pharisees for 31/2 years JESUS Preached. The Jewish community around Mary and Joseph were made to forget that Mary was pregnant before the Jewish customary marriage. Otherwise, she and the person who made her pregnant ought to have been stoned to death. How could they stone GOD'S HOLY SPIRIT?

Of course, without doubts, Joseph for having betrothed Mary would have been a victim of circumstances. He would have been stoned to death no matter how much he would have pleaded unless Mary produced another physical man responsible for her pregnancy. But you see, our GOD is A GOD of order and HE knew what HE was doing. Of old, HE had made it to be known and prophesied by Moses, David, Solomon, Isaiah, Jeremiah, Zechariah, Malachi, and even giving Prophet Isaiah the names of our savior. HE had prepared John to be amazingly born of very old people who were past delivery age to come and prepare for HIS Son JESUS. From the time of conception, GOD made it known; first to Simon, and Anna who righteously waited for the Holy Birth of Messiah in the Temple then to Mary, Joseph, Elizabeth, John's mother, the shepherds and finally to the wise men about the birth of our savior.

Really, we need to look at that wisdom of GOD and consider that there is no greater knowledge and wisdom with power than that. And that is why man without the help of the HOLY SPIRIT cannot comprehend the wisdom of GOD. With the wisdom of the miracles that GOD applied during the conception, and the birth of Our Savior LORD JESUS CHRIST on earth, we have enough evidence to make us believe and prove that; surely, our LORD GOD is able and very able to make all our miseries missiles to fight and destroy all our enemy's schemes and plans and assignments that he has assigned to his demons to destroy us. What we need to do is to believe and trust that GOD is readily willing to frustrate Satan on our behalf, Amen and Hallelujah! Yes! Let us not frustrate one another in any way, thinking that, "It is so and so doing me evil for him is my enemy."

<u>No! It's not your brother or sister:</u>

It is the spirit of the enemy, Satan behind that man or woman; because, the Jews would have hurt or killed Mary and Joseph if the devil was not removed from their way by our mighty GOD. Therefore, when you and I see things not working well, let us look at the source of our misery and know it is Satan and not that man or woman you call your enemy. And what is the medicine for that? Prayer of worship! Magnify the name of the LORD and let HIM alone be exalted, and HE will work miracles for you. 2 Corinthians10:3-6, "for though we walk in the flesh we do not war against the flesh: For the weapons of our warfare are not carnal but Spiritual and are Mighty through GOD to the pulling down of all strong holds of the devil our enemy: Casting down every imagination and every high thing that exalts itself against the knowledge of GOD, and bringing to captivity every thought to the obedience of CHRIST; and having in a readiness to avenge all disobedience, when your obedience is fulfilled." AMEN!

Faith is our Strongest Spiritual Weapon!

Fear is the devil's strongest weapon! It is the counterfeit of Faith. And both are

Contrary to each other, they can never agree or dwell in the same place; heart or mind.

FAITH, is our strongest weapon, substance and evidence that brings joy, peace, love, patience, courage, perseverance, comfort; hence victory. Fear brings anger then insecurity, timidity, hatred, sorrow, restlessness, discomfort; hence, victim of defeat. Therefore, in order that we may walk in the sea of miracles, we have to overcome fear and anger. Our miracles are on our way, only we should learn to be wise not to be overcome by anger when Satan sends his demons to enter our beloved people. Remember they are merely victims and the tools that he uses when he is tempting us.

CHAPTER 21

Anger is One of Number One Satan's Weapons

Devil knows if he can manage to make you live an angry life, he has overcome you completely. You have become his victim no matter how much you will proclaim to be saved. That is why we need to be Truly Born Again in the Blood of JESUS CHRIST so that we can overcome anger. When temptations come through other people it is easy to be angry at them and feel very bad about them. Satan at that time feels very happy and he knows he has held both parties captive. The one he is using to tempt you and you who are angry at your fellow person whom devil is using to bring the temptation to you.

Satan tries to bring you down using other people that come across to you. You will be thinking it is that person who is offending you, but it is that evil spirit behind everything. Devil has successfully deceived both of you that you are bad to each other. The enemy has lied to both of you; "Oh! You two cannot be happy together or even greet one another kindly, you are enemies!" From today you will know that this is a lie from your enemy and you can help your friend to learn the devil's secret. Please by GOD'S grace and mercy do it and you will overcome the devil greatly and make him feel miserable instead of you and your friend being miserable. While I say this, I know there some people who will hate you out of nothing. Actually for no reason at all, but make stories to paint you bad and dislike you and if possible make others dislike you. With such people, you may try prayerfully to make peace with them and fail, at that juncture, thank GOD for them and for yourself then forgive them and yourself of your feelings, prayerfully love them, peacefully and joyfully, keep off. Hebrews 12:14 says, follow peace and holiness with all men, v15 lest root of bitterness springing up trouble you.

Sometimes, it may not be possible to convince the other party, depending on the depth of devils' power on him or her; but with prayer by faith, and time to heal, the LORD will help you to get to your friend and help him or her to overcome that spirit of anger and hatred. And when approaching that other victim, go apologetically to your friend knowing that you have also been a victim of the same spirit. Nevertheless, there are some victims you cannot approach because they have fully sold themselves to the devil. You may fast for them if the HOLY SPIRIT leads you to do so but do not waste GOD'S precious time thinking you will change everybody. There are some people you cannot change or take away their hatred like David could not change King Saul even after demonstrating a lot of love to him by sparing his life three times. Your duty is to forgive such and go ahead as if they are not there. CHRIST JESUS with all HIS Love was not and is not able to because HE does not force HIS Power where it is not needed and appreciated. Neither did the Apostles change all that came their way, but do not allow the spirit of anger and hatred to enter in you. Forgive them for they do not know whom they are serving.

I learned a lot from one of my beloved brother who went to be with the LORD in 1996. Brother Titus Nkonge used to tell me if I am hurt by someone; "Mom, It's not that person; it's the spirit behind that person. The person is good and wonderfully made, but the spirit behind him is of the enemy. You need to forgive and pray for that person so that he can come to the LORD and that will be the end of him making you unhappy." As long as I stayed close in fellowship with this Brother whom we became a best family in his wedding, I never saw my brother angry. But I would see so many other brethren who were older than me in faith angry, and hateful. I too, even after such fellowshipping with my brother Nkonge, I would be angry of even very little things that do not matter at all. Little did I know that my brother had known the secret of managing the feelings that bring anger; and he had discovered and known the wisdom of GOD that is in CHRIST JESUS by the HOLY SPIRIT and had entered deeper in the LORD in HIS Anointing that cannot be defeated. Anointing that destroys the yoke, Isaiah 10:27. As much as I had observed my brother, you could hate Brother Titus Nkonge, but he would still love you. He never cared what others were doing or what they were saying about him. You could talk ill about him, but he would still love you and pray for you. But he was a very wise brother he would not open his treasures to his enemies just because GOD has given him peace with them like King Hezekiah. For that is one of the greatest lesson that young brethren need to learn from 2 Kings 20:12-17, and 2Chronicles 32:31. You love but know that there are people who are not of your KINGDOM and they are baptized with the spirit of deception and hate. Pray that our LORD GOD will keep such away from your dwellings in JESUS HOLY NAME AMEN!

I believe this is the kind of love and salvation that JESUS CHRIST brought to us. It has no captivity at all. It is a real salvation, here to set you free. Where nothing matters, and even what people fight for, you do not care about it, you only care about the relationship you have with JESUS CHRIST, and you love the others out of nothing good that they have done to you. Praise the Lord God Almighty in Jesus Holy Name! I am really learning through this book to be a real Christ Like believer. And I believe you too, will learn a lot and have all that you know about GOD confirmed in you. Many a times, I have read books of brethren and find some of the things said GOD has already taught me. HE only wanted to confirm to me what HE has already said to me. Likewise, you too you will find a lot that GOD has taught you and HE is confirming to you through this book.

We must strive to manage the anger so that devil does not get a weapon to fight us through the anger in us, and make us look and behave like him. We hate Satan and all his ways and properties, don't we? Yes we do! Personally, I hate Satan with all my heart and with everything that is within me. My sincere prayer is that; My Heavenly Father will enable me to live hating Satan and everything satanic throughout my life until I get to my eternal home Amen.

Through using other Beloved people, Satan wants to make those people and us captives of his anger by making them offend us, and by making we feel offended by them. I have gone through humiliation and hurt by most of the beloved people that GOD brought my way. Most of those people were brought to me by God so that I could be of some help to them in their difficult situations. When their problems got solved, they would start treating me like a filthy rag. Seeing how they are treating me, I would feel very bitter towards them, and feel hatred; instead of feeling pity for them, and knowing that; they were just captives of our enemy, that spirit of the devil behind them. But whenever I remembered what my Brother Titus Nkonge taught me, I would feel very sinful and pray for forgiveness and ask GOD to give me love for such people more than I ever loved them before. Sometimes, it used to take long for me to remember that "it is the spirit behind them."

However, now I know how to manage the anger and bring love out of the SPIRIT OF MY FATHER who is real love. GOD is love, and HE loves every one of us regardless. I love those who may have offended me in any way and I feel no offence. Even those who have been baptized in the spirit of hate, I forgive and love them but keep a distance and move on.

Let us learn to manage anger and turn it to love and we shall have Satan our enemy defeated and turn one of the biggest missiles that Satan uses to bring misery into a missile to destroy his plans over us; Amen! I thank GOD for bringing Brother Nkonge to live with us here on earth before HE took him back to our eternal home; for he taught me a treasure of knowledge that I cannot forget, and which I am now sharing with you. That teaching continued to linger in my mind and register inside of me and give me the desire to be even more anointed with the spirit of forgiveness and love.

Unholy Anger is the devil's weapon over us; we need to manage it and allow only the Holy Anger to come to us:

CHAPTER 22

When Managing Anger

Remember a well-managed anger can bring blessings:

There are several brethren in the Bible that went through hurtful and annoying situations that would have caused them to be terribly angry, but GOD helped them to control their anger, and manage it so well that instead of becoming a source of stress and destruction, it became missiles to destroy the miseries that it could have caused, and brought blessings. What Satan had meant for evil; if you allow GOD to use it, HE will use it for a blessing and for a message instead! AMEN!

Examples of those Bible Brethren that let GOD help them manage their anger were set for us so that we can learn from them how to manage anger and let it become missile instead of misery. And in JESUS HOLY NAME; it is possible to have your anger controlled if only you give GOD a chance to control it for you at that moment when you are well stricken by it. Devil wants us to be angry and keep hurting. He gives us many unreasonable reasons to why we should be angry. But our GOD wants us to rely on him so that he can keep us happy, that we might enjoy our loving GOD'S relationship. Our GOD Loves us so much that we cannot afford to stay miserable any more. We must be covered by HIS love, joy, and peace. By faith we can stay happy at all times. Anger is not a tool of joy, peace, love, faith, meekness, gentleness, goodness, longsuffering, and self-control, it is a weapon of mass destruction. When anger persists, it brings bitterness, bitterness births anxiety and resentment, which produces great stress; hence, depression leading to many complications like hypertension and many other medical and surgical conditions, finally, death.

Do you see why you and I should not indulge into the things that brings anger and bitterness? The biggest question here is, how can we keep away from such angering situations and occurrences?

The answer is:

First, Prayer of True Worship is the key to open the door of a calm mind. A humble and a contrite spirit enables better anger management. Sometimes, you need to just say a short prayer like, "O my Dear Lord God, help me here now. Do not let me fall, LORD, help me in JESUS Name, Amen." If the person who has brought the offense is approachable, tell her or him, politely that you're sorry, you really do not want to engage in that kind of talk.

It is important to learn how to have a remorseful heart with compassion before GOD and learn how to appear before the throne of Mercy with a humble and a contrite heart that the KING of Kings will never let anger settle into. GOD values all the hearts that are remorseful and compassionate. HE will never despise, but enrich and give HIS favor and Grace. Our GOD loves us so much that HE wants us to have everything good crowned by HIS Joy. But our enemy Satan prevents GOD'S people from getting our Father's blessings by keeping them angry about things that he, Satan, brings to us through his cunning ways. In it all, we thank our LORD JESUS CHRIST who died for us so that HE can remove us from eternal anger to everlasting Joy: by having that knowledge and understanding of our LORD GOD'S blessedness. With GOD'S wisdom, we are able to overcome the devil's miseries of anger and get GOD'S missiles to fight for our blessings.

You see, Daniel, Shadrach, Meshach, and Abednego never engaged themselves in anger and bitterness toward their traitors nor toward the King. Instead, they prayed, worshiped their true GOD and overcame with great victory. They never allowed themselves to be victims of anger and those Babylonians. If they became angry at Babylonians, they would not have been able to pray; hence, no victory.

The second King of Israel King David received his GOD'S missiles of remorsefulness and compassion with GOD'S passion to fight for his blessings.

David never let the miseries that his King, the first King of Israel Saul was trying to bring to him to take over by embracing the anger of Saul's threats. King Saul never gave David a moment to breathe without death threats. One thing that David had was the assurance of GOD'S abundance of life in him. He knew no one could kill him unless he had permission from GOD his maker. David had the wisdom to know that; his GOD has a good plan, and thoughts for him and a good purpose to have created him, and anointed and ordained him a King. Unlike King Saul, who forgot his calling and his anointing and ordination, and was filled by the spirit of pride bringing selfishness and jealousy; hence, murder spirit generated and filled him up. Surprisingly, both Kings were anointed by the same Prophet, Samuel.

GOD is all wise, HE knew if David were anointed by another Prophet; when Saul would be failing for treating his anointing with pride, and arrogance, he would blame the prophet that anointed him. And some of the weak people of Israel would say, "GOD did not give King Saul a good Prophet to anoint him with power."

You see, King Saul instead of seeing young David as potential future general of his army and know that their battles are GOD'S battles; he saw an opponent, and an enemy. After David killed Goliath, King Saul felt threatened instead of rejoicing in the LORD GOD who won the battle for them. King Saul had no eyes to see no one would have killed such giant with a stone. No! He saw a competitor and fear fell on him; hence, anger and bitterness until finally devil killed him without GOD. You see, everything started with fear, that "false evidence appearing real." Then when he was told by Samuel about his sins, King Saul got angered with Prophet Samuel instead of being remorseful. Then the bitterness made him do things against GOD'S command causing the loss of his anointing; hence, his family and the monarchy. Fear of losing brings anger and anger is a very expensive tool of the devil and I cast him away with his tools and I paralyze them in the Name of JESUS CHRIST My LORD AND My Savior, Amen!

By the way, King Saul was not a weak person at the beginning, 1 Samuel 11:5-11, & vs12-15

King Hezekiah in Isaiah 39:8; instead of being sorry for his actions, was angered at the prophet's report. His end and the end of Israel the northern kingdom was terrible, because, much as GOD had blessed King Hezekiah; (he felt lifted high when he became prosperous after the healing and the additional of 15 years) he never humbled himself before A Mighty GOD who revealed to Isaiah that the king had sinned.

When we look at those two great Kings; Saul was well described by GOD when Samuel the Prophet was sent to go and anoint him. But his end was not wonderful because of his response to his sins. Hezekiah was wonderful in all righteousness, but his final response to GOD'S servant made his end miserable and his sons and daughters were carried away captive. When we look at King David's sins that made GOD send Prophet Nathan to him, they were miserable and despicable. Adultery is scandalous, but the way King David treated the Prophet of GOD and his attitude towards his own sins before GOD brought him victory and joy thereafter. Psalms 51:17, a broken and contrite heart thou shall not despise O LORD!

We need our LORD'S kind of humility. CHRIST JESUS was humble to death. JESUS did not need to die. First, no one would have killed CHRIST at all. No power can overcome HIM. Therefore, HE freely and humbly gave HIS life for us. Some situations might come to us in a way that we may find ourselves in some circumstances that may cause us do something that would bring a shameful result. Instead of us fighting for what we call, "our rights", or protection of our ego it is better for us to apologize and be remorseful and cry to GOD for forgiveness. It helps a million times. Other times, we do not need to apologize but to move away from those who may cause us sin, but not argue with them.

<u>In the book of Nehemiah 5:6 we see anger well managed:</u>

Let us see this man of GOD who lived being a man; just like us and who surrendered his life for his nation. Nehemiah was angry at the opponents of the work of GOD when he saw how they opposed him to prevent him from doing the work that GOD had allowed him to do in Jerusalem; to rebuild the wall of Jerusalem. Nehemiah 6:9 says, "The opposition group led by Tobiah, and Sanballat weakened the builders by giving them a bad false report, but Nehemiah Prayed for GOD to strengthen his hands". In Nehemiah 6: 11-13 Nehemiah reasoned in the Lord his GOD and knew his position in the Lord, and refused the advice of the deceivers.

Likewise, when Satan comes to weaken our prayer hands so that we do not build a wall against him, we need to reason with prayer the more and worship the Lord Our GOD more than ever before. To be able to accomplish, we must be able to distinguish the voice of the deceiver the devil from the sweet commanding voice of GOD our King who has said, "Go ahead and build the wall and every material that you will need, the house of the King will supply." The building of the wall of Jerusalem by Nehemiah is symbolic of our building of the Spiritual wall for GOD. When our Lord GOD gives us HIS work to minister to others we need to know every task and the accomplishment is for Him, and His Kingdom for His glory.

There are many people who are not willing to do GOD'S work with you, and yet the Lord has given you a mission. Leave them alone and go ahead and GOD will give you people to work with you, Amen! In Nehemiah 6: 14, Nehemiah prayed that the LORD GOD would think upon his enemies, Tobiah, Sanballat, the prophets and the prophetess Noadiah. These people would have put fear in him to stop working for the LORD. It is good when we ask our LORD GOD to look at the demons and their agencies that want to weaken us from doing HIS work.

CHAPTER 23

Holy Anger And Evil Anger

The Holy Anger comes by the desire to protect the Name of Our LORD GOD and HIS Work from being destroyed by those who are caught up with pride and jealousy. One of the most successful ways that our enemy Satan brings to the children of GOD is anger through their acquaintances. Those who brought trials to Nehemiah and Daniel were people known to them, not strangers. They wanted to create fear and doubt in them; hence, spiritual disability. We need constant prayer against fear so that it will never take grasp on us and prevent us from getting control of anger. If we obey, we will never act foolishly. Nehemiah prayed, and stood boldly to build the wall.

In Daniel 3:17-18, we see fearless Believers of the Old Testament:

These three anointed servants of the Most High LORD GOD stood firm on the side of their GOD. The bold answer Shadrach,

Meshach, and Abednego gave to king Nebuchadnezzar made their Lord God Almighty happy. That answer allowed GOD to show HIS mightiness to king Nebuchadnezzar when HE rescued the three from Nebuchadnezzar's fiery furnace. These three men of GOD knew their GOD'S capability of saving them. They knew their relationship with their GOD was firm and their Lord God's love is divine, and they were not going to compromise to the fear; hence, anger. Instead of fearing death, they decided to use that circumstance to show the king that there is ONE who is greater than him. King Nebuchadnezzar was angered and he answered the three men in a hurry without thinking why they were so bold. He obeyed his people and acted in kindled anger that brought his people to death in the same fire they had built for the three men of GOD. Hatred had caused the Babylonians to be proud; hence, anger of the three foreigners being highly promoted in their nation. The thoughts of their hearts brought disaster to people that burned in that fire while throwing Shadrach, Meshach, and Abednego to their fiery fire. We know GOD saved HIS children out of that fire and out of the hands of the King as they testified. The power of positive testimony and power of a spoken word in the LORD moves GOD'S Actions.

In Daniel 6: We see Daniel himself has a teaching on how to control anger and be successfully successive as a true Christian too. This Daniel had just interpreted the finger writing on the wall to King Belshazzar; hence, pride could have encompassed him after such an accomplishment. He could have rebuked the other presidents and princes under him for putting an image up to be worshiped. Daniel knew that the statute was put up to ensnare him, but he never commented about it. He only went ahead to worship his GOD in the right manner as he always had. He knew vengeance was the LORD'S, and if GOD could not deliver him out of the hands of his enemies, he could not deliver himself. He very well knew his rise in the kingdom was miraculous and out of GOD'S grace and not by his might. Sometime men, GOD'S Creation, when we are raised in positions, we feel like we put ourselves in that position, and become very proud. Yes! I have done it! When and how?

Please Dear LORD help us as YOUR children not to be captured by spirit of pride and have mercy on me to stay me away from it. I hate that spirit of pride and any time I ever feel like it got me up, I feel very bad about it. It is a crafty spirit of Satan and it knows how to creep in; better be aware of its movements. By the way, the spirit of pride comes in very many fashions. Sometimes, we may not even notice it; only GOD who would reveal it to us so that we can repent it. King Saul of Israel never thought he was proud, but when GOD looked at him, he saw nothing good in him, but pride; and said, Saul was proud and disobedient.

Dear Lord our GOD, help and forgive me really in your everlasting mercy; for pride may not be known by the bearer unless you reveal it. Let us really pray against this spirit for it is even killing the Church. My Father, help us to ask your kind forgiveness and prevent the spirit of pride come to us, the body of CHRIST at any time.

But most of it all; help me Dear LORD MY GOD not to have the spirit of pride within me. LORD You know it and its manifestations, I do not know it very clearly. I need your help; for what we call pride sometime may not be, and what we call humility sometimes may not be humility; You alone Dear Lord,

You know everything and all that is good and best for us. Make me that which YOU desire in JESUS HOLY NAME I Pray and believe it's done Amen!

King David also became proud and counted the people of Israel, to see how much his nation had grown, thus provoking GOD to an anger that caused many men of Israel die. But when it was revealed to him, he repented, and GOD'S anger was withdrawn. Job is also another character that managed his anger wisely, he prayed and talked positively about HIS GOD and refused to curse him in the midst of his long-drawn-out miseries. Even when his three friends and the fourth younger friend Elihu proclaimed that Job was justified, Job insisted of enquiring of the LORD about his calamities, he praised the name of the LORD for all his miseries. In the book of Job; Chapters one and two says, in all these things, Job never sinned against GOD. Satan had predicted that after he was through punishing Job with all tribulations, Job would curse GOD to HIS face. But even after being tried through his wife, Job never cursed GOD. He only blessed the Name of the LORD his GOD. GOD was right with HIS testimony about Job's righteousness. Job knew GOD was right in everything HE did.

<u>Unmanaged anger becomes a good weapon for devil to use against the bearer:</u>

For in the presence UNGODLY anger there is no peace. GODLY Anger is called holy anger and it comes when fighting for righteousness sake. Genesis 4:6-8 Here, Cain was angered because GOD did not receive his offering. Anger in Cain created uncertainty following jealousy and fear; hence, bitterness entered in him and he slew his brother. If Cain had prayed and worshipped GOD instead, he would have managed anger well and saved his brother's life and his life too. When anger is not well managed it can bring a serious choler, hence rage and murder, as in Cain's case. Cain refused to hearken unto GOD'S advice and did whatever anger dictated him to do. Satan had known very well he had overcome Cain through his lies of giving Cain one of his properties known as jealousy that brought anger and murder. May our Dear LORD GOD help us to well manage the devil's weapon of unholy anger and take away the weapon of fear which brings jealousy that our enemy Satan tries to put in us! And it is in JESUS HOLY NAME, I pray, ask and believe, AMEN!

This is a Godly advice if you have been overtaken by anger.

You must die to self! CHRIST JESUS said, "If you want to follow me, you must deny yourself, take up your cross and follow ME!" Mark 8:34-38

Now, let's ask ourselves, how do we deny ourselves? This is the key to self-death!

It's not easy but with GOD it is possible to deny you the self and die in CHRIST JESUS. Just sincerely say, LORD JESUS, I need you more and more and thirst and hunger more and more to have only YOU, in my life. When it is, "no longer I that lives but CHRIST who lives in me," then you are really dead to self.

Unless you die to yourself, it is not possible to carry the character and the nature of a Born Again that JESUS described in John 3:3-8. Anger cannot be managed by the old man. Only a self-denied person can manage anger and that has to be a dead man in CHRIST JESUS. A totally committed surrendered man! Mark 8:34-38, Luke 9:22-27: for everything that is dead, it has no feelings. It's hard to offend a body in the mortuary.

Actually, the old man was poisoned by the enemy Satan at the Garden of Eden as he lied to them and put choler inside their bodies. According to the World English Dictionary Choler [kóllər] is a 14th century language via French colère from Latin cholera "bile" bodily fluid (see cholera), believed to cause bad temper or anger (archaic or literary): one of the four basic fluids of the body according to medieval medicine, thought to make somebody whose body contained too much of it prone to anger and irritability (archaic). Bile is physiologically a digestive fluid: it's a yellowish-green fluid produced in the liver, stored in the gallbladder, and passed through ducts to the small intestine, where it plays an essential role in emulsifying fats. Otherwise, why should the Almighty GOD create us with Choler, cholera in Latin tongue and Kholera in Greek? This Choler is characterized by bitterness, which brings feelings of bitterness and irritability in the brain; hence, anger demonstrating evil actions as a result. Literary speaking, we can see that this spirit of anger and bitterness is likened with Cholera which is an acute intestinal disease: "an acute and often fatal intestinal disease that produces severe gastrointestinal symptoms and is usually caused by the bacterium Vibrio Cholerae." "Illness caused by bile:" 1st reference, (Encarta ® World English Dictionary © & (P) 1998-2005 Microsoft Corporation. All rights reserved.)[14th century. Via Latin, "illness caused by bile" < Greek kholera < kholē "bile"] 2nd reference for Bile in Goggle and Wikipedia and many other translation reference dictionaries and books have similar meaning as: "History bodily humor: according to medieval medicine, one of the four basic fluids of the body humors, an excess of which was thought to make somebody prone to anger, and it's also known as bitterness, irritability, ire, vitriol, spleen, sourness, temper, wrath, anger, fury, and rage." Other descriptions of findings inconnection with body humor that controls, "Mood: a temporary mood or state of mind. "History body fluid: according to medieval science and medicine, any of the four main fluids of the human body, blood, lymph, yellow bile or black bile that determined somebody's mood and temperament" 14th century. Via Anglo-Norman < Latin, "body fluid" < humere "be moist"] Encarta ® World English Dictionary © & (P) 1998-2005 Microsoft Corporation. All rights reserved.

For sure, the real truth is: Only JESUS CHRIST in the new man, a true Born Again can neutralize that bitterness and irritability, and give sweet calm feelings even when things are not working the way we expected or the way we want them to be and are very bad looking and feelings are terrible. The HOLY SPIRIT OF JESUS CHRIST, THE VERY WORD THAT GOD USED TO CREATE ALL THINGS WILL QUENCH THAT BAD, BILE FEELING AND GIVE HIS JOY, PEACE, AND HIS LOVE TO ENCOMPASS YOU. Only, apply HIS principals of faith, believe, and trust and you will find yourself full of joy in the midst of your adversities.

According to the Word of GOD, I believe, this substance of deep yellow bile was not made and meant by GOD to cause anger or wrath and sickness in man that HE created into HIS own Image and likeness of righteousness and holiness. That body fluid was created in man as one of the digestive fluids to help in digesting fat for normal bodily utilization. And none of the four body fluids GOD created in man without proper good function physiologically. Therefore, mental irritability producing anger, or wrath following bitterness, resentment, hatred and all other products, comes as a result of man's general disobedience to GOD. Disobedience leads to the loss of GOD'S presence, without which we lose guidance on how to control our brains during overwhelming situations. Then devil actively with his deception kindles anger that stimulates our nerves to make every fluid production or secretion excessive for the body to bear it; hence, body defensive mechanism manifests in its best training. If you have trained or you have let the HOLY SPIRIT Train your body to worship and give GOD thanks and praise at all time, then you'll start worshiping instead of cursing then joy, peace, and love by faith will encompass you. If you have trained or you have let Satan train your body to anger and curses or physical fight, restlessness, anger, bitterness, curses and fight will swiftly get and command you to it. That is why OUR LORD JESUS SAID, "you/we shall know them by their fruits," Matthew 7:16-20

Here, I know some medical specialists, especially those who deal with nerves, hormones, and some kind of body fluids will raise eyebrows but I have done my research thoroughly such that a sitting for reasoning together is welcome.

Looking at it critically, Adam and Eve before they disobeyed and ate the forbidden fruit, it's never recorded that onetime they were angered such that they fought to dust until one kind elephant came to separate them. Never! Those guys were at peace all the time because they lived in fellowship with GOD worshiping HIM in Spirit and in Truth. There was no interference from Satan the devil. In fact, I look at anger or wrath as one of the worst generational curses that has been passed over and over from one generation to another from the spirit that entered Adam to Cain, Ishmael, and Esau to the ten sons of Jacob unto Judas to today's people. If we look at what wrath has done over all generations to destroy families here on earth, we shall feel indebted to repent and fight it in the Name of JESUS CHRIST until that spirit is completely defeated. Why not! If medicine can eradicate some viruses and bacteria that cause killer diseases; and they are all manufactured by the same spirits of the devil and released here on earth to kill GOD'S people. Yea, then we can also come together and Pray Hallowing our Father who Art in Heaven enough until HE feels honored to bring HIS Kingdom here on earth as it is there in Heaven. Amen! Why not! All that we need is to respect ourselves to show our LORD GOD love and honor that we have for HIM and HE will cause us to do exploits; Ezra 10:1-, Daniel 11:32, Daniel 1:4-21.

Daniel 1:8 says, "But Daniel purposed in his heart he would not defile himself with the King's food neither with the wine that he drunk; therefore, he requested the prince of the eunuch that he might not defile himself. Now GOD had brought Daniel into favor and tender love with the prince of the eunuchs. And the prince of eunuchs said unto Daniel, I fear my lord the king, who hath appointed your meat and drink: for why should he see your faces worse liking than the children which are your sort? Then shall you make me endanger my head to the king. Then said Daniel to Melzar whom the prince of the eunuchs had set over Daniel, Hananiah, Mishael, and Azariah: Prove thy servants, I beseech thee, ten days; and let them give us pulse to eat and water to drink." Now here, a Mustard Seed Faith is at work. From verse 13-21, we read of the victory that followed this agreement by faith. These four young men went to pray. They did not go to eat health and do gym. They went to worship their GOD who lives forever, the Creator of everything. Daniel knew, HE who created their bodies is able to keep them well fed with Heavenly food instead of contaminating the temple of the HOLY SPIRIT. They knew who they were and their relationship with their GOD. They would not give themselves be seduced by the king's food and authority. Do you know this king is the one who had carried even their king, the king of Israel into captivity, but Daniel and his 3 brethren never paid any thought to what the devil does: for they knew their GOD loved and cared for them. They knew their GOD could never leave nor forsake them if they reverenced HIM.

The demon that carries the sin of anger, wrath and rage has never been discovered as a serious sin to be searched from its root and be exposed by saints of the Most High LORD GOD and be cast out of the human race. It is the high time we need to come together and cast that spirit away together with its manifestation so that it will not continue to dominate the world. The world is already suffering from wrath. Hate has become the order of the day. Righteousness is becoming remote because the Sons of GOD are being swallowed by the world in their wrath. Divide and rule spirit is working day and night making even the children of GOD think why should they come together in unite and those are of that race and others are of that color and the others are of that language and others of that accent; forfeiting the truth of GOD in Psalm 133. Devil says, "I make sure you cannot come together rest you pray Your GOD, and the Blood of JESUS CHRIST come to your rescue!" The evil one has put his toe down for the body of CHRIST, but surely, if we know our GOD and his power, we shall do exploits, and make a change; Daniel 11:32, 12:1-4-5-13. We are supposed to work for our LORD GOD since it is still day time and make a tremendous change now so that our LORD GOD may prepare the Church for the Holy Bride of HIS Son JESUS CHRIST. THE LAMB of Redemption should now come as the LORD of Lords and the KING of Kings; Yes Jehovah, and Amen!

Anger, bitterness, wrath and rage, is too much and it has caused nation upon nations to live in hatred and problems battles and killings of all kinds; Galatians 5: 17-21, Ephesians 4: 29-31. Well, they may say it is Fulfillment of prophesies prophesied in the Old Testament and to the New Testament by Our LORD JESUS CHRIST, but prophesy comes from the mouth of GOD to warn us HIS people for HE knows when sin will increase and when HE will take HIS vengeance over it; Genesis 15:13-16. As generation that knowledge has greatly increased, we are supposed to seriously repent and pray since all GOD'S grievous prophesies are happening at our time. So that we may lead many to righteousness of GOD by repenting for them and crying that HE may have mercy and cause them repent their sins and receive JESU CHRIST

Let me say this, personally I know what anger, wrath and bitterness can do, and the damage it can bring. I am one of those people who suffered a lot from that demon of anger and rage. I hate it in JESUS HOLY NAME! But I worked on it day and night casting it out of me in the Mighty Name of JESUS CHRIST, the Name that is above every other name! And I know by the power of the Holy Spirit And The Fire OF GOD In Me It Is FOREVER gone together with Its Effect. the fire of the holy spirit Consumed And Defeated it Completely Out Of My life, my Body, My Spirit, and My Soul, And In Everything That

Is Within Me And all That Is Mine NEVER TO COME BACK AGAIN. I prayed In The Mighty Name of JESUS CHRIST My Lord AND BELIEVED! I overcame and I'm an overcomer by the blood of the lamb and the word of my testimony and received the fruit of the holy spirit as in Galatians 5:22-23, Ephesians4:20-28, if we keep the counsel of the Word of GOD we are overcomer.

It is easy to suffer stupid things from Satan without knowing that it is not the will of our GOD we have those evil manifestation of the devil in us. The old man is the only one that should carry devil's properties, but the new man should carry GOD'S Image and property that is in JESUS CHRIST by HIS Word. If we deny ourselves, take up the cross and follow JESUS CHRIST our Savior to die on it; if we hate and forget worldly things, then we shall have saved ourselves a lot of problems of the old man. Dying to self! Only by the Supreme Spirit of GOD can we be able to die to self. Self is the enmity of GOD'S Power. The enemy uses our bodies to yield and be subjected to self-feelings and image. Once we are subjected to our feelings and image, we cannot receive the Power of GOD to overcome the devil's suggestions while he is trying to lie to us. We must be saved and reject his lies like Moses at the Red Sea.

Stand still and see GOD'S Salvation today! The Egyptians you see behind you, you will never see them anymore, in JESUS Holy Name! Amen! You may not see how this red sea is going to separate and give a dry smooth road for you to pass through, but GOD knows how HE is going to get you through it. It may seem to be very hard, but remember the same GOD who killed the firstborn of Satan, and let you get out of the captivity that Satan had put you into; is the same GOD now who is surrounding you at this red sea. And GOD can see how the enemy is raging behind you. Do not be afraid, fear not, GOD knows how to finish your enemy and clear him out of your way. That financial mountain or sea is not greater than what GOD has done for you in the past, Amen! And Glory, Hallelujah!

Therefore, let us pray that HE kills our old self completely and put us on that cross where by our will crosses with HIS will. When we are dead to our self, we shall be able to worship GOD in the midst of our problems and put HIS name high above everything. And HE will equip us with HIS wisdom and knowledge to give us understanding and courage to wait on HIM. It is hard to wait without seeing, and yet you are being harassed by bills and other needs. But remember, during, and after JESUS CHRIST'S Death, HIS disciples were being harassed by a lot of fears of what was going to happen with them. They looked at their three years of being with HIM and saw nothing but a great failure. They saw how they lost their businesses and "precious time" so they thought, following this man who saved others but could not save Himself. At that moment, if you told our LORD'S first disciples that they will be known throughout the world as victors and be extremely famous as children of GOD, they would not have believed you. Now, they are forever rejoicing in heaven waiting to come to rule the earth for 1000 years with the KING of Kings and the LORD of Lords and thereafter in heaven they will enjoy life with CHIRST forever and ever, Amen!

After three days of their anxiously waiting, of course, it was a different story! To the Centurions that kept the sepulcher, they beheld HIS resurrection in the Mightiness of GOD as the earth shook with earthquake and tomb opened. And to HIS Disciples they beheld the Glory of CHRIST'S Resurrection and 40 days they conversed and ate with HIM before they show HIM taken to Heaven. And the Angel of the LORD physically appeared and talked to them of HIS coming again as the KING of kings and the LORD of lords. We too, if we die to self and receive CHRIST JESUS' death and resurrection, we shall be able to stand still and behold HIS glory as HE delivers us from every shame that the enemy wants to put on us.

Looking at the Word of GOD, a man who has died to self, as the Holy Spirit teaches us through our Brother Paul in 2 Corinthians 4: 7-14, "But we have this treasure on the earthen vessels, that the excellency of the power may be of GOD, and not of us. We are troubled on every side yet not distressed; we are perplexed, but not in despair; persecuted, but not forsaken; cast down, but not destroyed. Always bearing about in the body the dying of the LORD JESUS CHRIST that the life of JESUS might be made manifest in our body: For we who live are always delivered unto death for JESUS'S sake, that the life of JESUS CHRIST might be made manifest in our mortal flesh, so then death worketh in us, but life in you. We having the same Spirit of faith, according as it is written, I have believed, and I therefore have I spoken; we also believe and therefore speak; knowing that HE who rose up our LORD JESUS shall raise us also by JESUS."

That is all CHRIST wants you and me to do so that HE can take over our lives and use them for that purpose HE created us for. GOD created us so that we can worship him and live for HIS glory. When we live for GOD'S glory we no longer strive for the things of this world which are temporary, but for things that are not seen. 2 Corinthians 5:7 "we walk by faith not by sight:" For even though in this life, we need these things of this world; like, clothes, food, housing, and traveling aids like vehicles, we do not live for these things, neither do we live in them, we now live for CHRIST JESUS. For it is HIM that died for us so that we should through HIM have life and have it more abundantly, John 10:10. And it is by faith we can receive this abundant of life with all the other things we need for life. For we are saved by faith not by the good works that we had done, let's we boast. Human beings good works cannot save any one for the Heavenly Kingdom.

Faith gives us hope of life now and the life to come. Romans 8:24, "For we are saved by hope: but hope that is seen is not hope: for what a man seeth, why should he yet hope for? But if we hope for that we see not, then do we with patience wait for it." When we obey our GOD, and live according to HIS will, HE will turn all our messes into a messages of HIS Kingdom, and turn all our misery into missiles for HIS glory. Amen! May our Loving GOD bless everyone who will read this book and encourage those who are already in HIS will by CHRIST JESUS, and those who are going through some very difficult situations and are broken before HIM be comforted! And those who have not yet known or accepted JESUS CHRIST as their Savior and the only King of their lives, may they learn how to come into HIS Life and into HIS Kingdom and be GOD'S children, now and forever, Amen!

For "JESUS IS THE WAY, THE TRUTH, AND THE LIFE: No one comes to the Father" GOD in any other way, but by JESUS CHRIST We Enter Into Eternal Joy, Peace, and Love In GOD'S KINGDOM; Now and in life to come, John 14:6 & Galatians 5:22-23.

"For GOD SO LOVED the world that HE gave HIS only begotten SON JESUS CHRIST that whosoever believes in HIM should not perish but have everlasting life," John 3:16

Now that HE came, died and resurrected to save and deliver us from all evil; HE is coming again to receive us HIS believers to HIS Everlasting HOME! Revelation 22:20, Even so come LORD JESUS!

AMEN!

REFERENCES AND RESEARCH

Research: Libraries like John Hopkins University in Baltimore, UB and BCCC books and Dictionaries. Computer Dictionaries, Wikipedia and Goggle.

References: The Bible reference is from NKJV.

Other Non-Bible References: (Encarta ® World English Dictionary © & (P) 1998-2005 Microsoft Corporation. All rights reserved. 14th century. Via Anglo-Norman < Latin, Encarta ® World English Dictionary © & (P) 1998-2005 Microsoft Corporation All rights reserved. 2nd reference for Bile in Goggle and Wikipedia

Quotes: “You were not intended to bear them,” said Max Lucado in his Book, “Traveling Light: Releasing the Burdens You Were Never Intended to Bear.”

Quotes: “People ask me,” “What is the purpose of life?” “And I respond: In a nutshell, life is preparation for eternity. We were not made to last forever, and God wants us to be with Him in Heaven. One day my heart is going to stop, and that will be the end of my body-- but not the end me. I may live 60 to 100 years on earth, but I am going to spend trillions of years in eternity. This is the warm-up act - the dress rehearsal. God wants us to practice on earth what we will do forever in eternity. We were made by God and for God, and until you figure that out, life isn't going to make sense," Said Pastor Rick Warren. Rick Warren is the Pastor of Saddleback Church in California and the Author of highly sold "Purpose Driven Life," Book.

All Bible Verses from Genesis to Revelation from NKJV.

In past I read so many books of Christian writers and listened to several TV and Church Preachers and have gained knowledge and wisdom as I heard those teaching, brethren and co-workers in the ministry teach, counsel, and preach the WORD.

Just to mention a few Authors and Preachers that have encouraged my writing:

- Dr. Jay Adams, my Biblical Counseling Professor, Trinity College of Bible and Seminary University, Author of many counseling enlightening, encouraging mentoring books
- Dr. Charles Stanley, TBN Preacher, Author with counseling encouraging Teachings
- TBN Founder, Dr. Paul Crouch, Author, Encouraging Word "Tell that mountain to move and it'll move"
- Pastor Donnie McClurkin, Gospel Singer, TBN Host, Preacher with the Word and an Author
- Dr. Max Lucado, Author with counseling words in his books, especially, "Traveling Light"
- Pastor Joe Osteon and his wife, TBN Preacher, Pastor, Author, Encourager and Counselor
- Pastor John Hagee TBN Preacher of Prophetic Word of GOD and an Author

- Joyce Meyers TBN Preacher with counseling encouraging Word and an Author of many enlightening books
- Bishop TD Jakes, Preacher, Teacher, Mentor, and an Author of many encouraging, teaching and inspiring books.
- Rev. Reinhard Bonnke worldwide Gospel Crusade Preacher with signs and wonders of miracles following. He is an Author of encouraging books.